THE ROCKHOUND'S MANUAL

THE
ROCKHOUND'S
MANUAL

Gordon S. Fay

1817
HARPER & ROW, PUBLISHERS
New York, Evanston, San Francisco, London

LIBRARY OF CONGRESS CATALOG CARD NUMBER: 77–157080

STANDARD BOOK NUMBER: 06–011218–2

Acknowledgments

The author is indebted to many people and many organizations for much of the material which appears in this book. Special thanks in this regard are due the U. S. Geological Survey, the U. S. Bureau of Mines, the U. S. Bureau of Land Management, the U. S. Forest Service, *Mineral Information Service* (a publication of the California Division of Mines and Geology), and the many state geologists and other officials in government and private business who contributed information that was incorporated into this book.

Sincere appreciation is also extended to the Los Angeles County Museum of Natural History, especially to Miss Barbara Lowe, curatorial assistant, for her aid in the selection of the museum specimens which were photographed in color. The donors of many of the specimens photographed include Dr. M. J. Groesbeck, H. Henke, R. F. Meiklejohn, the Museum Foundation, W. C. Runyan, J. Smith, and L. Webb.

The color photographs were made by Armando Solis, as were the two black and white photographs credited to him in the body of the book. Many of the other photographs were furnished by the U.S. Geological Survey, and thanks in this particular regard are extended to Mr. Irvil P. Schultz of the Survey's Photographic Laboratory for his very efficient help in the selection of these photographs.

Table of Contents

A section of color plates follows page 146.

Chapter 1
The Rockhound Hobby

Rubies, sapphires, diamonds, jade, emeralds, gold—the list reads like a treasure trove from distant lands, yet these are only a few of the many minerals found in the United States by rockhounds, people who collect rocks and minerals as a hobby.

Gems such as diamonds and emeralds are relatively rare, and few rockhounds become rich at their hobby, of course, but most rockhounds consider this fact to be unimportant. The great rewards of this hobby come from such things as a pleasant and exhilarating day in the fresh air, away from the crowds, looking for mineral specimens which nature fashioned millions of years ago and which no other human eyes have heretofore seen.

Although most rockhounds regard the chance of financial gain as just another intriguing facet of a fascinating hobby, it is true that the chance of "striking it rich" is always present to some degree. As examples, a weekend tourist in Arkansas found a $75,000 diamond, a rockhound in Nevada almost literally stumbled over a deposit of opal worth $50,000, a boy in North Carolina uncovered a rich pocket of gem tourmaline, a trout fisherman in Maine discovered a valuable deposit of stream gold, and a housewife found a hill of jade in British Columbia worth millions of dollars.

Rockhounding in the United States

Most people are surprised to learn that many of the best mineral collecting areas in North America are in the states east of the Mississippi River. The typical photograph of a prospector panning for gold, for example, is usually taken on a stream in either California or Alaska, yet it is as easy, if not actually easier, to find gold in some eastern streams, all the way from Maine to Georgia. The New England states, New York State, Pennsylvania, New Jersey, and the southern states are actually heavily mineralized, and between all

1

of them they furnish an amazing array of minerals including gold, silver, copper, emerald, amethyst, beryl, tourmaline, diamond, rose quartz, smoky quartz, lepidolite, garnet, topaz, agate, moss agate, sapphire, and many more. As a matter of fact, some of the best mineral specimens ever found, and now in museums as prize specimens, were discovered while excavating for subways and skyscraper foundations in New York City!

The midwestern states have long enjoyed a deserved reputation as prolific suppliers of good specimens of agate, petrified wood, and fossils, but what is not generally known is that certain regions within these states are rapidly coming to the fore as prime collecting areas for many types of minerals. The variety as one travels this area is wide. For example, diamonds have been found in five of these states, and gold has been found in all of the midwestern states. Good specimens of various ore minerals abound in South Dakota, Minnesota, and Missouri. Native copper, sapphire, and garnet have been found in Indiana, along with gold and diamonds and many other minerals. Ohio and Kansas offer a wealth of quartz, pyrite, fluorite, geodes, opal, amethyst, moss agate, agate, petrified wood, and fossils.

The Rocky Mountain states and the Pacific Coast states are of course very heavily mineralized and they present a wide and colorful profusion of mineral specimens including metallic ore minerals, petrified wood, agate, sapphire, gold, topaz, jade, amethyst, smoky quartz, topaz, opal, fire opal, tourmaline, and beryl. The Pacific Coast states have the added feature of swiftly flowing streams discharging into the ocean, and the result is that many gemstones such as jade, agate, moss agate, and bloodstone can be easily found on some ocean beaches where the action of the waves has sorted the material for the picking-up.

The southwestern states—Arizona, New Mexico, Texas, and Oklahoma—for the most part constitute prime rockhounding territory. These states supply beautiful ore mineral specimens to the rockhound, along with such minerals as amethyst, obsidian, agate, petrified wood, turquoise, moss agate, garnet, opal, moonstone, topaz, and carnelian.

Hawaii is built up of volcanic rocks and consequently is

not endowed with very many minerals of interest to the rockhound, in contrast to Alaska where gold, jade, agate, fossils, jasper, thundereggs, amethyst, and many more minerals await the collector. Some companies in Alaska fly groups of rockhounds to jade claims, some of them north of the Arctic Circle, and then fly the rockhounds and their specimens back to Alaskan cities.

Mild winters make many of our states into virtual paradises for the collector in the field but the many facets of rockhounding also make the hobby into a year long activity, even in those regions which may have snowy winters. Many rockhounds enter their choicest mineral specimens in local and regional competitive mineral shows throughout the year. Thousands of rockhounds are attracted by the art of the lapidary, and in home workshops all over the nation they carefully cut and polish selected rock and mineral specimens into attractive objects and sparkling gems of high and often professional quality. Some rockhounds spend many informative and interesting hours at home or in local mineralogy classes as they study crystallography or analyze minerals by blowpipe (see Chapter 5) or by other simple analytical means. Growing numbers of rockhounds are *micromount* specialists (see Chapter 15) who mount specimens of microscopic size for study by means of low-powered microscopes.

Rockhound Clubs

There are approximately 1,000 rockhound clubs in the United States. Approximately 300 rockhound clubs are scattered throughout other countries such as Australia, Germany, England, Japan, Canada, South Africa, New Zealand, and Italy. Within recent years, the international flavor of the hobby has been sharply accentuated by activities such as "rockhound tours" from the United States to mineral collecting localities in other countries. Increasing numbers of rockhounds from other countries are now visiting the United States every year, also. Thus, the American Federation of Mineralogical Societies has launched Operation Rockhound International, a hospitality program whereby rockhounds visiting the United States may obtain information concerning collecting, localities, etc. The information is furnished by members of rockhound clubs in the United States and is communicated either by correspondence or in person. Several rockhounding magazines feature "swap corners" whereby rockhounds all over the world may trade specimens with each other.

Joining a rockhound club is an excellent way for a beginner to start the hobby. Most rockhound clubs hold meetings at fairly regular intervals, and club members typically take a keen interest in helping newcomers find and identify specimens. Lectures by well-known experts on phases of the rockhounding hobby including geology, mineralogy, and lapidary techniques are featured at many club meetings. A typical club is usually a member of a regional association such as the Eastern Federation of Mineralogical and Lapidary Societies. The official magazines of the regional associations are usually published monthly and they feature helpful articles concerning mineral collecting localities, collecting practices, lapidary instruction, and related activities.

Where Can You Look for and Collect Mineral Specimens?

A very basic fact concerning the problem of where you can and cannot collect mineral specimens is that all land in the United States is owned, and that there is no such thing as unowned land. A piece of land may look like the most abandoned and most desolate parcel of wasteland in existence. It may be in the middle of a forest which apparently has never been touched by man, or it may abut a highway which winds along a rocky and uninhabited shore. In these and any other cases, however, the land is owned. Much of the land in the western states and Alaska is owned by the federal government, while most of the land in the midwestern, eastern, and southern states is state-owned or privately owned.

Permission should, of course, always be obtained before collecting specimens on private land. Growing numbers of owners of private land throughout the United States are now charging admittance fees to rockhounds who wish to enter their properties for collecting purposes. These fees are usually very reasonable and sometimes include such services as having a lumbering bulldozer dig into and scrape off surface material while rockhounds walk slowly behind the machine, looking for specimens.

Regulations concerning rockhounding on state-owned land vary widely depending upon state laws, the type of land, whether parts of it have been set aside for recreational activities and for what types of activities, etc. As may be imagined, hiking through, say, a state park which was made into a state park because the land involved contained priceless dinosaur tracks would almost certainly prompt some inquiries from park officials if the hiker carried an assortment of hammers and chisels. On the other hand, some state parks are virtual rockhound meccas. Visitors to Blackburn State Park in Georgia, for example, are told how to and then actually do pan for gold. Fossil collecting is strongly encouraged in Hueston Woods State Park in Ohio (the fossils are approximately 500 million years old), and the state of New Mexico recently established Rockhound State Park for rockhounds.

Where some states expressly allow rockhounding in designated state parks, other states just as expressly forbid rockhounding in all state parks. Some states have no particular objection to rockhounding in state parks as long as there is no defacement of rock outcrops, etc. Laws regarding rockhounding on state lands other than state parks also vary from state to state and the rockhound should always check with the proper state agencies before attempting to collect specimens on any state-owned or state-controlled lands.

The collecting of mineral specimens, etc., *is not permitted in national parks or national monuments*. Much of the land in national forests, however, is open to rockhounding but the person who wishes to rockhound in a national (or any other) forest should always check with a ranger or forestry office to find out which areas are open to rockhounding. This is especially important during the summer and early fall months in some sections of the country as much of the forest land normally open to such recreational activities may be temporarily closed due to extreme fire hazard.

Some of the original public lands of the United States which are still under federal ownership have not been set aside for use as national forests, parks, reservations, and monuments, etc., and these lands, comprising almost one-fifth of the total land acreage of the United States, are "public domain," managed by the Bureau of Land Management. A new regulation, as a result of the magnitude of the rockhounding hobby, lists rockhounding as one of the permitted activities on the public domain. Most of these lands are in eleven western states and Alaska, with small acreages in the Midwest and Southwest. The "public land" states and their most recently determined acreages of public domain are given below.

Public Domain Acreage in the United States

State	Public Land Acreage
Alabama	1,158
Alaska	278,142,341
Arizona	12,925,990
Arkansas	2,367
California	15,222,261
Colorado	8,459,470
Florida	1,842
Idaho	12,172,725
Kansas	1,515
Louisiana	3,900
Michigan	4,133
Minnesota	41,749
Mississippi	1,614
Montana	8,226,377
Nebraska	7,923
Nevada	45,957,820
New Mexico	13,440,297
North Dakota	75,969
Oklahoma	9,609
Oregon	15,668,266
South Dakota	278,206
Utah	22,983,922
Washington	273,748
Wyoming	16,681,025
total	452,584,227

Recreation guides in the form of maps having much helpful information on them have been published for several of the above listed states by the Bureau of Land Management and these guides usually list, among other things, some of the good rockhounding areas on the federal lands in these states. There are specific times when specific areas of the land managed by the Bureau will be closed to public use, and the rockhound should check with the district manager of the area he proposes to work in to determine if the land is open to rockhounding. Recreation maps of some specific areas and more detailed information concerning the public lands may be obtained by writing to the appropriate Bureau of Land Management office or offices listed below.

Bureau of Land Management Offices

Alaska
   555 Cordova St., Anchorage, Alaska 99501

Arizona
   Federal Building, Room 3022, Phoenix, Arizona 85025

California
   Federal Building, Room E 2820, 2800 Cottage Way, Sacramento, California 95825

Colorado
   Federal Building, Room 14023, 1961 Stout St., Denver, Colorado 80202

Idaho
   Federal Building, Room 334, (P.O. Box 2237), Boise, Idaho 83702

Montana, North and South Dakota
   Federal Building and U.S. Courthouse, 316 N. 26th St., Billings, Montana 59101

Nevada
   Federal Building, Room 3008, 300 Booth St., Reno, Nevada 89502

New Mexico
   Federal Building, South Federal Place, (P.O. Box 1449), Santa Fe, New Mexico 87501

Oregon and Washington
   729 N.E. Oregon St., (P.O. Box 2965), Portland, Oregon 97208

Utah
> 125 South State, (P.O. Box 11505), Salt Lake City, Utah 84111

Wyoming
> Courthouse Building, 2120 Capitol Avenue, (P.O. Box 1828), Cheyenne, Wyoming 82001

Requests for information concerning location and status of public lands in Minnesota should be sent to the Montana office, and requests for information concerning public lands in Oklahoma should be sent to the New Mexico office of the Bureau of Land Management. Inquiries concerning public lands in Nebraska and Kansas are handled by the Wyoming office of the Bureau. Inquiries relating to public lands in Alabama, Arkansas, Florida, Louisiana, Michigan, and Mississippi should be sent to the Eastern States office at 7981 Eastern Avenue, Silver Springs, Maryland 20910.

The rockhound should check the location and status of the public lands with the appropriate Land Office very carefully, especially in the states east of the Mississippi River, before attempting to collect specimens. The public lands in these states are difficult to locate as the tracts are relatively small and may be without public access. The Land Offices can furnish details on other conditions which may preclude public use of the land.

The foregoing listing of approximately 42,000 acres of public land in Minnesota will be of interest to many midwesterners, and the land involved is itself interesting in that the portion administered by the Bureau of Land Management consists primarily of unsurveyed islands in the northern part of the state. An inventory is currently being made to determine the number and sizes of the islands and the stock of resources on them. Specific information concerning these islands may be obtained from the Bureau of Land Management office in Montana.

How to Find Mineral Collecting Localities

In addition to rockhounding magazines and the Bureau of Land Management recreation guides for some states, the rockhound has a number of other sources of information which will help him to locate good collecting areas in any state. Virtually every state offers reasonably priced state publications for sale which describe specific mineral occurrences within the state, and a list of such publications plus information on how to obtain them can usually be obtained in libraries. The U.S. Government Printing Office also offers similar material for sale and although the bulk of state and government publications of this sort presumes some knowledge of geology and mineralogy on the part of the reader, a growing number of states publish excellent and nominally priced booklets expressly for rockhounds. As a few examples, the Alabama Geological Survey has produced an extremely well done 100-page book on Alabama rockhounding which sells for fifty cents, the Indiana Geological Survey's publications of *Guide to Some Minerals and Rocks in Indiana* and *Let's Look At Some Rocks* sell for twenty-five and thirty-five cents, respectively, and the Division of Geology of the Florida Board of Conservation has authored *Guide to Rocks and Minerals of Florida,* price $1.00. Residents of Florida, incidentally, may also purchase, for an additional $1.50, a rock collection to which the guide is keyed.

In addition to such publications, many states now offer free printed material on rockhounding within a particular state. A list of the states offering such material, with descriptions of the brochures, etc., appears at the end of this chapter. Some of these publications are shown in Fig. 1.1.

Some states publish both free and nominally priced rockhounding material of excellent quality. As an example, the Pennsylvania Geological Survey offers three free educational booklets (see list at the end of this chapter) and also publishes two extremely helpful and well done paperback books for rockhounds. Bulletin G 33, *Mineral Collecting in Pennsylvania,* contains 164 pages, and Bulletin G 40, *Fossil Collecting in Pennsylvania,* has 126 pages. Both bulletins deal primarily with collecting localities but also contain basic and interestingly written information. Each bulletin costs fifty cents (plus a 6% sales tax for Pennsylvania residents only). (Incidentally, these two bulletins are not sold by the state geological survey but they may be purchased from the Division of Documents, 10th and Market Streets, Harrisburg,

Fig. 1.1: A wealth of free and nominally priced published material on rockhounding is available. Sources include the United States government, the various states, and chambers of commerce. (Photo by Armando Solis)

Pa. 17125, and checks made payable to "Commonwealth of Pennsylvania" must accompany orders.)

Keeping pace with the rockhounding hobby, there are now a number of travel guides on the market, each dealing with a particular section of the United States and describing how to get to various mineral collecting localities. Some of these publications are excellent. Maps are usually included, and brief descriptions of the minerals which can be found at a particular site are given. The most helpful of these rockhound travel guides also include some notations concerning the status of the land involved, that is, whether it is privately or publicly owned, where to get permission to enter the land, etc.

One method of finding mineralized localities is often overlooked by even experienced rockhounds. There are usually books, in the genealogy sections in libraries, which deal with the histories of particular towns and cities, including the histories of any mining and quarrying which may have been done scores or even a few hundreds of years ago. One rockhound who now lives in a now moderately populous section of Massachusetts was startled to thus learn that in the early 1900's there had been a small but fairly productive gold mine only a few miles from his present home. He and a friend found the brush-covered mine mouth the next weekend and triumphantly returned with specimens of gold-bearing quartz, one of which he presented to the astonished owner of the property who thus suddenly found out that he owned a gold mine.

Annotated lists of magazines and books which rockhounds will find helpful and interesting will be found in the Bibliography. Immediately following in the current chapter is a list of states which offer free printed rockhounding material, a description of the material offered by each state, and the addresses to which the reader should write, to obtain the material. A number of other states are preparing such information but only those states which are known at the present time to definitely have such material or have indicated that it will be available by the publication date of this book have been included.

States Offering Free Printed Rockhounding Material

Alaska

Write to: State of Alaska Department of Natural Resources, Division of Mines and Geology, Box 5-300, College, Alaska 99701.

Ask for: *Information Circular No. 9.* This circular lists rockhound dealers and rockhound clubs in Alaska.

Arizona

Write to: Department of Economic Planning and Development, Suite 1704, 3003 North Central Avenue, Phoenix, Arizona 85012.

Ask for: *Arizona Rockhound Guide.* An excellent guide with good color photographs of rocks and minerals. Tells how to get to good collecting areas, and includes a table of rock types.

Colorado

Write to: Colorado Department of Public Relations, 986 M, State Capitol, Denver, Colo. 80203.

Ask for: (1) *The Minerals of Colorado and Area Locations,* (2) *Colorado Gem Stones,* (3) *Colorado Fossils.* These are all good, (1) being a booklet, and (2) and (3) being single sheets.

Delaware

Write to: Travel Division, Delaware State Development Department, 45 The Green, Dover, Delaware 19901.

Ask for: Information on rockhounding

Idaho

Write to: Idaho Department of Commerce and Development, Room 108, Capitol Bldg., Boise, Idaho 83707.

Ask for: (1) *Gems and Locations* (brochure), and (2) *Idaho Camping Guide Map.* The title of the brochure is self-explanatory. The map shows rockhounding areas and describes the minerals which can be found in each location.

Illinois

Write to: Illinois Department of Mines and Minerals, 112 State Office Bldg., Springfield, Illinois 62706.

Ask for: *Guide to Rocks and Minerals of Illinois,* by Illinois State Geological Survey. An excellent 40-page booklet which includes identification charts, good drawings, and the geologic history of Illinois.

Not available in quantity. One to an organization, only. Individual requests cannot be honored.

Iowa

Write to: Iowa Conservation Commission, Department of Information and Education, 300 Fourth St., Des Moines, Iowa 50319.

Ask for: Existing material on state parks in Iowa which offer rockhounding information.

Kansas

Write to: The University of Kansas, State Geological Survey, Lawrence, Kansas 66044.

Ask for: (1) *Kansas Rocks and Minerals.* This is an extremely attractive and well-done 64-page booklet. *Mailing charge ten cents.*

(2) *Surface Features of Kansas.* A map showing in pictorial manner the chief topographic features of Kansas. Has explanatory text. Size of map is 23″ × 26″. *Mailing charge ten cents.*

(3) *Stories of Resourceful Kansas. Pamphlet 1. Featuring The Kansas Landscape.* Interesting and well-illustrated 42-page booklet dealing with Kansas geology, much of this from the standpoint of what can be seen from highways. No charge.

Note: A booklet on fossils, similar to *Kansas Rocks and Minerals,* is "in the works" and may be available by the time you read this, so ask about the fossil booklet, too. All of these Kansas publications are outstanding and the booklet on fossils will be of the same quality.

Maine

Write to: Maine Geological Survey, Department of Economic Development, State Office Building, Augusta, Maine 04330.

Ask for: *Maine Mineral Collecting.* This is a pamphlet which describes Maine minerals, where they can be found, and gives some field tips.

Michigan

Write to: Michigan Tourist Council, Stevens T. Mason Bldg., Lansing, Michigan 48926.

Ask for: Free material on rockhounding. This is what you get:

1. *Michigan's Colorful Minerals.* Excellent color photographs of minerals.

2. *Michigan Beach Stones.* Brochure. Good descriptions and color photographs.

3. *Collecting Minerals in Michigan.* A 24-page booklet. Includes field tips, locations, descriptions of minerals, and the general geology of Michigan.

4. *Guide to Michigan Fossils*. A 24-page, profusely illustrated booklet. Includes descriptions of fossils, fossil-collecting localities, field tips, and general geology of Michigan.

Minnesota

Write to: Minnesota Department of Economic Development, 57 West 7th St., St. Paul, Minnesota 55102.

Ask for: Brochure on rockhounding. Describes Minnesota gemstones and minerals, and lists collecting localities.

Montana

Write to: Advertising Department, Montana Highway Commission, Helena, Montana 59601.

Ask for: Rockhounding brochure. Describes general locations of gemstones, etc., and lists the museums in Montana having rock and mineral displays.

Nebraska

Write to: State of Nebraska, Game and Parks Commission, Lincoln, Nebraska 68509.

Ask for: *Discover Nebraskaland*. This pictorial booklet contains a one-page description of gemstones and gemstone locations in Nebraska. Even though it doesn't contain much about rockhounding, write for the booklet, anyway. The color photographs are more than worth it.

Nevada

Write to: Department of Economic Development, Carson City, Nevada 89701.

Ask for: *Nevada Rock Hunting*. Informative brochure. Maps are included.

New Hampshire

Write to: New Hampshire Division of Economic Development, Concord, New Hampshire 03301.

Ask for: *Some Pointers On Mineral Collecting In New Hampshire*. Tips on collecting New Hampshire minerals. This brochure does not list locations but does list several books which should be helpful in finding abandoned feldspar and mica mines in pegmatite dikes (pegmatite dikes are the "homes" of the best tourmaline and beryl crystals). Also lists New Hampshire mineral shops.

New Mexico

Write to: Department of Development, State of New Mexico, 113 Washington Avenue, Santa Fe, N.M. 87501.

Ask for: One-page description of Rockhound State Park. Park is near Deming.

North Carolina
Write to: Travel and Promotion Division, Department of Conservation and Development, Raleigh, N.C. 27602.

Ask for: Kit of rockhound material. This includes material from chambers of commerce in rockhounding areas in the state, plus Information Bulletin No. 137 which describes gemstone (ruby, sapphire, etc.) occurrences in North Carolina.

North Dakota
Write to: North Dakota Travel Department, State Capitol Grounds, Bismarck, N.D. 58501.

Ask for: *North Dakota Tourist Information Directory.* This directory includes rockhounding tips and collecting localities. North Dakota is also a "happy hunting ground" for Indian artifacts, buffalo skulls, deer horns, etc.

Ohio
Write to: State of Ohio Department of Natural Resources, Division of Parks and Recreation, 913 Ohio Departments Building, Columbus, Ohio 43215.

Ask for: *The Fossils of Hueston Woods.* An attractive and profusely illustrated 16-page booklet on the fossils of Hueston Woods State Park (approximately 50 miles from Columbus). Also has information on geologic history of this section. Fossils drawn are natural size, for the most part. Map shows best locations for collecting fossils in the park.

Oregon
Write to: Oregon State Highway Department, Highway Building, Salem, Oregon 97310.

Ask for: *Oregon Rocks, Fossils, Minerals, Where to Find Them.* Concise and excellent brochure which describes specimens which can be found, the areas where they are found, and how to reach these areas. Maps included in brochure.

Pennsylvania
Write to: Bureau of Topographic and Geologic Survey, Main Capitol Annex, Harrisburg, Pennsylvania 17120.

Ask for: (1) *Common Rocks and Minerals of Pennsylvania.* An illustrated and extremely informative 27-page booklet.

(2) *Common Fossils of Pennsylvania.* A profusely illustrated booklet of 18 pages.

(3) *Pennsylvania Geology Summarized.* A very attractive and informative 17-page booklet.

Rhode Island

Write to: Rhode Island Development Council, Executive Department, Roger Williams Building, Hayes Street, Providence, Rhode Island 02908.

Ask for: The several sheets on Rhode Island minerals and gemstones, plus the paper on the state mineral and the state stone.

Note: With the above material, a small sample of *cumberlandite* is also usually sent, an intrusive igneous rock once used as an iron ore in the state, and a small sample of *bowenite*, a gem mineral which resembles nephrite jade.

South Dakota

Write to: Department of Highways, Travel Division, Pierre, South Dakota 57501.

Ask for: Available material on rockhounding. At time of writing, a brochure on rockhounding also seems to be forthcoming.

Utah

Write to: Utah Travel Council, Council Hall, Capitol Hill, Salt Lake City, Utah 84114.

Ask for: *Utah Fact Book.* In addition to listing recreation areas and campsites, etc., contains a brief description of gemstone localities, plus some field tips.

Virginia

Write to: Department of Conservation and Economic Development, Division of Mineral Resources, Natural Resources Building, Box 3667, Charlottesville, Va. 22903.

Ask for: List of companies selling rocks, minerals, and fossils in Virginia.

Wisconsin

Write to: University Extension, The University of Wisconsin, Geological and Natural History Survey, 1815 University Avenue, Madison, Wisconsin 53706.

Ask for: (1) *Mineral and Rock Collecting In Wisconsin,* and (2) *Fossil Collecting In Wisconsin.* Well-written pamphlets, with excellent field tips for finding and collecting specimens.

Chapter 2

Maps, Tools, Equipment, and Field Tips

Maps commonly used by rockhounds vary from simple road maps to topographic maps, largely depending upon whether the rockhound is going to stay near mapped roads or is going to do some exploring. Once at a potential or actual collecting site, the rockhound selects the tools and equipment which he will use, his choices depending mostly upon field conditions and personal preference. Most of the tools and equipment used in rockhounding are simple, and in many instances consist of items which can be found about the house or which can be made from inexpensive materials.

Much more important, of course, than the possession of tools and items of equipment is the knowledge of how to properly use them. Some field tips concerning such usages are given in this chapter while other suggestions are given in Chapter 6 and in other pertinent chapters. The current chapter also takes up the important subject of "field manners."

Maps and How to Use Them

Maps are popularly thought of as aids in helping us to get from one place to another on at least fairly good roads, but anyone who has been rockhounding for any length of time has probably had more than one occasion to use topographic, and possibly geologic, maps. Essentially, a topographic map shows the configuration of the ground by means of printed *contour lines* which represent *contours*. A contour is an imaginary line on the ground along which all points are at the same elevation. A geologic map is commonly overprinted on a topographic map and shows different rocks by means of colors and colored patterns.

17

Many rockhounds are more or less familiar with the uses of both topographic and geologic maps but there are probably few, even experienced, rockhounds who realize what a wealth of information concerning possible mineral localities can often be obtained from even simple road maps. This particular use of maps involves stream drainage patterns and is explained in Chapter 6.

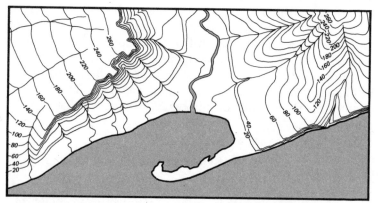

Fig. 2.1: The upper drawing shows a river valley between two hills with the sea in the foreground. The lower drawing is a topographic map of the same region. (Courtesy U.S. Geological Survey)

Topographic Maps. Fig. 2.1 shows the relationship of the contour lines on a map to the actual topography of the ground. Notice that the elevations given on the contour lines in this particular map are all multiples of twenty feet. The vertical spacing of contours as they appear on a map is the *contour interval;* thus the contour interval of this particular map is twenty feet. Contour intervals are chosen so that the topography will be clearly, and as precisely as possible, delineated. Imagine, for example, the appearance of the map of Fig. 2.1 if a contour interval of five feet had been used instead of a contour interval of twenty feet. The cliff shown would be represented on the map by contour lines printed so closely together that they would appear as an almost solid mass of ink.

A brief study of Fig. 2.1 demonstrates these important points concerning topographic maps:

1. Assuming the same contour interval throughout the map, the steeper is the slope the more closely spaced are the contour lines. Steep slopes are therefore represented by closely spaced contour lines, gentle slopes by widely spaced contour lines.

2. Contour lines do not cross. If two contour lines did cross, this would mean that the point of crossing has two different elevations. This is impossible except in the rare instances of overhanging cliffs, etc.

3. Where contour lines cross streams or valleys, the contour lines form more or less rounded V's which point "upstream" toward higher elevations. The V's formed where contour lines cross ridges point downslope along the ridges.

Map Scale. The scale of a map may be expressed as (1) an equality stated in different units, (2) a representative fraction, or (3) as a graph, or bar scale. As an example of an equality stated in different units, the scale of a particular map may be printed on the map as "1 inch = 100 feet." This means that a measurement of one inch on the map represents a distance of 100 feet on the ground. Expressed as a representative fraction, the same scale is 1:1200, that is, a measurement of one unit on the map represents a distance of 1200 of the same units on the ground. The bar scale needs no explanation, this being the way in which scales are expressed on most road maps. Ground distances scaled from maps are of course horizontal, and not slope, distances.

Maps and the Magnetic Compass. Despite what may be thoroughly understood about such things as map scale and contour lines, maps will not be of much help in the field unless you can determine where you are on the map and can "point" the map in the right direction. For this reason, rockhounds, hunters, fishermen, etc., should know how to use the magnetic compass in conjunction with maps.

The north-seeking end of the compass needle points toward *magnetic north,* and depending upon where you are in the United States, magnetic north will be either to the west or east of *true north.* This is always true unless you happen to be on a certain irregular line which runs in a roughly north-south direction in the eastern part of the United States, and whose location slowly but constantly changes. On this *agonic line,* the directions of true and magnetic north coincide. East of the agonic line, the compass needle points west of true north. West of the agonic line, the compass needle points east of true north. A topographic map will usually show the directions of true and magnetic north for a given year in a particular region, the angle between the two norths being called the *magnetic declination.* Near this diagram will usually be found a statement concerning the numerical value of the annual change in declination for the region covered by the map. In the contiguous United States, the annual change in declination is only a few minutes and its effects may be disregarded if a fairly recently published map is used.

One fact which definitely is of importance, however, is that the compass should not be used in the vicinity of masses of iron, or near electrical fields. When using the compass, stay at least sixty yards away from high-tension power lines, twenty yards away from cars, trucks, etc., ten yards away from telegraph wires, telephone wires, and wire fences, and one yard away from hammers, chisels, etc.

How To Find Out Where You Are. Let us suppose that you are driving along a road and that you want to find out where you are. We will assume that you are traveling in fairly open country so that, after getting out of the car, you note a nearby area from which the surrounding topography can be seen. Once in this area, place the unrolled topographic map on a flat area, possibly on a rock, preferably at waist height or higher. Place the compass on the line on the map which represents the direction of magnetic north, usually shown by a half arrowhead. Adjust the position of the compass so that the "N" and the "S" on the compass are both directly above the magnetic-north line, the compass "N" being closest to the half arrowhead. Now carefully rotate the map, being careful not to dislodge the compass, until the north seeking end of the compass needle is directly over, or points to, the half arrowhead. The map is then oriented, that is, it is "pointing" in the right direction.

Next, select two ground features which preferably are at about right angles to each other from your position and which can be located on the map. Place, say, a pencil on the map so that one edge of it passes over one of the points selected on the map. Using this point as a pivot, sight along the pencil edge and swing the pencil about this point until your line of sight also passes through the corresponding feature on the ground. Draw a line along the edge of the pencil. Repeat the procedure for the other point. The point of intersection of the two lines is your location. Actually, the angle involved does not have to approximate a right angle but the accuracy of the method does increase as the angle approaches the value of ninety degrees. Shallow angles of less than forty-five degrees should be avoided.

Notice that if you orient the map close to a road, etc., which you can locate on the map, only one line need be drawn. Its intersection with the map representation of the road, ridge, stream, etc., will fix your position. The method of drawing two lines to fix your position, however, can be used in territory which is entirely unknown to you and where, often, nearby topography does not immediately seem to correlate with anything on the map.

Using the Watch as a Compass. A watch can be used to determine the approximate direction of *true* north and south. The method can be used in any region between the Tropic of Cancer and the Arctic Circle, and can therefore be used in the contiguous United States, throughout most of Canada, and in that part of Alaska below the Arctic Circle.

To use the watch as a compass in the above described regions, point the hour hand of the watch at the sun. A north-south line will then pass approximately midway between the hour hand and the "12" on the watch, if the watch is keeping standard time. If on daylight saving time, the north-south line will be approximately midway between the hour hand and the "1" on the watch. If there is any doubt concerning which is north and which is south, remember that the sun is to the east of a true north-south line before "sun" noon, and is to the west of the line after "sun" noon. Note again that this method determines the direction of *true* north and south and it should also be again stated that the method is approximate.

Geologic Maps. A detailed discussion concerning geologic maps is not within the scope of this book but some fundamental facts concerning geologic maps should be understood before attempting to use them.

The two most used symbols on geologic maps are those used to denote strike and dip. The *strike* of a stratum (or vein, or fault plane, etc.) is the map or compass direction of a horizontal line on the stratum, while the *dip* is the vertical angle between the stratum and a horizontal plane. The dip is measured perpendicular to the strike.

All of this usually seems rather confusing at first, but strike and dip and the relationship between them can be easily understood by holding, say, a closed book at any angle with the top of a table or desk. The book represents a portion of a rock stratum. Now hold a pencil on the upper cover of the book so that the pencil is parallel with the desk or table top. The pencil is a "strike line." Place a coin or some other small flat object flat on the book's upper cover, just below the pencil (or on any imagined horizontal line) and let the object slide. It will slide down the "dip line" and, of course, the steeper the dip angle the faster the object will slide.

Fig. 2.2 shows two strata, each in a geographically and topographically different area. The strata have the same strike and dip, but notice how the topography of the surface affects the outcrop pattern on each map. This relationship between the structural features of strata, etc., is extremely important and should be carefully noted by anyone using geologic maps.

How to Obtain Maps. The various states publish maps, some of which may be of value to rockhounds. The purposes of state-published maps vary so much, however, that the rock-

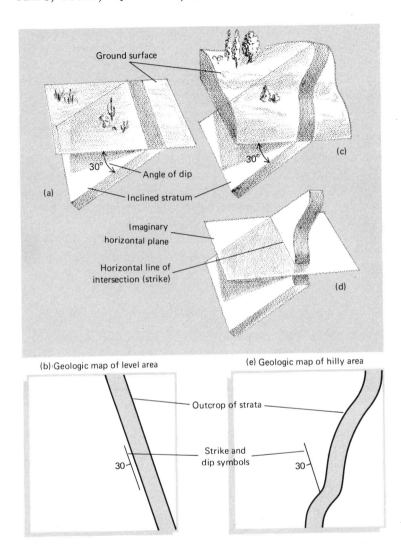

Fig. 2.2: Geologic map fundamentals. Notice how surface topography affects the pattern of rock outcrop. [From Dennis P. Cox and Helen R. Cox, *Introductory Geology: A Programmed Text* (San Francisco: W. H. Freeman), copyright © 1965]

hound should first determine just what he wants to know about a particular area, and then contact the proper state agency.

Some, but not all, U.S. Geological Survey offices sell their topographic maps across the counter. Topographic map indexes of all the states, and information regarding the purchase of both geologic and topographic maps, may be obtained by writing to "U.S. Geological Survey, Branch of Distribution," at 1200 South Eads Street, Arlington, Virginia 22202, or at Denver Federal Center, Denver, Colorado 80225. Topographic maps are also sold by private agencies such as map stores, some surveying companies, and some bookstores. Maps of national forests, and detailed information on these areas, may be obtained by writing to "Forest Service, U.S. Department of Agriculture," Washington, D.C. 20250.

Tools and Equipment and How to Use Them

The tools used by experienced rockhounds are largely a matter of preference governed by experience, but the beginning rockhound is faced with the fact that he doesn't really know what tools and items of equipment to get. Actually, this question is very easily resolved as the tools and items of equipment needed in rockhounding are few in number and are easily obtained. Some of these are illustrated in Fig. 2.3.

Rock Picks and Rock Hammers. The basic tool and thus the "badge" of a rockhound is a rock pick or rock hammer costing between five and ten dollars. Many beginning rockhounds, having heard that a hammer of some kind is used in the field, are inclined to go on their first field trip with a hammer which has perhaps been borrowed from the garage tool chest. Although several more or less pleasant hours may be spent in pounding away at rocks with, say, a carpenter's hammer, a common net result is that the beginner has nothing to show for his pains except some battered and fractured pieces of what might have been good specimens. Rock picks and rock hammers, on the other hand, are expertly designed and weighted to accomplish a maximum of desired results with a minimum of effort. The chisel edge of the

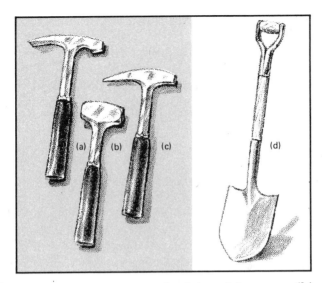

Fig. 2.3: Some rockhounding tools. (a) rock hammer; (b) rock pick; (c) rock-cracking, or "crack" hammer; (d) miners' shovel.

rock hammer is somewhat helpful in regions where rock tends to split along definite planes, such as planes of stratification, but the rock pick is generally preferred by rockhounds as the more all-around tool.

Chisels and Gads. A measure of care and varying amounts of what might be called "field craftsmanship" must sometimes be employed to extract a mineral specimen in one piece. *Rock chisels* are used to split rocks in desired directions. *Gads,* tools which come to a point at one end, are used to force rock apart. Hammers of some type of course supply the driving force for chisels and gads. Heavy hammers of the sledge variety are sometimes used to break up rock by themselves but their indiscriminate use has ruined many a good specimen, and they should be used only when absolutely necessary.

Basic Equipment. Safety goggles should always be worn if there is any chance of rock or steel fragments entering the eye. A pair of work gloves will be found to be a welcome item of equipment when handling jagged rock material, or when using hammer and chisel, etc. Incidentally, the number of flying rock chips can be materially reduced by holding the chisel with a gloved hand close to the rock, rather than nearer to the top of the chisel. Tissue paper and newspaper for wrapping specimens, a bag for carrying specimens, and a notebook and a pencil for recording mineral identities and locations should all always be carried into the field.

Other Tools and Equipment. As basic as the above described tools and items of equipment are, the tools and equipment actually used in the field may range from none at all, as in the case of hunting for wave-concentrated gemstones on a beach, to a variety which seemingly defies general description. During a rockhound field trip to a collecting spot, for example, a number of rockhounds may be working over the rock rubble on a steep hillside with shovels, rakes, and screens. One hundred feet away from them, another group of rockhounds may be flat on their stomachs, exploring crevices in the hillside with an assortment of tools ranging from kitchen spoons to long steel bars. Down at the foot of the hill, near a stream, a few gem-minded rockhounds might be enthusiastically pumping kitchen sieves up and down in the water, sorting the heavier minerals in the sieve from the lighter.

A beginning rockhound would be understandably confused by such a variety of hardware unless he realizes one simple fact: every tool and piece of equipment being used is being used to either (1) transport, (2) break, or (3) sort material, or aid in those processes. Thus, there is a maximum of only three main processes involved, these being transporting, breaking, and sorting. This is a simple but an extremely important point, for now the rockhound can select his own tools and equipment on a logical basis, and may even want to invent a few tools and pieces of equipment for himself.

The time-honored method of moving rock material is, of course, by shovel. Shovels used in rockhounding may be either the long-handled or the short-handled "miners'" shovel. No matter which kind may happen to be favored by a rockhound, all rockhounds agree on one thing: the blade of the shovel should come to a near or rounded point. It is almost impossible to dig down into rock fragments or gravel of appreciable size with a shovel whose blade is straight and square-ended. The writer's personal preference, perhaps because of mining experience, is for the short-handled shovel.

As strange as it may seem to some, especially in this age of automation, there is an art to shoveling, and the rockhound who is going to do much shoveling can make his work much easier by learning correct methods. Assume, for example, that you are shoveling heavy stream gravel, that you are using a short-handled shovel, and that you are right-handed. Put the tip of the shovel into the gravel, at a shallow angle, and then stand so that you are facing in a direction nearly at right angles to the handle of the shovel, your left side toward the shovel. Grasping the shovel with both hands, bend the knees and move the shovel handle downward until it is touching your left leg above the knee. Now lean forward and dig into the gravel with a combination downward and forward thrust, most of which is furnished by your weight as you lean forward. Push against the shovel handle with your left leg whenever necessary to exert leverage. As the blade of the shovel moves into the gravel, bend the knees more and increase the forward lean until a full load is obtained. If this is done correctly, the shovel handle will be in almost constant contact with the left leg, and with varying amounts of pressure. This method, of course, has several variations.

The carbide lamp is another old mining stand-by which, in addition to the short-handled shovel, has been adopted by many rockhounds. The type of carbide lamp designed to be held in the hand is best for most rockhounding purposes. Carbide lamps are not expensive and their reflectors throw a wide circle of good illumination. Rockhounds commonly use carbide lamps while working in caves and mines, and the lamps are also fine for illuminating such openings as rock crevices in hillsides, etc. Carbide lamps have the further advantage that their flames can be adjusted to leave a dark smudge on rock surfaces, thus an interesting looking spot can be quickly marked for future reference with a rockhound's personal "petroglyphs." The flame jet of a carbide lamp will tend to plug up with deposits from time to time, and for that reason a thin wire should be permanently attached to the lamp so that the jet may be cleaned out whenever necessary. This is important, as it is usually impossible to find anything in the field which is thin enough and also strong enough to clean out the jet.

Most rockhounds probably do not realize it, but when they pry rock apart, or pry mineral specimens from rock, they are using a mining process which is known in many mining regions as "barring down." When a miner "bars down" he inserts the pointed end of a steel bar into a rock crevice, crack, or joint and pries rock material apart. The bars used for prying in rockhounding are of course smaller than the bars used in mining but what they lack in size they make up for in the way of variety. Pry bars used by rockhounds encompass practically everything from hand weeders, through automobile lug wrenches, to bars made especially for rockhounds and sold by rockhound supply companies. Some rockhounds adapt crowbars, etc., to their needs, but whatever is used, leverage is the important thing and for that reason the sharpened end or ends of the bar should be angled to the rest of the bar.

Screening. Still another mining process which has been adapted to rockhounding is that of *screening*. Screening is a simple but effective method of sorting rock material according to size so that a given amount of material will vary between a minimum size and a maximum size, these sizes having been determined beforehand. In Montana, for example, the famous sapphires of that state are often found in streams, with placer gold. To recover the sapphires and the gold, the gravel in one particular sapphire-gold placer mine is passed through or retained on screens of decreasing size of mesh. The first screen allows the normal maximum-size sapphires to pass through but holds back particles of larger size. The material on each of the screens, except that on the first screen, is then run through a sluice box. As the particles in the sluice box at any one time are therefore all about the same size, the sluicing operation effectively concentrates the particles according to their specific gravities.

Various screening methods based upon the same principle are used by rockhounds but these methods all have the same objective: to get rid of the particles of undesired size and retain those of desired size for examination or further processing of some type. Screens used in rockhounding can be massive and built on the spot, or at the other end of the spectrum, they can consist of a "nest" of small screens which are held in the hands and shaken back and forth.

Screens are very easy to build. The wire used should be galvanized and should have a square mesh, however. If, as often happens, the material to be screened contains a considerable amount of clay or dirt, the material should be cleaned with water. If a box screen is being used to screen out and retain, in the screen, particles of desired size, the box screen may be immersed in water and shaken back and forth, and up and down. The material on the screen should be moved back and forth on the screen with a downward pressure, and any balls of clay or mud should be broken up, as gemstones are sometimes found in such balls. Material may also be cleaned by pouring water onto the material on the screen, and at the same time moving the rock fragments and pieces back and forth on the screen as described above. If the work is being done near a stream, it is usually possible to place the end of a length of garden hose upstream, in the water, and thus have a supply of water which can be hosed onto the gravel.

If you are screening through more than one screen, do not be in too much of a hurry to throw away the "worthless" material on a "reject" screen. Some years ago, as a visitor to the sapphire-gold placer mine in Montana previously described, the writer, wanting to get more experience in this form of mining, volunteered to help in running a batch of gravel through the entire process. With visions of gold nuggets in his mind's eye, he was just about to toss away a piece of "worthless" material on the upper screen when the miner working with him suddenly yelled, "No!" What had been nearly discarded proved to be one of the largest, most cornflower-blue sapphires found in three years of operation at that mine!

Similarly, don't be in a hurry to discard the material which has passed through your finest screen. For one thing, the material could contain gold. One thing is certain: the material will contain crystals some of which will be the size of a pinhead, or smaller. The chances are that some of these crystals can be made into micromounts (see Chapter 15). Micromount enthusiasts are always keenly interested in obtaining such concentrates. In general, the smaller a crystal, the more perfect it is, and a tiny crystal of a particular mineral will often sell for much more than a hand specimen of the same mineral.

Cone Sieves. An interesting method of retrieving gemstones from dirt and gravel is practiced in several countries including Brazil, Ceylon, and Venezuela. The process, little practiced in the United States although it is extremely efficient, involves the manipulation of a cone-shaped screen or sieve in water. In Ceylon and some other areas, the cones are commonly made of wood, while in Venezuela the gem miners use cones which are made from wire-mesh screen mounted on two-foot diameter circular wooden frames. The average rockhound will probably not go to the trouble of building such a sieve but, as the reader has already no doubt concluded, a rockhound becomes rather expert at improvisation and substitution, and cone sieves are no exception. The depth of a cone sieve should be approximately one-third of its base diameter, and it so happens that many stores sell wooden planters, wicker baskets, and "coolie hats," etc., some of which are of just about the right shape and of about the optimum size of "mesh." A large kitchen sieve may also be used, although the amount of gravel which can be processed by it at one time is necessarily less for the simple reason that a sieve does not look anything like a real gem-concentrating cone sieve except near its bottom. For best results, therefore, a kitchen sieve should be filled with gravel only to the point where the maximum depth of gravel in the cone thus formed is approximately one-third of the diameter of the "base" of the gravel cone.

As to the operation of the sieve, let us suppose that we are using a large kitchen sieve which has been charged with gravel all of about the same size, the sizing having been done by either screening or hand sorting, or both. Assume that the sieve is beneath a water surface—in a stream, for example—and is motionless. If we now suddenly thrust the sieve downward with sufficient speed, every rock and mineral particle will momentarily remain exactly where it was but will then immediately start settling toward the bottom of the sieve. Imagine, somewhere in the gravel, a light particle which is side by side with a heavy particle. As we suddenly move the sieve downward, both particles, for a split second, are still side by side, but then the heavy particle will move or at least tend to move downward through the water at a faster rate than does the light particle. The same thing is happening all throughout the material in the sieve, and thus the heavy particles will gradually move toward the bottom of the sieve as the sieve is pumped up and down in the water.

Actually, of course, the particles in the cone sieve are touching one another most of the time and thus there is little, if any, free fall. Rather, the process essentially becomes one of particles colliding, and sliding and rolling past one another. Every time the sieve is plunged downward, however, all of the particles at rest are again momentarily suspended and then the heavier particles again work their ways beneath the lighter particles. To speed up this downward motion of the heavier particles, the sieve should be shaken occasionally from side to side as it is pumped up and down.

After a few minutes of this up-and-down-and-sideward motion, the contents of the sieve can be flipped over onto a flat surface. The heavier minerals will be on the top of the cone of wet material. It is a good idea at this point to put the upper one-third of the wet material into a pan and examine the material carefully. Even though nothing interesting may be immediately visible, you can either pan or sluice (see Chapter 7) this material for gold and possibly overlooked gemstones, etc.

Safety

Rockhounding, like all other outdoor activities, has its safety rules and precautions. Although specific field procedures relating to safety will vary with actual situations, the more important precautions are discussed below.

Before leaving on a trip, the rockhound should make sure that a first aid kit and plenty of water are stowed away in the vehicle. Necessary repair tools should be inspected for both quantity and working order before leaving, and extra fan belts should be taken along.

Go on collecting trips with a companion or with a group, especially when going into rough or sparsely inhabited areas. When you do go into such an area, tell someone—the local police or sheriff, for example—where you are going and when you expect to be back. Always take maps and compasses along with you, and know how to use them. If you are going to go into poisonous-snake country, wear boots and *carry* a snakebite kit with you; don't leave it in the car. If you go into the desert, always go with at least one other person, and in at least two cars. When traveling alone in strange territory, travel on mapped roads—not on trails—and always stay within sight of your car.

Quarries and highway construction projects, etc., are often good mineral collecting sites but be sure to obtain permission before entering such areas. Even if you have obtained previous permission to work in such places, verify, just before entering such sites, that no blasting is going to be done while you are there. Blasting schedules are usually rigorous but they can be changed. Do not enter old mines unless you know the mine, or have someone along who does. Be extremely careful around any kind of abandoned mine property. Such places are often very dangerous even for experts. In addition to such hazards as cave-ins, brush-hidden shafts, rotted ladders, and steep ore chutes, abandoned mines commonly contain gas which is often concentrated in deadly pockets. Don't try to be your own miner, either, by digging hillside excavations or small caves, etc., in which you plan to work. This is a dangerous procedure. Don't rely on your timbering to prevent a cave-in unless you are an expert miner and, in general, *never* work in a place where there is an overhang of rock or soil directly above you. Also, when on a slope, never work directly above or directly below anyone else.

Outdoor Manners

Private Property. Within past years, several good, privately owned mineral collecting areas have been closed to entry because of the actions of a few people. Permission to enter private property is a courtesy on the part of the owner but unfortunately such courtesies have sometimes been returned by damage to property, and littering. When on private property, leave gates and fences as you found them, open or closed, and do not drive your vehicle off the roads on the property unless you have obtained permission to do so. Before leaving any area, be sure that you have not left litter behind.

It's Your Land. In addition to essentially the same common-sense rules of behavior which should be observed on private land, the use of public land, such as state parks, state recreational areas, county recreational sites, national forests, "public domain," etc., involves a few additional outdoor manners. First of all, of course, when on public land, find out officially if and where you can rockhound. Remember that you cannot collect mineral specimens, etc., in national parks or in national monuments. When camping, keep a clean camp. When leaving, leave a clean area. Be sure that any fires are out. If you are aware of vandalism on either private or public property, report it promptly. Treat public campsites, picnic areas, and all types of public lands as if they were part of your home. They are. It's your land.

Chapter 3
Minerals and How They Form

Man's earlier speculations concerning the origin and structure of minerals have ranged all the way from the idea that minerals such as quartz were permanently frozen ice to the livelier idea that minerals reproduced sexually. By the beginning of the twentieth century, however, scientific investigation had outstripped inventive speculation, and the structural similarity of crystals of a given mineral plus other characteristics were accepted by scientists as strong if indirect evidence that minerals must have an orderly atomic structure. No one had really proved it, however, and there matters stood until 1912 when von Laue, a German scientist, using X-rays, photographed the atoms within a mineral specimen.

Von Laue's "photographs" were actually complex diffraction patterns whose analyses required extensive calculations involving light theory, but the results were indisputable: the atoms of the specimen were arranged in a three-dimensional, geometric, repeated pattern. Since 1912, every one of the over 2,000 minerals found on earth has been similarly "photographed" many times and in many parts of the world, and always with the same results: a given mineral has an orderly and unique arrangement of its component elements (see Fig. 3.1).

The Chemical Composition of Minerals

Most minerals are compounds. Quartz, for example, has the chemical formula SiO_2 which means that, in quartz, electrically charged atoms, or *ions*, of silicon have united with oxygen ions in the numerical ratio of one silicon ion to two oxygen ions. Some elements such as copper, silver, and carbon, in addition to occurring in combined form as compounds can also occur by themselves alone as minerals.

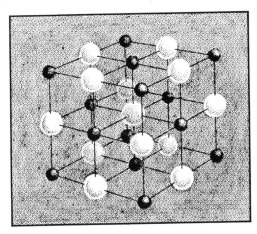

Fig. 3.1: Schematic diagram of sodium (smaller) ions and chlorine ions in the mineral halite (table salt).

It might seem that a given mineral must have a definite, fixed chemical composition and this, in general, is true. The chemical composition of some minerals, however, can vary somewhat. *Scheelite*, for example, an ore mineral of tungsten, is usually described as being calcium tungstate. Usually, however, scheelite also contains some molybdenum. As the amount of molybdenum increases, the amount of tungsten decreases in the mineral in order that the mineral remain in chemical balance. As the operation involved is an in-place substitution of one element for another, the internal crystal structure remains essentially the same and the external characteristics such as crystal shape therefore change little if at all. Thus two pieces of scheelite exhibit the same surface characteristics but they may have different chemical compositions. Minerals which can vary in this manner in their chemical compositions and still maintain the same crystal shape, etc., are said to be members of an *isomorphous series*.

Definition of a Mineral: Crystal Form

Having now looked into the interior world of minerals we can give a definition of a mineral. Assuming that we are talking about minerals which we find in the field, and not man-made minerals, we can say that *a mineral is a naturally occurring, inorganic substance possessing a fixed, orderly atomic arrangement of its component elements, and having a chemical composition which is fixed or which varies within known limits.*

With such an almost inflexible, locked-in program guiding its growth it is little wonder that a given mineral will tend to assume a characteristic *crystal form* as it solidifies. Galena (lead sulfide), for example, commonly crystallizes in cubes while quartz typically forms hexagonal prisms. When crystals do form, then, they are the outward expressions of internal atomic structure. If there are relatively few atoms involved, the crystal is small. If there are relatively many atoms involved, the crystals are large. For a given mineral, however, the atomic arrangement is the same whether the crystals are microscopic in size or five feet long.

Theory and the Rockhound

Admittedly, anyone who finds an excellent mineral specimen, especially one which looks as if it may be valuable, is not going to enthuse too long over the fact that what he has found is a particular, three-dimensional array of atoms. Rather, the rockhound is faced now with the very practical problem of identifying his discovery. This, however, is exactly the point where theory and practice meet.

Most minerals found by the rockhound can be identified by observing and testing their physical properties, and these physical properties depend upon one thing: the atomic arrangement involved. As each mineral has a unique arrangement of its component elements, its physical characteristics are unvarying, or they vary within known limits, and this fact is the basis of mineral identification in the field. This means, for example, that whether a certain mineral is found in Oklahoma or in Tibet, the results of the field tests made upon that mineral will identify it—assuming, of course, that the particular specimen is identifiable by field tests alone.

Crystalline Structure

It is important to note that the term "crystalline" does not mean that actual crystals must be visible in a specimen.

Good crystals, as a matter of fact, are relatively rare items compared to the vast amount of mineral material which occurs without apparent geometric form. In either case, however, crystals or no crystals, a given mineral has the same fundamental arrangement, or pattern, of its elements. Thus when we say that a specimen is "crystalline" we mean only that it has the orderly atomic arrangement of component elements which is unique to that mineral, and we do not mean that the specimen is necessarily in a crystal shape of some kind.

Some mineral material is composed of microscopic grains, the unique atomic pattern of the mineral being present in each grain. To the unaided eye and even under high magnifications, the substance appears noncrystalline but the atomic pattern is revealed by the electron microscope. Such a substance is said to be *cryptocrystalline*, an example being agate.

Mineraloids are substances which look like and are often grouped with minerals, but mineraloids have an amorphous, or noncrystalline, structure as is evident when viewed under high-power microscopes. *Opal* is a mineraloid.

Why Minerals Crystallize: Ionic Bonding

Atoms are the building blocks of all matter, and a simplified picture of an atom is that of a *nucleus* consisting of *protons* and *neutrons*, and a number of *electrons* which are traveling in various orbits, or *shells*, around the nucleus (see Fig. 3.2). Each proton has a positive (+) electrical charge and each electron has a negative (−) electrical charge. Each neutron is electrically neutral, that is, it has no charge. Each electrically uncharged atom must therefore have the same number of electrons as protons.

For some reason (no one really knows why) a given atom with eight electrons in its outermost shell is "stable." Neon, for example, has eight electrons in its outer shell and is "inert." On the other hand, an atom which does not have eight electrons in its outermost shell will, if possible, gain, lose, or share electrons in order to achieve an outermost shell containing eight electrons.

Suppose, for example, that a sodium atom and a chlorine

atom approach each other. Sodium happens to have one electron in its outermost shell and eight electrons in the next shell. Chlorine has seven electrons in its outermost shell. The magic number of eight electrons in the outermost shell can be achieved for both atoms if the one electron in the outermost shell of sodium jumps across to the chlorine atom. It does this. The sodium atom now has a new outermost shell containing eight electrons, and the chlorine atom also now has eight electrons in its outermost shell. Both atoms have attained "stability," in that there will be no further exchange of electrons.

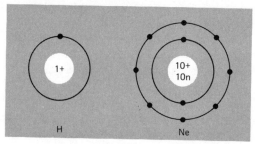

Fig. 3.2: Diagrammatic representation of the hydrogen (H) and the neon (Ne) atoms. For chemical and electrical equilibrium, an atom must have as many electrons (−) as protons (+). The number of neutrons (n) may vary, resulting in *isotopes* of a given element.

The atoms, however, are now electrically charged. The sodium atom has lost an electron and is now charged positively (+). The chlorine atom has gained an electron and is now charged negatively (−). Both atoms are now *ions*, that is, electrically charged atoms. Since oppositely charged particles attract each other, the ion of sodium joins with the ion of chlorine and the result is sodium chloride, or common table salt. Most inorganic compounds are formed by such "ionic bondage."

With that as a background, let us now consider what happens when molten rock crystallizes. Suppose that we heat some sodium chloride to a temperature where the sodium chloride becomes completely molten, which means that the sodium and chlorine ions have separated from each other because they have been literally wrenched apart by the movement imparted to each ion by heat. As long as we keep applying sufficient heat to the molten material, the ions of sodium and chlorine will be kept moving around so rapidly they will not be able to bond together by electrical attraction. Imagine, though, that we now remove the source of heat. As the molten material cools, the movement of the ions becomes less and less until, finally, the electrical attraction between the ions begins to appreciably affect the motion of the ions. In answer to this growing control, the ions jockey into position while the solution is still completely liquid, the solution then becomes "mushy" as crystals start to take form, and finally crystallization as a solid takes place. Most minerals are crystallized from molten rock solutions in much the same way in nature except that, in the usual molten rock solution, different minerals usually crystallize at different times. These crystals will then tend to sink, rise, or remain in the same place in the solution depending upon several factors including the specific gravities and the viscosities involved.

Methods of Crystallization

The rockhound who finds a good mineral specimen in the field may understandably not be too concerned about the origin of the specimen. On the other hand, there is nothing quite like finding a good specimen and being able to mentally reconstruct the history of the specimen, from its birth (often millions of years ago) to its discovery. Also, an understanding of the various methods of crystallization is basic to understanding why certain minerals are found in certain rocks and rock structures, etc. Conversely, such an understanding will greatly help the rockhound who is searching for a particular mineral since in knowing how that mineral crystallizes, the possible areas of logical search are greatly reduced.

Crystallization Due to Evaporation. Some minerals dissolve easily in water and upon evaporation may form as a crust on, say, the bed of a "dry" lake. Borax is such a mineral.

Crystallization From Hydrothermal Solutions. The last great stage in the underground cooling of *magma*, or molten rock, includes the release of *hydrothermal solutions* from the magma. These essentially hot-water solutions often carry metallic and other elements in solution into the surrounding rock. Here, deposition in solid form takes place because of reduction of both pressure and temperature, and chemical reaction with the wall rock. Of interest to the rockhound is that hydrothermal solutions also find their way into cracks and fissures to form *pegmatite dikes* (see Chapter 6). Gemstones found in pegmatite dikes include beryl, aquamarine, topaz, tourmaline, ruby, smoky quartz, and sometimes emerald.

Crystallization From the Gaseous State. Some elements can exist in gaseous form; thus, minerals such as sulfur and some iron minerals are often found deposited around volcanic vents. Of much more importance to the rockhound, however, is the fact that gases play an important part in the formation of some of the larger crystals of gemstones in pegmatite dikes and in some cavities (see Chapter 6).

Crystallization From the Molten Condition. A major method of crystallization from the molten condition has already been described in this chapter under "Why Minerals Crystallize." It is worth pointing out, however, that settling of crystallized material in magma chambers has resulted in some of the world's most spectacular concentrations of heavy metals such as platinum and chromium.

Crystallization By Metamorphic Action. *Metamorphism,* that is, a change in rock structure, also commonly involves the formation of new minerals. *Muscovite,* the common light-colored mica, for example, is readily formed when rocks fairly close to the surface of the earth are subjected to certain types of stress. Metamorphic minerals can be formed in a number of ways, by heat, pressure, and chemically active fluids or by any combination of these, the three agents of metamorphism.

The Crystal Systems

Mineral identification often becomes a simple matter if a mineral specimen includes one or more well-formed crystals. There are six *crystal systems,* the *crystallographic axes* of each system being imaginary straight lines. There are six basic figures and it is convenient for our purpose to imagine that each crystallographic axis in a particular figure connects the centers of opposite faces of that figure. For example, one of these basic figures is the cube, and in the isometric, or cubic, system there are therefore three axes, all of equal length, and all at right angles to each other.

It must be emphasized that these basic figures are merely conveniences to help us in determining the crystal system to which a particular specimen belongs. Actually, many crystals look as if the "original" edges on a given basic figure have been wholly or in part beveled, the resulting edges then having been beveled, and so on. The lengths and

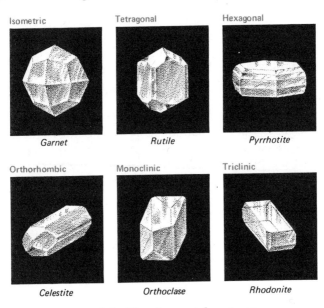

Fig. 3.3: The six crystal systems

directions of the crystallographic axes, however, remain the same as they were before this "beveling" occurred. The six crystal systems and their characteristics are shown in Fig. 3.3 and are described below:

1. Isometric system. The basic figure is a cube. There are three axes, all of the same length and all at right angles to each other.

2. Tetragonal system. The basic figure is a prism with four rectangular (but not square) sides, and two square bases. The crystal faces meet at right angles. The two horizontal axes are equal in length and the vertical axis is longer or shorter than the horizontal axes. (Butter and margarine are packaged in individual, tetragonal shapes.)

3. Hexagonal system. The basic figure is a six-sided prism with hexagonal bases. The sides meet the bases at right angles. There are four axes, three of these being in one plane and equal in length. The other axis is longer or shorter than the three co-planar axes and is perpendicular to them. (An unsharpened drawing pencil is an example of the basic figure of the hexagonal system.)

4. Orthorhombic system. The basic figure is a rectangular prism. The three axes are of different lengths and are all at right angles to each other. (This book, when closed and placed flat upon a table, could represent a basic figure whose vertical axis is shorter than either of the two horizontal axes.)

5. Monoclinic system. The basic figure has six faces, and three axes of unequal length. Two of the axes are at right angles with each other. The third axis is inclined to the plane of the two other axes. (The basic figure may be represented by placing a telephone directory on a table and then exerting a sliding pressure so that the binding edge is not vertical. In this position the non-horizontal axis of the thus-formed basic figure joins the centers of the covers and is non-vertical. This axis is perpendicular to one of the other axes but is inclined to the third axis.)

6. Triclinic system. The six faces of the basic figure are parallelograms. There are three axes of unequal length, all inclined to each other. This system can get rather involved but, fortunately, relatively few minerals crystallize in the triclinic system.

Twinning

Every now and then the rockhound will find a specimen which appears to be made up of two similar crystals which have apparently grown together as *twins*. The twins may seem to penetrate each other or they may be joined along a contact plane. In either case, the twins share a common region with each other and thus share a common atomic arrangement in this area. Twins do not therefore form in random manner but, rather, the angles at which they twin and penetrate each other are controlled by the atomic arrangement. Thus *staurolite* (see Fig. 3.4), a mineral which is commonly found twinned, usually occurs as twins in the form of either a cross or an X.

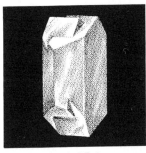 

Carlsbad Twin   Staurolite Twin

Fig. 3.4: Examples of twinning

Pseudomorphs

Pseudomorphs—minerals which have the crystal form of other minerals—are the impostors of the mineral world. These "false forms" may develop in several ways. A garnet, for example, may be altered to a mineral called *chlorite* but still retain the crystal shape of the garnet. Other types of pseudomorphs are formed by the original material of a crystal being replaced by an entirely different mineral, or by mineral material "coating" a crystal.

A *paramorph*, a type of pseudomorph, results when a mineral rearranges its atomic pattern with no change in composition or crystal form. The result is, of course, that there is now a new mineral in an already existent crystal shape, another of mineralogy's equivalents of "new wine in old bottles."

Mineral Classification

Minerals can be classified in a number of ways but one particular method suits the purposes of the rockhound extremely well since the method is based upon the chemical and physical properties of minerals. The classes in this system follow:

1. Those elements which may occur alone as minerals. Examples: gold, silver, arsenic.

2. The sulfides. Example: pyrite, or iron sulfide, one type of fool's gold.

3. The oxides. Example: hematite, an iron oxide and the chief ore mineral of iron.

4. The halides. Example: halite, or sodium chloride, common table salt being sodium chloride.

5. The carbonates. Example: calcite, calcium carbonate, the constituent mineral of limestone.

6. The nitrates. Example: niter, or potassium nitrate, used in making explosives.

7. The borates. Example: borax, a compound of sodium, boron, and oxygen, with water.

8. The sulfates. Example: gypsum, or calcium sulfate plus water, used in making plaster of Paris, wallboard, etc.

9. The phosphates. Example: apatite, a common rock-forming mineral and the mineral which represents the hardness of five on the Mohs hardness scale.

10. The arsenates and vanadates. Example 1: mimetite, a lead-chlorine arsenate, sometimes used as an ore mineral of lead but rarely as an ore mineral of arsenic. Example 2: vanadinite, a lead-chlorine vanadate, sometimes an ore mineral of vanadium.

11. The tungstates, molybdates, and uranates. Example 1: scheelite, calcium tungstate, a major ore of tungsten. Example 2: powellite, calcium molybdate, an end member of the calcium tungstate-calcium molybdate series. Example 3: carnotite, a bright yellow ore mineral of uranium, a uranate.

12. The silicates. Example: orthoclase (feldspar), a potassium aluminum silicate and a common rock-forming mineral.

Chapter 4

How to Identify Minerals in the Field

A good crystal is often just about all that is needed to identify a mineral but this happy state of affairs does not occur as often as it might for the average rockhound. The crystal shapes of specimens, or on specimens, found in the field are commonly far from perfect and there are many times when any recognizable crystal form in a specimen is entirely lacking. There are, however, physical tests and other observations which can be made upon a mineral specimen. These tests and observations are quickly and easily made in the field, and their results, more or less mechanically analyzed by a set of determinative tables such as appear in Chapter 16, will usually lead to a quick identification of most of the minerals that the average rockhound is liable to find. The use of the determinative tables is explained just before the appearance of the tables themselves, in Chapter 16.

Suggested Equipment for Field Tests

The following items are suggested for the physical testing of mineral specimens in the field:

1. pocket magnifying glass
2. knife (such as a pocket-knife)
3. copper penny (shiny)
4. small, hard-steel file
5. small piece of quartz
6. small piece of unglazed porcelain
7. small bottle of hydrochloric acid

The pocket magnifying glass is for studying characteristics such as mineral habit and crystal form. The knife, penny, file, and quartz are used for testing *hardness,* as will

45

be explained later in this chapter, and the piece of unglazed porcelain is for testing the *streak* of minerals. The small bottle of hydrochloric acid is used for a chemical test rather than for a physical test, of course, and constitutes a quick and effective way of determining, in most cases, whether a specimen is a carbonate of some kind. Most carbonate minerals which will be found will effervesce, that is, show a distinct bubbling action when a little hydrochloric acid is dropped upon them.

Mineral Habit

If a particular mineral is found to occur time after time in the form of, say, a radiating cluster of needle-like crystals, we say that this is a *habit* of this particular mineral. If another mineral typically occurs as a kidney-shaped mass, this is a habit of that particular mineral. Thus we have *mineral habit,* an extremely important aid in the identification of many minerals, especially when the crystal system of a specimen found in the field cannot be determined by inspection.

Mineral habit and human habit are alike in that both are affected by environment and heredity. The "heredity" of a mineral is, of course, its unique atomic structure while its "environment" refers to the conditions prevailing when a particular specimen of that mineral crystallized. A mineral which solidifies in a cavity obviously has a better chance to form good crystals than does the same mineral solidifying under more cramped conditions, and in this latter case the mineral may solidify, as sometimes happens, into a rather peculiar looking mass in which no crystals at all can be seen. In either case, crystals or mass, the mineral has assumed its habit for given conditions.

As there are a number of mineral habits, there are a number of names to describe these habits. Some minerals typically occur as a crust composed of crystals which may be of any size, from very small to large. Such a crust is called a *druse* and the surface is said to be a *drusy surface* (see Fig. 4.1).

The term *acicular* is used to describe needle-like crystals, such as those of rutile seen in *rutilated quartz,* while asbestos has a *fibrous* habit. In some minerals, the fibers tend to curl and the habit is therefore called *hairlike.* Incidentally, probably not many people realize that the fibers of minerals such as asbestos are in reality pieces or combinations of long, thin crystals.

Strangely enough, some minerals occur as thin crystals so tightly packed together that the resulting surface of the mass is smooth to the touch, and rounded. Rounded masses vary in size, depending upon the numbers and sizes of

Fig. 4.1: Small crystals of barite (*left,* dark) are perched on, or form a *druse* on, a cleavage surface of coarse calcite. *Drusy* is one kind of mineral habit. Cleavage surfaces represent directions of relative weakness in atomic bonding. This sample came from a mine in the state of Washington. (Photo by M. G. Dings, U.S. Geological Survey)

crystals and grains, and their positions, and may therefore be *botryoidal* (looking like a cluster of grapes), *reniform* (kidney-like), or *mammillary.*

Some minerals often crystallize in a geometric, criss cross pattern, or lattice work, of crystals and are said to thus occur in a *reticulated* habit. Whereas eye-catching reticulation is characteristic of only a few minerals, a seeming antithesis to reticulation, the solid-appearing *tabular* habit, is common, for example, in the micas. The statement, often seen in texts, that mica and some other similar minerals "commonly occur in tabular form" means that these minerals are commonly found in tablet-shaped (flat and relatively thin) masses.

Minerals which, like mica, occur in sheets or leaves which can be separated are *foliated* and, if the leaves are very thin, the term *micaceous* is sometimes used. A tree-like crystal pattern such as occurs in some agates (landscape agates, for example) is a *dendritic* pattern. A mineral which seems to be in the form of grains is *granular* while mineral material which is so firmly packed together that grains are not evident is said to be *massive*.

Other Physical Characteristics of Minerals

Minerals possess a number of physical characteristics which, in addition to the characteristic of mineral habit are used in the identification of minerals. Some of these other characteristics are, as in the case of mineral habit, determined by inspection. Others are determined by simple tests carried out upon a specimen.

Luster. Reflected light affects the appearances of the surfaces of some minerals in different ways, thus some minerals have different *lusters* than others. The luster of a mineral may be *metallic, submetallic,* or *nonmetallic.* Most minerals can be recognized as having either a metallic or nonmetallic luster, but once in a while along comes a specimen which seems to have some sort of an intermediate, or submetallic, luster. Few minerals actually do have a submetallic luster, which is just as well as it is difficult to describe a submetallic luster and even to remember what it looks like unless the rockhound encounters it a number of times.

There are several varieties of nonmetallic luster. Asbestos and some other fibrous minerals often have a *silky* luster while minerals like talc which demonstrate a good cleavage very often show a *pearly* luster. Some minerals, an example being sphalerite (zinc sulfide), have a characteristic *resin-*

ous luster. Milky quartz often has a *greasy* luster, as do some other minerals, while regular quartz usually has a *vitreous,* or glassy, luster. Many other minerals, tourmaline for example, also have vitreous lusters. A luster like that of a diamond is an *adamantine* luster.

Color. The color of a mineral depends not only upon the basic atomic structure and composition of the mineral, but also upon impurities which have nothing to do with the formal structure and composition of the mineral per se. Specimens of a given mineral which has a metallic or a submetallic luster usually have just about the same color; thus color is an important and easily applied aid in identifying such minerals. Care must be taken, however, to determine the color of such minerals, that is, those having metallic and submetallic lusters, on a freshly broken surface as some minerals possessing these lusters often tarnish, and quickly at that.

Whereas the color of different specimens of the same mineral having a metallic or submetallic luster tends to be the same, the color of a given mineral having a nonmetallic luster often varies widely—sometimes even wildly—from specimen to specimen. A classic example is quartz, which occurs in almost any hue. Some minerals with nonmetallic luster even show changes of color within one particular specimen. Some tourmaline, for instance, abruptly changes color near one end of a crystal, the colors often involved being green and red.

Some minerals exhibit "opalescence," a brilliant play of colors due to interference of light as it is reflected from the surface of the mineral and from layers immediately below the surface. Similar play of color due to this "thin film effect" can be seen in soap bubble films, oil spots on pavements, and so forth.

The play of colors seen in some minerals such as labradorite (see Chapter 11) is apparently due to the presence of twinning planes which cause light interference. A similar effect may be seen by sighting along the face of a 33⅓ rpm record toward a light and moving the record slightly up and down until the play of color is seen.

An interesting fact concerning the color of minerals is

that a number of minerals having nonmetallic luster, and this includes many gemstones, change color upon being heated to certain temperatures and many retain the new color permanently. This is how, for example, quartz suddenly becomes some kind of "topaz" and, unfortunately, is then often sold as topaz. A few minerals even change color when sufficient pressure is skilfully applied to a specimen.

Cleavage. As the constituent atoms of a given mineral are arranged in a unique and orderly fashion it would seem logical to expect that the mineral would become "unglued" in a limited number of orderly ways. Suppose, as an example, that we strike a crystal of calcite a sharp blow with a hammer. Now, if calcite has an atomic pattern such that the bonding force between its atoms is appreciably stronger in some directions than in others we would expect the calcite to break in the directions of relative weakness, and such breaking along theoretically flat, smooth planes is called *cleavage*. In some minerals, however, the relative strengths of the atomic bonding in different directions is such that these minerals demonstrate poor cleavage or no cleavage at all. In setting up determinative tables such as those in Chapter 16, then, we can establish two main categories concerning cleavage: minerals which show good cleavage, and minerals which show no prominent cleavage. Thus, by noting the cleavage characteristics of a mineral, we have greatly narrowed down the search for that mineral's identity.

Fracture. A number of minerals, rather than cleaving, will *fracture*, the difference being that where cleavage is a controlled break, fracture is a random break which as often as not will break across rather than always with the atomic pattern. A shell-like, or *conchoidal*, fracture is characteristic of many glassy-appearing minerals, quartz being an example (see Fig. 4.2). On the other hand, the fracture of a mineral such as hematite (an ore mineral of iron) may be either conchoidal, *uneven*, or *earthy*. An *irregular* fracture is the same as an uneven fracture. A fracture which is rough and sharp like that of some metals is *hackly*. Knowing the kind of fracture possessed by a specimen can be a big aid in the determination of the identity of the specimen as "fracture" is an important item in determinative tables.

Fig. 4.2: An Indian artifact made of flint. Flint, quartz, and many other minerals exhibit *conchoidal fracture*, well illustrated by this specimen. (Courtesy of North Dakota Travel Department)

Hardness. One and one-half centuries ago, in 1822, a German mineralogist named Frederick Mohs originated a scale by which the relative hardnesses of minerals could be used as an aid in mineral identification. The Mohs hardness scale is as follows:

1. talc	6. feldspar (orthoclase)
2. gypsum	7. quartz
3. calcite	8. topaz
4. fluorite	9. corundum
5. apatite	10. diamond

A mineral of a given hardness can scratch all minerals of lesser hardness. For example, suppose that a rockhound finds a mineral which can scratch quartz and can be scratched by topaz. The mineral must have a hardness of somewhere between seven and eight. The scratch-hardness test is based upon the use of smooth surfaces, a point which should be noted since the grains on a rough surface can be crushed by the pressure of a point of sufficient hardness and thus form a false scratch.

The hardness scale is somewhat misleading as it would appear by inspection that, for example, diamond is as much harder than corundum as corundum is harder than topaz. Actually, corundum can be much more easily scratched by diamond than can topaz by corundum. Other, but minor, departures from proportionality between numbers and hardnesses on the scale exist throughout the scale.

Due to their particular atomic arrangements, a few minerals have a different hardness in one direction than in another direction. An example of a mineral which shows this characteristic is kyanite, an aluminum silicate which is used as a refractory and also is often of good gem quality. The hardness of kyanite in the direction of its longest crystallographic axis is 5 but its hardness across the long axis is 7.

Although the hardnesses of minerals may be approximately determined by a set of minerals from the Mohs scale, many rockhounds make up their own inexpensive set of hardness "points" as indicated near the beginning of this chapter. Finger nails have a hardness of about 2½, a copper penny a hardness of approximately 3, a steel knife a hardness of just about 5½, depending upon the steel, a hard steel file a hardness of approximately 6½, a piece of quartz a hardness of 7, and a piece of carborundum has a hardness of 9. Other than finger nails, the rockhound has some choice as to how many of these items he will bring along with him but, as previously indicated, the penny, the knife, the file, and a piece of quartz will see frequent use.

How to Make Hardness Tests. There are several procedures to follow in making a hardness test, the first being to observe the obvious precaution of not marring a good specimen by a disfiguring scratch. Another point is that in determining the hardness of a mineral, the mineral should be tested in several directions in the event that the mineral, like the already mentioned kyanite, has more than one hardness. Next, hardness should always be tested on an unaltered surface as the hardness on a weathered surface can easily be several points below the true hardness as determined for the unaltered mineral. The next precaution has already been mentioned: test for hardness on a smooth, not a rough, surface. Finally, be sure that the mineral which is apparently scratched during a hardness test is actually scratched, and that the apparent scratch is not just a streak of crushed mineral material or a metallic streak from a penny, file, or a knife point. Although these procedures and precautions are logical and simple, the hardness test is often incorrectly performed, and one wonders just how many potentially interesting and possibly valuable discoveries have been summarily rejected by an incorrectly conducted hardness test!

Tenacity. Because of differing internal structures and compositions, minerals demonstrate several types and degrees of *tenacity,* or firmness in holding together when subjected to certain tests. If a mineral has a number of planes along which slippage can easily take place, the mineral will usually flatten beneath a blow and is thus said to be *malleable.* Gold is an example of a malleable mineral.

Some minerals are extremely *brittle* and literally fly to pieces when struck with, say, a hammer, or when a small piece of the mineral is pressed against a hard surface with something like the flat of a knife blade. A *ductile* material is one which can be drawn out into the shape of a wire, and a *sectile* mineral can be cut with a sharp knife. A *flexible* mineral can be bent without breaking. An *elastic* mineral can also be bent without breaking but an elastic mineral can also return to its original shape once the deforming force is removed, a property which is not implied in the word "flexible."

Streak. Many different minerals having metallic or submetallic lusters appear to have much the same color but the *streaks* of such minerals are often very different. The streak of a mineral is obtained by rubbing the mineral on a *streak plate,* a piece of white, unglazed porcelain. Some kinds of unglazed bathroom tile make good streak plates.

Streak is an important aid in mineral identification, especially where metallic and submetallic lusters are involved, and streak by itself is sometimes enough to identify a mineral. Hematite, for example, an ore of iron, sometimes forms black crystals but such crystals are relatively rare and not too many rockhounds would immediately recognize them as being hematite. The tell tale red streak always given by hematite, however, is usually enough to solve the mystery.

What really happens during the streak test, of course, is that the part of the mineral rubbed against the streak plate is powdered during the operation, and the streak is therefore a long, thin line composed of powdered mineral. Minerals having hardnesses greater than that of the streak plate will leave no streak at all. In general, such minerals have a nonmetallic luster. Minerals having nonmetallic lusters and whose hardnesses are less than the hardness of the streak plate usually have a white or nearly white streak.

Translucency. Some minerals are *translucent* in that at least some light passes through them, and some minerals are *transparent*, like transparent glass. A truly *opaque* mineral allows the passage of no light at all.

Specific Gravity. When we say that the specific gravity of a mineral is 2.7 we mean that a given volume of that mineral is 2.7 times the weight of an equivalent volume of water. The specific gravity of a mineral may be determined by weighing a sample of the mineral in air and then in water, being very careful in the latter operation that no bubbles of air are clinging to the sample. The specific gravity may then be calculated by this equation:

$$\text{specific gravity} = \frac{\text{weight in air}}{(\text{weight in air}) - (\text{weight in water})}$$

Knowing the specific gravity of a mineral is very helpful in identifying the mineral, but it has no doubt already occurred to the reader that beam balances, etc., are not standard items of field equipment, because of their size. Most rockhounds, however, after some experience with specimens of different sizes and specific gravities, are able to closely estimate the specific gravity by "hefting" a specimen, that is, by holding the specimen in the hand and moving the hand up and down a few times. At the same time the rockhound is "sizing up" the specimen by eye, noting its volume and anything else important, such as the amount of matrix rock around or attached to the specimen. The process probably seems highly unscientific to those who have not developed this skill, but it works and works well.

The Relationship Between Specific Gravity and Density. The specific gravity of a substance is expressed in numbers without attached units, but the *density* of a substance is expressed in terms of weight per unit volume. As an example, the average specific gravity of rocks near the earth's surface is 2.7. To find the density of these rocks, we multiply 2.7 by the weight of one cubic foot of fresh water, that is, 2.7 $\times$ 62.4 = 170 pounds per cubic foot.

Thus, one cubic foot of average crustal rock weighs approximately 170 pounds (the "170" is of course approximate and not exact), and we can say that the density of crustal rocks is 170 pounds per cubic foot. If we wished, we could also express the density in terms of pounds per cubic inch, grams per cubic centimeter, and so forth.

In the above example, we knew the specific gravity of a substance and calculated its density. Suppose that we already know the density of a substance and want to know its specific gravity. For example, the density of a certain type of rock is 187.2 pounds per cubic foot. The specific gravity of that rock is found by dividing "187.2 pounds per cubic foot" by "62.4 pounds per cubic foot." Notice that the units disappear, leaving "3.00" as the specific gravity of that kind of rock.

Fluorescence and Phosphorescence. Several kinds of radiation, including ultraviolet radiation, have the capability of displacing the electrons in certain minerals so that these minerals glow with visible light as the electrons return to their original orbits. If the glow ceases as soon as the irradiation of the mineral is stopped, the mineral is *fluorescent*. If the glow disappears gradually, the mineral is *phosphorescent*. Ultraviolet lights are used in prospecting for some ore minerals, and displays of fluorescent and phosphorescent minerals are striking features in many mineralogy museums.

Thermoluminescence and Triboluminescence. The variety of fluorite known as *chlorophane* will commonly glow with a green light (best seen in complete darkness) upon the application of heat. Minerals which glow upon the application of heat are said to be *thermoluminescent*. Some minerals will "flash" with light when stroked or hit with a metal point and some, milky quartz for example, will often emit flashes of light (again, best seen in complete darkness) if two pieces of the mineral are briskly rubbed against each other. The phenomenon of emitting light upon stroking, hitting, or rubbing is called *triboluminescence*.

Magnetism and Electricity. Whether you find any gold (see Chapter 7) on a particular field trip, save the black sand from the riffles of the sluice box and the bottom of the gold pan. Let the sand dry and it will be found that this sand is strongly attracted to magnets and to most steel knife blades. Also, when sprinkled over a paper (white, preferably), the sand will arrange itself to outline the force field of the magnet. Any mineral which is attracted to magnets is said to be *magnetic*.

Pyroelectricity results when some minerals are heated. When a crystal of tourmaline is heated, for example, the crystal develops a positive electrical charge on one end and a negative charge on the other. It is sometimes possible to develop these charges by merely leaving a crystal of tourmaline in the sun. That the charge actually exists can be shown by picking up small bits of paper, etc., with the crystal.

Some minerals demonstrate the property of *piezoelectricity*, the development of oppositely charged poles in a crystal by the application of pressure. Tourmaline exhibits this characteristic also, and an interesting application of this phenomenon is described in Chapter 9, at the beginning of that chapter.

Radioactivity. Some minerals are *radioactive*, that is, their individual atoms are breaking up as evidenced by the emission of alpha, beta, and gamma radiation. Such minerals can be best found in the field by using instruments such as various forms of Geiger counters, scintillometers, etc. Incidentally, if you want to add a sample of uranium-bearing rock to your collection, just go outside and pick up any rock. You now have a sample which you can truthfully label as "uranium-bearing rock" because all rocks found on earth contain at least some uranium. If a sample has an appreciably high enough content of uranium, however, the presence of uranium can be established by a simple test outlined in the next chapter, Chapter 5.

A Word About Testing

If you find a specimen which you want to keep but cannot immediately identify, above all don't ruin the specimen by destructive or disfiguring tests and thus become long on knowledge but short on anything attractive to show for your work. If you find such a specimen and you suspect that it could easily be marred or broken while you are trying to identify it, wrap it up carefully and have an expert identify it later. In the meantime, put it in your collection and enjoy it in the same condition in which it was formed millions of years ago, or at least in the condition in which you found it.

Chapter 5

Mineral Identification by Blowpipe

Every now and then, mineral specimens are found which, according to the information in determinative tables such as those in Chapter 16, might be any one of two or three different minerals. At other times, the rockhound might be collecting in a region where he may wish to know if a particular sample of rock contains a metal such as, say, gold, silver, lead, or copper. In such cases of mineral identification or analysis, the *blowpipe* will usually and quickly settle the problem.

In addition to its use in the field, many rockhounds know *blowpipe analysis* to be an extremely fascinating facet of the rockhounding hobby, to be engaged in at almost any time. Many rockhounds spend many pleasant hours at home, or in mineralogy clubs, rockhound clubs, evening classes, etc., with the blowpipe, testing and identifying specimens which they found on the previous weekend or during the past summer. One of the most amazing things about blowpipe analysis is that all of the supplies and equipment needed for a very efficient laboratory can be put into a container about the size of a shoe box.

Blowpipe Equipment and Supplies

The blowpipe is merely a tube, usually from seven to ten inches long, which tapers to a curved, smaller end (see Fig. 5.1). The smaller end of the blowpipe is inserted in a small flame, and a blast of air through the blowpipe affects the flame in two ways: (1) the flame is bent into a direction in which it can be conveniently used, and (2) the heat of the flame is greatly increased. A third fact that the flame is thus also made longer is of no direct importance in our work in itself.

The flame used for blowpipe work may be that of a Bunsen burner, an alcohol lamp, or a candle, although better results are usually obtained by the beginner from either a Bunsen burner or an alcohol lamp. When in the field, the gas for a Bunsen burner may be conveniently obtained from disposable cylinders of gas made expressly for campers. *Forceps* or *tweezers* with, preferably, stainless steel or similar tips, are needed to pick up small pieces of minerals to be tested and to hold these pieces in the flame for fusion and flame coloration tests.

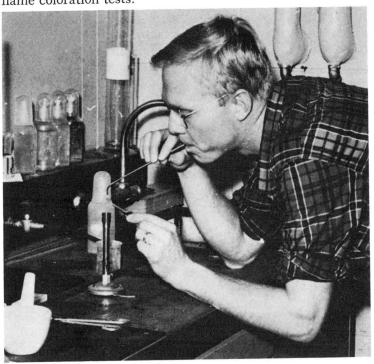

Fig. 5.1: Geologist operating a blowpipe. Blowpipes are used in mineral analysis and identification. (Photo by W. C. Walker, U.S. Geological Survey)

For some tests the mineral is crushed or powdered and then placed upon a *charcoal block* where it is then heated by the blowpipe flame. Charcoal blocks for this purpose are sold by mineralogical supply houses, and although any good, non-decrepitating charcoal may be used, the purchase of several "professional" blocks is recommended.

Platinum wire is required for flame coloration and borax bead tests, and two three-inch lengths of wire are suggested. A handle may be attached to each wire by fusing the end of a small glass tube, about four inches long and one-fourth of an inch in diameter, over one end of the wire. One wire should be used only for flame tests, and the other for bead tests. These tests will be explained later in this chapter.

Upon being heated by the blowpipe flame, some minerals become magnetic, hence a small *magnet* (or a knife whose blade is magnetized, or a magnetized screwdriver, etc.) will be needed to test for magnetism. If a magnet is to be purchased, the horseshoe magnets often sold in toy stores for about twenty-five cents will be satisfactory.

A *pestle* and *mortar* of some kind are needed for crushing mineral samples. One of the easiest and least expensive ways to meet this requirement is to use, for the mortar, a steel pipe cap of the type used in plumbing. For the pestle, a short piece of pipe can be used onto which has been screwed a smaller pipe cap. This solution is not only financially painless, but it has the further advantage that different arrangements of pestles and mortars can be used for different situations. For example, for brittle, hard minerals, the grinding head of the pestle can be just slightly smaller than the interior diameter of the pipe cap used for the mortar, in order that an appreciable portion of the sample does not fly out of the mortar.

The *reagents* used in blowpipe work are to some extent a matter of individual preference, but *borax* and *sodium carbonate* are basic. As these are used in dry form, they may be kept in either glass or cardboard containers. The most important wet reagents are *hydrochloric acid* and *nitric acid,* and these acids should always be kept in tightly stoppered glass bottles, the stoppers also being made of glass. It is very desirable that the bottles also be equipped with glass dropping-tubes with bulbs. Any reagents should be plainly marked, on their containers, with their correct names.

The list of reagents may be added to as the rockhound wishes, but the equipment and supplies already described will be found sufficient to perform qualitative tests on almost any mineral which the rockhound is liable to find with the exceptions, of course, of infusible oxides and silicates. In these cases, however, the identities can usually be established by the use of determinative tables (see Chapter 16). For convenience, the list of equipment and supplies already discussed is given below:

Equipment and Supplies for Blowpipe Analysis

Blowpipe
Bunsen burner, alcohol
   lamp, or candle
Forceps or tweezers
Charcoal blocks
Platinum wire

Mortar and pestle
Magnet
Borax
Sodium carbonate
Hydrochloric acid
Nitric acid

How to Use the Blowpipe

Fig. 5.2 shows why one part of the flame is called the *reducing flame* and another part is called the *oxidizing flame*. The oxidizing flame is the hotter of the two flames. Essentially, the reducing flame is the almost invisible inner portion of the flame, and it is due to this inner position that combustion in this part of the flame is incomplete. Thus, the reducing flame will act to take oxygen from oxidized substances. The outer portion of the flame, however, literally and figuratively has oxygen to burn, and a substance placed in this part of the flame will tend to take on oxygen. The points of maximum oxidation and reduction are shown in Fig. 5.2, and substances which are to be either oxidized or reduced should be held in the flame in the places indicated in the figure.

For a good oxidizing flame, the tip of the blowpipe should be just inside the whole flame. For a good reducing flame, the tip should be just outside the flame. To maintain a steady blast of air indefinitely, it is necessary to keep a constant supply of air in the mouth and to breathe in through the nose while blowing through the blowpipe. Many readers who at this point may try out this procedure by blowing out through pursed lips while at the same time trying to breathe in through their nose might conclude that the whole thing is impossible. The secret, however, is to keep the checks pressing in on the air in the mouth as air is breathed in through the nose. This can be done by deliberately distending the cheeks. Most people can learn this knack after some practice, but some who apparently never do learn it, settle for taking as deep a breath as possible and hoping that something significant in the way of a reaction will happen before they run out of breath. Some of these rockhounds, however, admit that they are apparently able to see reactions even when there aren't any, after such an eye-popping blast. All in all, it is well worth the time to learn how to maintain a steady flame for an indefinite period of time.

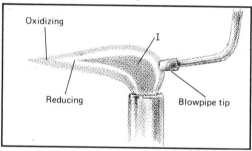

Fig. 5.2: Blowpipe flame. I is the inner blue cone, R is the reducing flame, and O is the oxidizing flame. Mineral fragments to be oxidized or reduced should be held at the proper places indicated.

Blowpipe Tests and Mineral Identification

Books on determinative mineralogy, and some determinative tables, include descriptions of the reactions of pertinent minerals during one or more blowpipe tests. For example, some minerals melt more easily than do others and minerals therefore exhibit varying degrees of *fusibility*. Some minerals will color a flame distinctively in *flame coloration* tests, and some minerals will distinctively color beads of fused borax in *borax bead* tests. By means of simple *charcoal block tests*, samples of many metallic minerals can be reduced to little buttons of metal which are easily identified.

Other charcoal block tests cover part of the charcoal block with coatings, or *sublimates,* whose colors and positions on the block are often all that is needed to identify the chief elements in a number of minerals. Under the blowpipe flame, some minerals *swell, decrepitate,* seem to *bubble,* or just *glow.* All of these phenomena are important as is a possible characteristic *odor.* As an example of the latter, an arsenic mineral usually gives off a strong garlic-like odor when roasted in the blowpipe flame. This same odor, incidentally, can be obtained in the field with minerals such as arsenopyrite by smartly hitting an edge of the sample with a knife blade or file, etc., as if trying to make a spark, and then quickly smelling the specimen.

Effervescence. Although not properly a blowpipe test as such, *effervescence,* a bubbling action, is characteristic of the carbonates when tested by dropping a small amount of hydrochloric acid onto a sample. This is an extremely easy test to perform, of course, and it should always be one of the first tests made.

Fusibility Tests. Whether a given mineral is "easily fusible," or "fusible with difficulty," or "infusible," (terms used in determinative descriptions of minerals), often considerably narrows down the various possibilities of mineral identity. The test for fusibility is done by holding a small splinter of the mineral in the blowpipe flame, using tweezers, or by placing a sample of the mineral on a charcoal block and then heating the sample with the blowpipe flame. If the mineral to be tested for fusibility could be a sulfide, it is in general a good idea to use the charcoal block rather than the tweezers. The reason for this is that many sulfides, in addition to fusing readily, give off characteristic fumes and thus may also deposit characteristic coatings on the charcoal.

It is important to know that the fusibility of a particular specimen depends not only upon the composition of the mineral but also upon the size and shape of the piece being tested. Therefore, small, thin fragments should be used and such conclusions as "fusible with difficulty" should be based upon the rounding of a thin edge of the fragment when subjected to the blowpipe flame.

Some minerals will *decrepitate,* that is, tend to fly into

pieces in the flame and if this happens some of the sample can be powdered and placed in a small, shallow depression at one end of the charcoal block. A depression of convenient size can be made by holding a coin edgewise against the face of the charcoal and then rotating the coin while pressing it down against the block. The powder should be carefully heated with the blowpipe flame, to try to get it into one single mass. If the powder blows away under the blast, it can be moistened with water (saliva is even better) to hold it together until the powder forms a sort of a crustlike mass which can then be held by tweezers in the blowpipe flame, for the fusibility test.

The method described above of powdering a mineral and then placing it in a shallow depression in the charcoal block, with moistening of the powder whenever needed, is also more or less standard procedure for the sublimate test, to be described later in this chapter.

Flame Coloration Tests. In some cases, *flame coloration* tests can be made by directly applying the blowpipe flame to a splinter or a powder of the mineral being tested. It is also sometimes possible to color the unaltered flame, that is, without benefit of blowpipe, by holding a splinter of mineral in the flame. If such tests do not give a noticeable flame coloration, however, this does not necessarily mean that a particular mineral does not have a distinctive flame coloration effect. It is therefore good practice to first powder a sample of the mineral and then moisten the powder with acid. Once the powder is moistened with acid, the blowpipe flame may be directed against it, and any flame coloration noted.

The easiest way to perform the test, however, is to dip about one inch of platinum wire into the moistened powder so that some grains of wet powder cling to the wire. The wire is then brought into contact with the almost invisible edge of, say, an alcohol lamp flame. Some minerals will thereupon color that part of the flame for a time which may vary from that of a flash to a rather lengthy time of coloration. Either a Bunsen burner or an alcohol lamp is recommended, as a candle commonly burns with a yellowish flame, and this color is capable of masking colors, especially those of short duration. A few grains moistened with hydrochloric acid may be tested first and then, if there is no coloration, repeat the test with grains moistened with sulfuric acid.

If it is at all possible that the sample contains arsenic, it should be first powdered and then roasted in the oxidizing and then in the reducing flame, before using the platinum wire. This process should be carefully repeated several times, being especially careful not to fuse the sample. Unless all the arsenic is thus removed, the arsenic will react with the platinum wire and make the wire extremely brittle. If the mineral contains sodium, the yellow color of the sodium flame is pervading and very persistent and can mask the flame colorations due to other elements. In such a case, if the only color evident is the yellow color of sodium, other tests, such as a borax bead test, should be made. The following table describes the colors imparted to a flame by some elements and phosphates.

Flame Colorations

Color	Element
scarlet	strontium
bright red	lithium
yellow red	calcium
yellow	sodium
yellow green	barium
green	boron
emerald green	copper
bluish green	phosphates
greenish blue	antimony
light blue	arsenic
violet	potassium

Borax Bead Tests. For the borax bead tests, use the platinum wire which is not used for the flame coloration tests, and shape the free end of the wire into a closed loop by wrapping the wire-end around a match or similar object. The mineral to be tested must be in powdered form and, again, if the presence of arsenic is possible, the powder should be roasted as previously explained.

To perform the borax bead test, the loop in the wire is

heated by the blowpipe flame and is immediately dipped into some borax. Some borax will stick to the loop which is then heated by the flame again until the borax on the loop is fused. The first few such fusions gradually build up to a bead by adding to a growing "skeleton" of borax clinging to the wire, and finally a bead of borax will fill the loop. The bead is heated and then placed in contact with the powdered mineral so that a few grains of the mineral cling to the bead. The bead is then heated in the *oxidizing* flame, allowed to cool, and its color noted. Then the bead is heated in the *reducing* flame, again allowed to cool, and its color noted again. Following is a list of borax bead colors associated with certain elements, each color being that of the bead when *cool.*

Borax Bead Test Colors

Oxidizing Flame Color	Reducing Flame Color	Element
green	green	chromium
blue	blue	cobalt
blue	opaque red brown	copper
yellow	pale green	iron
red violet	colorless	manganese
colorless to white	brown to dark brown	molybdenum
reddish brown	opaque gray	nickel
colorless to white	brown to brown violet	titanium
yellowish brown	green (bead is also fluorescent under ultraviolet light)	uranium
green	yellowish to green	vanadium

Tests for Sublimates and Metal Buttons

Some minerals, upon being blowpiped, give off characteristic fumes which collect on the charcoal block as *sublimates,* or coatings, of various colors. The test for sublimates can be made by placing a sample of powdered mineral in a shallow depression near one end of the charcoal block and then blowpiping the sample. Some minerals do not require powdering, fragments being satisfactory in these cases, but, in general, time can be saved by first powdering the mineral to be tested.

In testing for a sublimate, a metal button will sometimes form under the reducing flame, aided by the reducing effect of the glowing charcoal. Thus, some minerals will form a sublimate, some a metallic "button" (a small globule of metal), and some will form both. If no metal button is formed, add an amount of sodium carbonate at least equal to that of another powdered sample of the mineral, and try again to obtain a button with the reducing flame. Any metallic button thus obtained will be in or toward the center of the fused sodium carbonate. After cooling, the metal button and the sodium carbonate can be separated by hammering (carefully) on the entire mass after it is removed from the charcoal block. The following table lists the sublimates and buttons associated with certain metallic elements as they may occur in either pure or combined form, the latter of course being the most common form of mineral occurrence. A "volatile" sublimate is a sublimate which disappears under the reducing or oxidizing flame, as the case may be.

Sublimates and Buttons of Some Metals

Sublimates and/or Buttons	Metal
The sublimate is white and volatile and forms some distance away from the sample.	arsenic
The sublimate is white and volatile and close to the sample.	antimony
A yellow sublimate forms near the sample, and a white sublimate some distance from the sample.	bismuth
Button or other shape is formed when powdered mineral is heated with sodium carbonate. Button is malleable and turns from red to black as it oxidizes.	copper
Fuses easily and forms metal button.	gold
No sublimate and no button due to this element. Will not fuse but small pieces of minerals containing this element become magnetic after heating.	iron

Forms sublimates like those of bismuth. Also will usually give a metal button, even without using sodium carbonate. — lead

Forms a sublimate which is white yellow when hot and white when cold. Another sublimate may form as a reddish band near the sample. The white and white-yellow sublimates are volatile in the oxidizing flame and turn azure blue in the reducing flame. — molybdenum

Fragments will not fuse but upon heating in the reducing flame become weakly magnetic. — nickel

Forms a sublimate which is white and volatile. Reddish cast typically on outside of sublimate. Sublimate gives blue color to reducing flame. Fumes have strong odor, something like horse-radish. — selenium

Fuses into white button or some other form of pure metal which can be dissolved in nitric acid. Addition of hydrochloric acid to the solution makes a curdy, white precipitate. — silver

The sublimate formed is thick, white, and volatile. Sublimate gives blue-green color to reducing flame. — tellurium

The mineral cassiterite is fusible with difficulty on charcoal after thoroughly powdering and mixing with sodium carbonate. Forms very small particles of metal. — tin

Sublimate is formed if about twice as much sodium carbonate as powdered mineral is used. Sublimate is yellow when hot and white when cold. Sublimate turns green if moistened with cobalt nitrate and heated. — zinc

Chapter 6

How to Find Gemstones and Minerals

There is an old saying that people are known by the company they keep, and much the same thing can be said about minerals. As an example, some minerals are commonly found occurring together while other minerals almost never occur together. Even more important from the standpoint of the rockhound, a given mineral is usually associated with only one or two types of rock as far as good specimens are concerned, and even the mere ability to recognize a rock as being a particular one of only three major classes of rocks will almost infinitely increase the rockhound's competence in the field and his pleasure in the hobby. Any discussion of how to find gemstones and minerals therefore begins with an explanation of how to recognize the rocks in which these gemstones and minerals occur. Notice that the determinative tables in Chapter 16 include rock-type occurrences associated with various minerals and gemstones.

The Composition of Rocks

Any rock is solely or largely composed of minerals and most minerals are silicates, that is, some combination of silicon and oxygen with one or more of the metallic elements. Oxygen and silicon together comprise 74 percent of the weight of the earth's crust. In order of abundance, the metallic elements aluminum, iron, calcium, sodium, potassium, and magnesium furnish another 24 percent. Thus only eight elements are responsible for 98 percent of the weight of the earth's crust.

Even more astonishing, and because of the preponderance of silicates and the relatively large size of the oxygen ion, more than 90 percent of the volume of crustal rock is occupied by oxygen. Therefore, when we look at, say, a towering mountain range, nine-tenths of what we "see" is oxygen, the gas we breathe! Having thus cleared up at least 90 percent of any sense of mystery which may have been in the reader's mind concerning the makeup of rocks, we can now look at a few kinds of rocks, those in which, in general, the rockhound will look for gemstones and mineral specimens. There are three main kinds of rocks, *igneous, sedimentary*, and *metamorphic*.

Igneous Rocks

Molten rock material is called *magma* and magma is presumably formed at depths within fifty or so miles of the earth's surface, probably principally because of heat furnished by the radioactive decay of certain minerals in the earth's crust. Any magma contains gases. Probably due to a combination of gas pressure and pressure from the surrounding rock, magma makes its way upward through cracks and fissures, and sometimes even apparently forces itself into solid rock. If a magma forces its way to and onto the earth's surface, the magma is *extrusive* and is a *lava*. If the magma solidifies beneath the surface it is *intrusive*.

Classification of Igneous Rocks. There is a certain danger in classifying some rocks as either extrusive or intrusive since, for example, a magma which extrudes very slowly upon the surface will form just about the same type of rock as will a magma of similar composition which solidifies only a small distance beneath the surface. For this and other reasons, rock classification is commonly based upon composition and *texture*, that is, the appearance of the rock due to its granular structure.

Actually, the texture of an igneous rock is, in general, closely associated with where the magma cooled in relation to the surface. Grains and crystals which are forming in a magma which is solidifying at some depth below the surface of the earth will cool slowly and will therefore, in general, grow to relatively large size as compared to grains which grow in a magma closer to the surface. There is, of course, a more rapid heat loss near the surface and this means that grains and crystals will "freeze" while of intermediate or fine size. Thus, the classification of igneous rocks by texture not only allows us to more quickly identify a rock, it also more or less tells us where a particular rock was formed, in terms of distance from the surface.

A conclusion that coarseness of texture increases with depth of solidification is, in general, correct but other factors such as viscosity of a particular magma sometimes notably affect this general relationship. Also, some igneous rocks are made up of larger crystals, and sometimes pieces of rock, in a matrix of much smaller grain size. These rocks are also treated in the following discussion.

Composition and Occurrences of Igneous Rocks. It has probably already occurred to the reader that the texture of an igneous rock is not too easily seen, say from a car, while the color is usually evident. This leads us to the point that igneous rocks of the same color and chemical composition can have very different textures, depending upon whether they are essentially intrusive or extrusive rocks. Furthermore, a set of given rocks having different colors and different compositions, but with about the same general grain size, can all be essentially either extrusive or intrusive. This may seem to lead to all sorts of complications in the identification of igneous rocks, but it actually makes things very easy as, for example, in this arrangement of six major igneous rocks:

Rhyolite	**Andesite**	**Basalt**
Granite	**Diorite**	**Gabbro**

In the above arrangement, the two rocks in each vertical column have the same chemical composition and the same general characteristics of color. The rocks in the left-hand column are light-colored, those in the right-hand column are dark-colored, and those in the center column are intermediate in color. The three rocks in the top horizontal row are essentially "extrusive" in that they show a fine-grained groundmass, while the three rocks in the bottom row are "intrusive" at depth and show a coarse texture.

A wealth of information can be obtained from such a tabular arrangement of rock types. For example, granite is formed at depth but the same magma, solidifying on or near the surface of the earth, forms rhyolite. Diorite is formed at depth but the same magma forms andesite at or near the surface of the earth, and a similar relationship holds between gabbro and basalt.

The table can also be used in another way. Suppose that we want to know something about andesite, for example. We immediately see that andesite is the extrusive equivalent of diorite and is therefore fine-grained. The table also tells us that andesite is intermediate between being light-colored and dark-colored, and that its composition is somewhere between that of rhyolite and basalt. Therefore, if we know the composition of rhyolite and of basalt, we know the composition of the fine-grained minerals for which we will look in order to identify a rock as andesite. The compositions of these key igneous rocks will be presented later in this section.

Intrusive igneous rocks are commonly found in *sills, dikes,* and in deeper structures known as *batholiths,* the igneous rock being the main component part of these structures. Thus, *sills* are essentially tabular (tablet-shaped) masses of fairly fine-grained rock formed after magma forced its way between and parallel to layers of host rock, and solidified in that position. *Dikes* are tabular igneous rock formations which cut across the layering of the host rock (see Fig. 6.1). *Batholiths* are huge masses of intrusive igneous rock without a known floor and, supposedly, their magma, most of which later solidifies underground, furnishes the molten rock material for volcanos. In addition to being "reservoirs" for volcanos, batholiths are associated with many of the major mining regions of the world, many ore deposits occurring in the peripheral zones of batholiths. Batholiths can be of tremendous size as shown by the fact that the Sierra Nevada Mountains of California were in large part faulted out of a great batholith which is known to have a map-view area of at least 25,000 square miles. Most batholiths are composed of granite-like rocks.

It is evident that the texture of the rock formed near the

Fig. 6.1: A dike of igneous rock cutting sandstone (sedimentary rock) in New Mexico. (Photo by N. H. Darton, U.S. Geological Survey)

bottom of a great batholith will be much coarser than that of rock formed near the top of the batholith, but every now and then we find a rock with a texture which consists of coarser grains or crystals, or *phenocrysts,* in a groundmass composed of much finer grains. Such a texture is said to be *porphyritic,* and it can be caused by crystals forming at depth in a batholith or some other type of magma chamber or conduit, the crystals then being carried in still-molten magma to a position closer to the ground surface where the molten magma freezes with a finer texture. If the phenocrysts constitute at least 25 percent of the rock, the rock is a *porphyry.* Thus a granite in which phenocrysts form at least 25 percent of the volume of the rock is a *granite porphyry*.

Kinds of Igneous Rocks

Granite and Rhyolite. *Granite* (see Plate 1.A) is an intrusive rock and is composed of approximately 70 percent feldspar, 20 percent quartz, and 10 percent dark minerals. These dark minerals are *ferromagnesians*, minerals consisting principally of iron and magnesium. *Rhyolite* is the fine-grained equivalent of granite, that is, the magma which forms granite at depth would form rhyolite as an extrusive.

Basalt and Gabbro. *Basalt* (see Plate 1.B) is essentially extrusive, fine grained, and dark in color. Basalt consists of about 50 percent plagioclase feldspar (see Chapter 11) and 50 percent ferromagnesians. Common *traprock* is basalt. A magma which would form basalt would form *gabbro* as an intrusive rock. Gabbro is, of course, coarse-grained.

Andesite and Diorite. *Andesite* is extrusive and fine-grained and is intermediate between rhyolite and basalt in both composition and color. About 98 percent of the lavas are andesites and basalts of some kind. The intrusive equivalent of andesite is *diorite* (see Plate 1.C).

Peridotite. *Peridotite* is a coarse-grained intrusive rock which is something like a gabbro but contains less silica than does a gabbro. Peridotite is the host rock of diamonds and is mainly composed of the mineral *olivine*.

Pegmatite. *Pegmatite* (see Plate 1.D) is a very coarse-grained rock which is often found near the edges of large igneous intrusions. The chief minerals in pegmatite are feldspars and quartz, but rockhounds are interested in pegmatites chiefly because some pegmatites contain outstanding specimens of gem minerals such as tourmaline, beryl, topaz, and some varieties of spodumene. Tin minerals, zirconium minerals, and uranium minerals are also found in some pegmatites. Pegmatites commonly occur as dikes (see Fig. 6.2).

Other Igneous Rocks. (Obsidian.) We could, of course, set up other classes of igneous rocks in addition to those already discussed. For example, we could say that a rock which is intermediate in composition between a granite and a diorite is a *grano-diorite*. In general, however, most of the igneous

Fig. 6.2: A pegmatite dike cutting Precambrian gneiss in Colorado. (Photo by J. R. Stacy, U.S. Geological Survey)

rocks liable to be found by a rockhound can be placed in one of the categories already described.

Obsidian, however, usually puzzles the person who finds it for the first time. Also known as *volcanic glass* (see Plate

1.E), obsidian results when a granitic magma cools so rapidly that a non-crystalline, glassy structure results. This, of course, would normally happen only on or near the earth's surface. Although obsidian is usually dark in color, it has the same chemical composition as a granite and is translucent on a thin edge. Obsidian is discussed further in Chapter 12.

Sedimentary Rocks

Rocks at, or near, the surface of the earth are subject to weathering, and weathering operates to both decompose and disintegrate rock over a period of time. At this very minute untold numbers of rock particles which have weathered away from parent rock masses are moving in streams all over the world, toward lakes and oceans and seas, to be deposited on top of thick layers of other rock particles. Eventually, and principally by a combination of pressure furnished by the weight of overlying sediments and cementation accomplished by cementing material carried in solution by circulating water underground, some of these particles will be bonded together to form a *sedimentary rock*. Sedimentary rocks formed in this manner often show a layered, or bedded, appearance due to differing grain size, color, composition, etc. Material which later becomes sedimentary rock can also be transported and deposited by glaciers and by wind. Some kinds of sedimentary rocks can also be formed by chemical precipitation and other processes.

Sandstone. *Sandstone* is primarily made up of sand grains which have been cemented together. Contrary to popular useage, the word "sand," in geology, refers to size rather than composition. In other words, although "sand" is usually thought of as common quartz sand, a sandstone may be composed of sand-sized grains of any material which is strong enough to be bonded together as a rock. Thus, a sand can consist of small pieces of feldspar or of small pieces of an iron oxide, the latter being the "black sand" of placer gold mining.

Sandstone (see Plate 1.F) is extremely easy to identify. The sand grains are usually very visible to the unaided eye, and many of the surface grains can often be rubbed off by hand. Sandstone usually fractures around the sand grains and not through them, and it also commonly fractures along bedding planes which may or may not have been visible before the fracturing.

Conglomerate. A *conglomerate* is made up of rounded stones, ranging from gravel to cobbles in size, and a matrix of cementing material into which the rounded stones have been cemented, the cementing material being of much finer texture than the overall pattern of the rounded pebbles. If the stones in the "cement" are angular in shape rather than rounded, the rock is called a *breccia*.

Shale. *Shale* (see Plate 2.A) is composed of particles of clay and silt which have been compressed and cemented into rock. Unlike the constituent particles in sandstone and conglomerate, the shale particles are so small that they usually cannot be seen without the aid of a microscope. Shales can be of almost any color, and many shales will tend to split into thin, parallel layers. A shale will commonly grade into sandstone in nearly the same plane, and it is also common to see a sequence of alternating sandstone and shale layers and beds in road cuts and on the sides of valleys, etc.

Limestone. *Limestone* is principally calcium carbonate. Some limestone is fine-grained and was chemically precipitated from ocean water. Other limestones are built up by lime-secreting organisms such as coral and some algae (see Plate 2.B) while still other limestones are made up of the fragments of shells, etc., which have been cemented together.

Dolomite. *Dolomite* differs chemically from limestone only in having more magnesium and a fixed chemical composition. Actually, then, dolomite is a mineral as well as a rock. Differentiating between a limestone and a dolomite in the field is a simple matter: limestone will effervesce when cold hydrochloric acid is applied to it and dolomite will not effervesce unless it is powdered first.

Metamorphic Rocks

A metamorphic rock is one which has been formed from another rock, usually by a combination of heat and pressure far beneath the surface of the earth. In addition, chemical fluids play an important part in some types of metamorphism although heat and pressure are the chief agents of metamorphism for the metamorphic rocks to be described in this section of the book.

Slate. If a shale is subjected to sufficient heat and pressure, the minute particles of clay in the shale will alter to mica. As might be expected, the mica and other flakes so formed will tend to be parallel to one another. As also might be expected, the two wider sides of each flake will be approximately at right angles to the direction of pressure. This orientation of the flakes may or may not be parallel to the original bedding planes in the shale but, in any event, a *slate* has been formed, and the orientation of the flakes now determines the direction of cleavage in the slate (see Plate 2.C). The individual flakes of mica and other "flat" minerals are so small in a slate that they cannot be seen as flakes, but it is the mica, etc., which furnish the dull luster on the cleavage surfaces of many slates. Slate can also be formed from some fine-grained rocks other than shales.

Phyllite. If a slate is subjected to further metamorphism, a *phyllite* may be formed. The only observable difference between a slate and a phyllite is that, due to increased metamorphism and further development of minerals such as mica and chlorite, a phyllite shows a silky sheen on parting surfaces.

Schist. Like slate and phyllite, *schist* is a foliate rock in that many varieties of schist show definite cleavage patterns as a result of metamorphism. Schist is commonly the result of the metamorphism of phyllite which, of course, means the formation of even more mica and similar minerals. Actually, mica is so prevalent in some schists that these rocks are known as *mica schists* (see Plate 2.D). Schists are recognized as such by the fact that in any schist, flat plates of minerals such as mica, chlorite, talc, or hematite are easily seen with the unaided eye. Although cleavage of course tends to take place parallel to the orientation of these flat crystals, other minerals usually also form and some of these minerals are significantly three-dimensional. For this and other reasons, the cleavage surface of a schist is typically rather wavy instead of being straight as in, for example, a slate. In addition to being formed from metamorphic rocks of a lower grade of metamorphism (for example, phyllite), schist can be formed from any igneous or sedimentary rock, one result being that there are many varieties of schist. Another result is that in traveling through a region which has been subjected to widespread metamorphism, schists of some kind or other are usually the dominant rocks.

Fig. 6.3: Banded gneiss in North Carolina. The exposure of rock is approximately two feet high. (Photo by A. Keith, U.S. Geological Survey)

Gneiss. A combination of heat and pressure may be sufficient to metamorphose rocks such as sandstone, granite, diorite, and gabbro into a *gneiss*. Gneiss (see Plate 2.E) has a coarser grain structure than either slate or schist and, as shown in Fig. 6.3, has a banded appearance. Gneiss often has wavy, and often contorted, layers of alternating light-colored and dark-colored minerals. Unlike slate and schist, gneiss does not exhibit well-defined cleavage, and when broken, it is just about as liable to break in one direction as any other.

Serpentine. *Serpentine* is a term used for both a rock and a mineral. We would therefore suspect, doing a little analytical thinking, that serpentine is formed in and from a rock which is very rich in one particular mineral. *Dunite* is such a rock and it consists almost entirely of the mineral *olivine*. Upon metamorphism—in this case, metamorphism brought about by high-temperature gases and fluids—olivine changes to greasy-feeling serpentine (a magnesium silicate with water), and the rock dunite also largely becomes serpentine. Thus "serpentine," without qualification, could mean either a rock or a mineral. Serpentine is usually greenish in color. A variety, *chrysotile*, is the best asbestos. The occurrence of jade (see Plate 6.C) is associated with that of serpentine (see Plate 6.D).

Marble. *Marble* is formed by the metamorphism of limestone and, sometimes, dolomite. Pure marble is snow white and is coarsely crystalline. The marble used for building-facades, etc., usually contains impurities of some kind, resulting in various areas within the marble which are often of different colors. Marble shows no cleavage.

Quartzite. *Quartzite* is metamorphosed quartz sandstone whose original cement has been metamorphosed to a much harder and more binding material, to the extent that a fracture in quartzite takes place through the grains, rather than around the grains as is usual in almost any sandstone. Quartzites are usually light-colored and often have a vitreous or near-vitreous luster.

Contact Metamorphism

There are several different types of metamorphism, but one, *contact metamorphism*, brings about the formation of some important gemstone and ore mineral deposits which can be recognized with relative ease.

Contact metamorphism operates like this: Consider a magmatic intrusion at depth. The temperature of the magma is, say, approximately 1300°F. The magma is forcing heat into the surrounding rock, and high-temperature gases and fluids are moving, under great pressure, into the rock. Some rock near the contact of the host rock and the magma will be metamorphosed by heat alone. As an example, the rock near the magma may be metamorphosed into a *hornfels*, a hard, compact, dark-colored (usually black) rock. Also, new minerals are commonly formed as the high-temperature gases and solutions force their way through the rock surrounding the magma, and some of these new products are often extremely important ore minerals and, in some cases, gemstones. In any event, metamorphism has occurred near the contact of the intrusion and the host rock, hence the term "contact metamorphism."

How and Where to Look for Gemstones and Minerals

The desirability of seeing, studying, and handling as many rocks and minerals as possible before looking for minerals in the field cannot be overemphasized. The next step is to be able to recognize the various kinds of good mineral hunting grounds, and some of these places, incidentally, may have been bypassed by thousands of people until some rockhound who applied a little geology came along.

A classic example of this occurred recently in Iowa, in a sand pit. Would you look for gold in a sand pit? One rockhound did, knowing that the sand had been deposited in the geologic past in water, a fact which was apparent from the layering in places. In addition to sand, gold is also transported and deposited in many streams (see Chapter 7), and the rockhound therefore sampled the pit. Today, rockhounds visit this pit regularly and, if they hit a good layer, can pan about twenty cents worth of gold out of a shovelful of Iowa sand.

Pegmatite Dikes. The origin of pegmatite dikes and their importance as the hosts of several kinds of gemstones have already been discussed in this chapter. The next question, then, is how to find and identify pegmatite dikes.

First, in metamorphic and igneous rock regions, unusual-appearing small ridges, valleys, or other depressions which seem to exist for no apparent cause often signify the presence of a pegmatite dike. To illustrate: some pegmatites are relatively resistant and weather out as ridges while other pegmatites are relatively soft and may form depressions in the surface of the ground. Still other pegmatites, buried some distance below the surface, with no pegmatite at all visible, will collapse in one or more places and form what appear to be "pot-holes" whose bottoms and sides are covered by a mixture of soil and vegetation. Such depressions should be investigated (making sure, of course, that you are not dealing with something like a caved mine-shaft) as cavities in pegmatite dikes which have been found in this manner have furnished some of the most spectacularly beautiful and most valuable mineral specimens ever discovered. In addition to museum-quality specimens of gemstones such as tourmaline, topaz, and beryl, some pegmatites furnish a variety of rare minerals.

Trees often grow in the depressions in the tops of pegmatite dikes for, apparently, two good reasons. First, the soil formed from the weathering of a pegmatite dike is usually suitable for tree growth and, second, the trees can literally gain a foothold in the cavities and their surrounding cracks. So, apparently solid rock with trees growing in it should be literally looked into, as should an expanse of rocky soil in which trees are growing in an unusual manner or pattern.

Veins. Some solutions leaving the parent body of magma carry with them certain metals in dissolved form, the metals later being deposited in the intruded rock, usually as compounds. The solutions carrying the metals are hydrothermal —hot water—solutions and they typically migrate into fissures, solidify, and thus form *veins*. Most ores of copper, mercury, silver, lead, and zinc are found in such veins, as are many ores of gold and some of tungsten. In some places, the mineralized material may not completely fill the vein, resulting in a cavity called a *vug* (see Fig. 6.4). Museum-quality crystals of minerals such as quartz, pyrite, chalcopyrite, and other ore minerals are often found in such cavities.

Veins rarely exceed widths of more than a few feet but they are often very extensive in their other dimensions. The wall rock of a vein typically shows evidence of metamorphism and this fact can sometimes be used to locate veins which are not visible. As an example, the succession of minerals leading away from the sides of a hydrothermal vein is often quartz, white mica, clay minerals, and unaltered rock, in that order. Conversely, when one finds this succession of minerals in rock, it indicates that a hydrothermal vein of some kind may be nearby, near the quartz and mica.

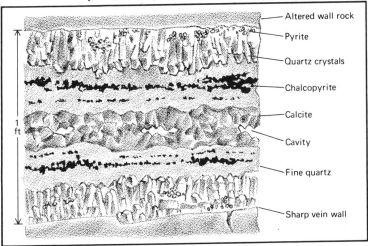

Fig. 6.4: A banded vein. Note that the minerals occur in definite sequence, in bands. Veins like this, with this sequence of minerals, are often formed within a few hundred feet of the earth's surface. (From Dennis P. Cox and Helen R. Cox, *Introductory Geology*, copyright © 1965)

Miarolitic and Amygdaloidal Cavities. As a lava flow cools, gas is released and many hardened lavas thus contain a number of cavities, known as *amygdaloidal cavities,* in which good mineral specimens are often found. Amygdaloidal cavities are not restricted to lavas but are sometimes also found near the margins of dikes and sills. Beautiful crystals of quartz (including amethyst), various kinds of zeolites, and crystals of calcite are often found in these cavities.

A *miarolitic cavity* is a crystal-lined cavity in a rock such as a granite, that is, an intrusive rock. These cavities were formed during solidification of the magma and may range in size from the most common size of about one inch in diameter to that of a few feet in diameter. Miarolitic cavities in granite often contain excellent crystals of quartz, topaz, tourmaline, and beryl; thus granite quarries are good hunting grounds for such minerals, especially if miarolitic cavities are evident.

This latter might seem to be in the realm of wishful thinking. Actually, however, there are usually quite a few cavities of some type or other which have been exposed by the quarrying of granite and, even if no actual cavities are evident, they can often be found by doing a little detective work. Not even many experienced rockhounds know that the grain size of the host rock is much larger near the edges of a miarolitic cavity than it is farther away; hence a roughly circular pattern of larger grains in the host rock grading away from the larger grains to smaller grains may outline the position of a hidden cavity. The smaller the cavity, of course, the closer it would have to be to the rock surface, to form a distinguishable pattern of different-sized grains. Another possibility is that the cavity has already been removed in rock blasted from the present quarry face. A happier thought is that a large pattern of different-sized grains on the quarry face may mean a large cavity just inside the face.

Stream Gravels. Stream valleys are often excellent places in which to look for gold and durable minerals such as gemstones. For century upon century, streams have been cutting through rock, the valley sides have been weathering, and minerals have been sliding into the streams, concentrating in certain places in those streams. These places are in general places where the stream's velocity decreased, with varying degrees of abruptness. In these places, the heavier particles stopped but the lighter particles continued their journey downstream.

These lighter particles are in general particles of the common rock-forming minerals such as quartz and feldspar. Most gemstones are heavier than these rock-forming minerals, so gemstones tend to collect in these deposits along with heavy metallic minerals of which gold, tungsten minerals, and tin minerals are examples. How to look for gold in stream deposits is explained in Chapter 7. The search for and the extraction of gemstones in stream deposits are discussed in pertinent chapters.

Contact Metamorphic Areas. Contact metamorphic zones are frequently excellent places in which to look for good mineral specimens. As to how to recognize such zones, if we are in an area where limestone changes to marble, sandstone to quartzite, or slates and shales to hornfels, we can assume that we are in an area of contact metamorphism.

Contact zones in which limestone is the altered rock frequently contain ore minerals of copper, lead, or zinc, and also fairly commonly contain cavities into which project crystals of quartz, garnet, and some other minerals. Some metamorphosed limestones contain sapphire, ruby, and emerald.

If exposed on the surface, a contact metamorphic zone is easily recognized because the line of demarcation between the igneous rock and the metamorphosed rock is, remarkably, almost inevitably sharp and well-defined. Some non-visible contact zones can sometimes be located by sudden changes in types of vegetation, the reason being that certain types of plants will grow rather profusely over certain kinds of mineral deposits but not over others.

Hillsides, Road Cuts, and Quarries. Hillsides, road cuts, and quarries are often described as "windows into the geologic past," and it is true that they often constitute prime collecting sites. Some of the most successful agate hunting is done on steep hillsides, especially after a good rain, and road cuts and quarries have furnished many fine mineral specimens. It is essential, however, that certain common sense procedures be rigidly observed in such places.

First, of course, it is necessary that responsible permission of some kind be obtained before rockhounding in a road cut or quarry. Some states do not allow rockhounding in road cuts while other states do, and some states do not have any laws, one way or the other, concerning rockhounding on state-owned or state-controlled land. As the state geologist of one of these latter described states put it, however, probably no one would object to collecting of samples, as such, but the destruction of rock formations or the defacing of outcrops would be regarded as a serious matter in his state.

Rockhounds who wish to enter quarries are advised to read that part of Chapter 2 dealing with that subject, and follow the outlined procedure. In a quarry, the rockhound should look for exposed cavities, the quartz-mica-clay sequence which may indicate the nearby presence of a vein, unusual grain patterns in the rock which may indicate cavities, and fillings in joints and fissures. Above all, when rockhounding in a road cut, quarry, or on a hillside, never work directly above or directly below anyone else, or even approximately so.

Gravel Pits. Gravel pits are often good collecting localities for agates, petrified wood, and other specimens. One of the best ways of "working" an operating gravel pit is also so easy that some hobbyists might hardly consider it to be "rockhounding." This method is merely to get permission to visit the workings from time to time, and inspect the piles of reject material for specimens. The smaller material may contain gemstones such as garnets while the larger material often includes good pieces of agate, petrified wood, flint, chert, jasper, etc. The sand commonly contains gold and in some regions the local gravel mining companies are also the greatest gold producers in the area. There is little doubt that many gravel pits (and sand pits) throughout the United States will become meccas for gold-seeking as well as gemstone-seeking rockhounds as soon as some one does some panning in these places, as witness what happened in the Iowa sand pit. Be very careful, however, when working in these places. *Never,* for example, tunnel into the side of a gravel pit or sand pit so that there is sand or gravel over any portion of your body. This precaution is applicable to all situations of course, including tunneling into "solid ground," but sand and gravel-rich sand are especially notorious for caving without any warning.

Rock Folds. Over a long period of time, rock layers can be folded into an undulating, wavelike structure. The crest of a rock wave is called an "anticline" and the trough is known as a "syncline." Just as a flexed eraser will finally crack and break, cracks also develop in anticlines and synclines. If the pressure and heat are sufficient, the sedimentary layers being folded will change into schist and gneiss, and hot solutions will work their ways through the cracks in the folding rocks and interact chemically with the rock. This results sometimes in cavities literally lined with crystals of various sizes, of quartz and other minerals.

Gemstone-studded cavities of this type are known variously as "Alpine vugs," "Alpine veins," and "Alpine cavities," as this type of cavity is a favorite and much-sought collecting site in the Swiss Alps. For some reason, perhaps due to the relative lack of mountain climbers in the United States, few such cavities have been reported in this country. If, however, all United States rockhounds could see a nineteenth-century drawing of one of these Swiss Alp cavities as visualized by an artist of that day, mountain climbing would almost certainly gain at least a few more practitioners in this country. The drawing referred to depicts a group of men— a dozen or so—in a large, torch-lighted cavern festooned with mammoth crystals of smoky quartz. Some of the miners are prying away at big crystals lying on the floor of the cavity while the remaining miners, gazing upward, seem to be trying to decide whether to pry down some more "mine-run" crystals about six feet long or whether to go after some crystals approximately ten feet long!

Mines and Mine Dumps. For those tempted to explore old abandoned mines and around old mine workings: *don't!* As pointed out in Chapter 2, old mines and old mine workings are, commonly, extremely dangerous places, especially for the uninitiated. Even recently abandoned mines are dangerous for the non-miner because of ore chutes and winzes (underground shafts), etc., which to those unfamiliar with mines usually seem to be scattered helter-skelter throughout the mine, in a dangerous manner. If, however, a rockhound can visit a mine, either a working mine or a nonworking mine which is in good condition, with an expert who knows the mine, there are few rockhounding experiences which will be remembered with more enjoyment, especially if some good specimens are found.

As to mine dumps, it is almost anyone's guess as to what parts of a dump will furnish the best specimens. Probably as good a method as any to attack a dump is to sample it at random, digging fairly deep holes here and there in random locations until something interesting is found. Several more holes at the same elevation as that of the find may then be dug around the dump. If nothing is found in these holes, a trench can be dug between the holes. If nothing is found in the trench, the whole process may be repeated at the discretion of the rockhound and his muscles.

Ant Hills and Animal Burrows. One of the least known methods of finding mineral specimens is also one of the easiest, and many times one of the most productive. It consists of inspecting and testing the material which ants and other animal life bring to the surface of the earth. Ants, gophers, prairie dogs, and moles, etc., are very busy miners and they move a tremendous amount of dirt and rock to the surface. Some ants, for example, tunnel to depths of fifteen feet and a single ant nest can consist of a labyrinth of tunnels and passages and rooms going to a depth of fifteen feet, and spread over more than one acre. Some excellent gemstones have been found in ant hills and, as a matter of fact, some old-time prospectors have made it a habit to pan out ant hill material in a new region, as a good way in which to get an idea as to what may or may not be in the area.

Rock Types and Stream Drainage Patterns

Suppose that you find yourself on an unfamiliar road and you wonder what kinds of minerals there may be on the journey ahead. It would be impossible to come up with precise names of minerals, of course, but if the kinds of rocks ahead were known we would then have some idea about the possible kinds of minerals in those rocks. So, not having a geologic map of the area, you look at your road map. More precisely, you look at the streams on the map which are close to your proposed route.

In many instances, the drainage pattern of streams in an area is strongly controlled by the underlying rock. A *dendritic* ("tree-like") pattern, one of the drainage patterns shown in Fig. 6.5, usually forms in regions underlain by massive rock, either igneous or metamorphic, or by uncontorted sedimentary strata. If igneous, it could be almost any kind of igneous rock but if it is metamorphic rock, it prob-

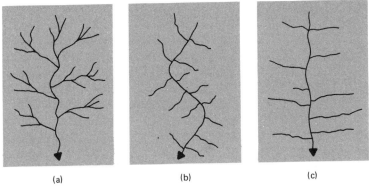

(a)   (b)   (c)

Fig. 6.5: Stream drainage patterns: (a) dendritic; (b) rectangular; (c) trellis.

ably is something like a gneiss, since schist is foliated and not massive; or it could be marble, but probably not slate, and so on with our analysis.

A *rectangular* drainage pattern is usually associated with joints and faults in massive rocks, or with metamorphic rocks such as schists whose foliation controls the pattern. Thus, a rectangular pattern next to a dendritic pattern on the same watershed might indicate the presence of a zone of contact metamorphism.

A *trellis* pattern is often associated with alternate bands of strong and weak rocks. This pattern is very common where sedimentary rocks have been folded and the main rivers have cut through the folds, an example of this being the Appalachian region of the United States.

How to Remove Specimens from Rock

The first thing to remember about extracting a specimen from rock is to not be too much of a perfectionist, and the second is to take advantage of whatever cracks, joints, and so forth that there may be, which will aid in the extraction. If the specimen, whether attached to some matrix rock or not, can be removed by careful prying, don't worry about the fact that it may not look exactly like a hand-trimmed museum specimen. Just be thankful, label the specimen, wrap it up, and put it in your collecting bag.

Whether or not a rockhound wishes to include some matrix rock with a specimen often depends on whether he wants the specimen for a collection or for lapidary use. If the latter, and if the specimen is not too deeply embedded, it may sometimes be removed, whole, in the field by using chisel, hammer, and, of course, safety goggles. When using chisel and hammer for this purpose, always chisel *away* from the specimen and never toward it, and do the work very carefully. If the specimen is deeply embedded, a channel may be chiseled at a safe distance around the specimen and then deepened until it is at least as deep as the width of the rock "pillar" at its top. The pillar can then be chiseled through at its base, the ease of this particular operation depending mainly upon how strongly the chisel was slanted in the deepening of the channel. Fossils may be removed from rock in the same manner. Also, if it is desired to remove a fossil from rock in the field, without any host rock, chip *away* from the fossil and never toward it.

If a specimen is in a carbonate rock, it is sometimes possible to loosen the specimen from the rock by applying hydrochloric acid to the matrix material, around the specimen. Before using this method, make sure that the specimen itself is not going to be attacked by the acid, perhaps by applying some acid to similar material of noncollection quality.

Chapter 7

Gold

Gold (see Plate 2.F) is one of the earliest known metals and it has been prized throughout much of the world for thousands of years. It was largely the desire for gold and eternal life which spurred on the alchemists of the Middle Ages. The alchemists believed that gold could be made from other metals, and some believed that once this was done the secret of eternal life would also be known. At least a few of these experimenters arrived at the conclusion—usually one of their last—that drinking a solution of gold and lead would give them everlasting youth.

Strangely enough, the belief of the alchemists that gold could be made from other metals was, by itself, correct. Today, for example, an unstable form of gold can be made from platinum and iridium by "smashing" atoms, but just as the alchemists did, we still get our gold from the ground.

In addition to its use as a standard for the value of money, gold is a key material in many activities. Approximately three-fourths of the gold used by United States business and industry is used in dentistry, jewelry, and various art forms. Much of the remainder is used in defense and aerospace work where, for example, gold platings on the external parts of the vernier rocket engines of the Apollo spacecraft maintained those engines at safe operating temperatures as the spacecraft coasted toward the moon. A considerable amount of gold is also used in electronic accounting and other business machines.

Gold in the United States

A mental picture popularly associated with searching for gold is that of an old-time prospector and his burro plodding along beneath a Western sky. Actually, the first gold rush in the United States was not in California but was in Georgia, in 1828, and since then gold has been found in most of the fifty states. Despite the fact that many of these discoveries were unimportant from an economic view, gold was once mined commercially in such states as Massachusetts, Pennsylvania, and North Carolina. As a matter of fact the latter state was our leading producer of gold until the soft, yellow metal was discovered in quantity in California. Right now, some of the world's best samples of stream gold are being found by rockhounds in our New England, middle Atlantic, and southern, as well as our western states.

Is It Gold?

The two minerals most commonly mistaken for gold are fool's gold and yellow mica. Gold itself is soft and yellow, and has a specific gravity of 19.0. Gold is also malleable, and it is essentially the combination of gold's softness, weight, malleability, and sectility which makes it easy to identify. Conversely, quick tests on something like fool's gold or yellow mica will immediately show it not to be gold. These tests are so simple and so definitive that it seems almost unbelievable that, as actually happened during the early days of the California gold rush, at least one ship was hastily loaded with fool's gold and mica-bearing rock and sent back to New York.

Technically, fool's gold may be either of two minerals: *pyrite* (a sulfide of iron) or *chalcopyrite* (a sulfide of copper and iron and a major ore mineral of copper). Similarly, yellow mica may be one of several micas. If the specimen is large enough, one very simple field test will usually suffice to determine whether a particular piece of "gold" is actually gold or some form of fool's gold or mica. Pyrite (see Plate 3.A) is hard and brittle while chalcopyrite (see Plate 3.B), or "copper pyrites," is soft and brittle. Mica is also soft and it breaks up easily, due to its cleavage characteristics. Gold is soft, but it is also malleable and sectile. Thus, if the point of a knife blade of normal hardness is applied with some force to a specimen, as if trying to cut into the specimen, pyrite will not even scratch. Both chalcopyrite and mica, however, are easily cut and the resulting loose particles can be crushed into many more particles by applying pressure with the flat of the blade. Gold is easily cut too, of course, but it will flatten under pressure and will not break up as do chalcopyrite and mica.

The specimen to be tested is commonly a small particle, however, and in such a case the pocket magnifying glass should be used to observe just what does happen under the point of a knife or pin. Assuming that the particle is on a flat surface, scrape at it with the "flat" of the point and with some force as if trying to make it "stand on end." Pyrite will tend to "jump" under this pressure, away from the point, or may even fracture and fly apart, while chalcopyrite and mica will immediately break up into many smaller pieces. Gold will flatten under such pressure but it will not break up into the many smaller pieces characteristic of both chalcopyrite and mica under pressure, when the tested specimen is small. Under a sliding pressure, a small piece of chalcopyrite will smear into a greenish-black streak in a gold pan while a small piece of mica will commonly form a yellow smear on the bottom of the pan. This yellow smear, by the way, is often taken as evidence by the inexperienced gold-seeker that what has been found is gold which has thus demonstrated its malleability. A little judicious scraping of such smears, however, shows that they are made of myriads of tiny particles.

The type of mica (see Plate 3.C) most often mistaken for stream gold, strangely enough, is mica which was originally much darker in color but which weathers to a yellowish color, the yellow being much more pronounced when the mica is wet. When dry, the mica is almost white. This, incidentally, is the glittering yellow material which is constantly being scooped out of streams and brought home as "gold" which, as it usually turns out, mysteriously loses its golden color somewhere on the way back. Thus this mica can be identified as such, even without a knife and a magnifying glass, by merely allowing it to dry.

The simplest test of all for the identification of gold is the one used by experienced prospectors who observe the luster of the mineral in more or less direct light and then in the shade furnished by holding the hand over the specimen. Fool's gold and mica lose most of their "shine" in the shade while the luster of gold remains almost the same. The test requires a little practice, however, and the beginner should supplement it with the knifepoint or pinpoint test outlined above.

Gold in Veins

If one is to believe the many stories of early western gold prospecting, a good number of major gold strikes resulted because of a seeming affinity between burros and gold veins. One such strike was supposedly made when a burro came limping back into camp with a gold nugget in his hoof, another when an angry prospector, retrieving a hammer which he had thrown at a rapidly departing burro, found the hammer stuck into a vein of gold, and so on. One story even tells of a prospector finding his strayed burro standing motionless and staring at a gold vein, like a hunting dog pointing game.

The typical gold vein, however, is a far cry from the still-popular image of an easily recognized and spectacular display of golden brilliance. Factually, the gold in a gold vein is usually not visible except upon close inspection—and sometimes not even then—unless the deposit is exceptional. This is the first thing for the seeker of gold veins to realize.

Gold which occurs in veins is typically of hydrothermal origin, that is, it has been deposited from a hot, watery solution which escaped from a body of magma (see Chapter 6). The typical gold vein is a *fissure* vein, where an already existent joint or fissure in rock has been filled by a hydrothermal solution which solidified in the fissure. Also in opposition to the popular idea of a gold vein as a kind of a gleaming, ribbon-like structure, many gold veins are actually disjointed vein fragments rather than being one continuous vein structure.

No matter what their size, fissure gold veins vary in color from white to a deep reddish brown. Most of the material in a fissure gold vein is commonly quartz, hence a possible white appearance to the vein. Hydrothermal deposition of gold is almost always accompanied by iron in some form also being deposited in the vein. Weathering of this iron produces "rust" stains and thus the color of the vein may be anywhere between the light color of quartz and the reddish brown of iron oxide. Practically speaking, any vein found on or near the surface of the earth which does not have rust stains probably does not have any gold in it either.

Gossan. Iron often occurs as sulfides in gold veins, and upon weathering these sulfides decompose to form iron oxide (this is where the stains come from) and sulfuric acid. The sulfuric acid thus formed is capable of leaching out some of the remaining metals, such as copper, by taking them into solution and carrying them downwards to the water table where, by a process of *secondary enrichment*, the metals are often redeposited.

Gold, however, is not dissolved by sulfuric acid, nor is quartz, and the result is that a porous rust-stained outcrop of quartz may be found which may contain an appreciable amount of gold, much of it in the pore spaces into which gold has fallen. Thus the gold seeker should always be on the lookout for these porous, iron-stained rock structures of *gossan*, also known as *eisenhut* or *iron hat*. When investigating such exposures it should be remembered that the porosity results from the solution of sulfides in the vein. Therefore, even if the vein does not contain gold, it may contain either copper or silver, or both, or some other metals. Furthermore, the gossan itself may be almost totally barren of values of a particular metal and overlie a rich concentration of, say, copper at the water table.

Gold Is Where You Find It. The old saying that "gold is where you find it" is sometimes applicable when looking for vein gold for the reason that gold deposited from hydrothermal solutions does not always end up in what can properly be called veins. For example, gold carried in hydrothermal solutions may deposit around hot springs and it also sometimes deposits in or against carbonaceous shale. Gold has also been found clinging to such things as grass roots which, apparently, happened to grow into a weathered vein. One of California's first gold strikes resulted when a Mexican laborer, working near Los Angeles, pulled up a wild onion and found gold among the roots.

Natural Gold Alloys. In nature, gold often alloys with other metals. Gold often alloys with silver, for example, and this particular alloy is usually easily recognized by its whitish-yellow color and its heavy weight. Gold also commonly alloys with tellurium to form *gold tellurides* which, although recognizably heavy, do not have the yellow color of gold. When these tellurides are heated, however, the tellurium—related chemically to sulfur—comes off as a thick smoke while the gold collects on the outside of the sample, in globules. Curiously, gold tellurides sometimes weather naturally to form a gold powder known as *mustard gold*.

Placer Gold

Gold is one of the heavy minerals which is found in natural, mechanical concentrations called *placers*. In general it is much easier to find stream gold than it is to find vein gold which is still in the vein. This is easily understood when we consider a stream cutting through a valley on whose sides there happen to be several gold-bearing veins which are covered by soil, rock, etc. It would be virtually impossible to find these veins directly, but nature for perhaps thousands of years has been weathering and eroding those veins and moving some of the particles downhill and into the stream. The concentrations of gold particles take place in certain favored areas and it is in these places that the gold seeker searches. In other words, logic alone can be used to find possible placer gold sites while the discovery of a gold vein is largely—as far as the amateur is concerned, at least—a matter of sheer hard work.

Tracing Float. It is sometimes possible to find a gold vein by tracing particles of placer gold, or "float," upstream to the place where the float disappears and then investigating the sides of the valley in that area. As to how far float should be traced upstream when it does not disappear, it is often written that gold particles become more rounded the further downstream they are carried and that therefore the valley sides should be searched wherever the float is angular, in order that no veins be missed. The fact is, however, that small particles of gold can be carried for considerable distances downstream without showing much rounding, and in many streams tend to remain angular in shape. This brings up the fact that if gold particles are numerous enough to trace upstream and are also large enough to show rounding, many goldseekers would be satisfied to collect all of this available wealth, at least before spending any time on looking for a vein, very possibly without success.

In general, finding a vein by tracing float is a difficult procedure and requires work and some knowledge of placergold geology. For example, the float in a present stream bed may have come from a vein which is now deeply buried by a landslide, etc., or it may not be coming from a vein at all. As one possibility, it may have come from a portion of a former stream bed now high above the valley floor, that is, from other placer deposits. For those who have the time and patience, however, tracing placer gold to its various sources can be a very interesting and sometimes financially rewarding activity, and one method of prospecting for gold-bearing quartz veins is illustrated in Fig. 7.1.

Fig. 7.1: Prospecting a hillside for gold. Beginning at point 1 samples were taken at fifty-foot intervals. The best prospect was found at point 8. Samples were then taken as represented by + until the crest of the hill was reached. In this case the vein was rich but did not crop out. (Courtesy of Mineral Information Service, California Division of Mines and Geology)

Fig. 7.1 could represent either the area in a stream valley to which float was traced and then disappeared, or a hillside which is prospected "from scratch," literally and figuratively. In any event, the objective is to find out if there is a gold vein on the hill and, if so, its location. To start, holes are dug down to bedrock, near the base of the hill and about 50 feet apart, and the dirt found near bedrock is panned for gold (panning is described later in this chapter). Suppose that the prospector finds "colors" in several holes. He determines which hole seems to have the most colors, climbs to a place about twenty feet higher above this hole, and digs another line of holes parallel to the first line. The dirt near bedrock in these holes is tested by panning, the richest of these holes is thus determined, and the procedure is repeated until the source of the gold is found. This is called the "postholing" method of prospecting.

Placer Locations. Gold particles and other heavy particles which are being moved by water will tend to come to rest wherever the velocity of the water appreciably slackens. Such places include regions of sudden lessening of the stream gradient, the upstream faces of boulders, those places where a smaller stream enters a larger stream, pools beneath rapids, cracks in boulders, pot-holes in boulders or in bedrock, and natural riffles in bedrock. Incidentally, and for some reason for which there seems to be little explanation, natural riffles in bedrock which more or less parallel the direction of stream flow seem to be more effective than cross-flow riffles in trapping gold.

One fact which seems to be unknown by many hunters of placer gold is that places where streams once ran, but are now relatively high and thoroughly dry, often furnish much richer gravel than the present channels of streams. In looking for placer gold, therefore, also look in those spots where the stream once ran and where its velocity must have slackened. Stream terraces—flat areas which represent former stream bottoms—are logical places in which to look for placer gold.

Whether digging gravel in a present or former stream channel, "gold goes deep" and the important thing is to get down to bedrock—and even further, if possible. This latter is sometimes made possible in the case of now-dry areas by cracks in the bedrock which can be pried open with a tool such as a pick or a bar. In such a case, all rock which is pried up should be scraped or brushed clean, the material thus dislodged being subsequently tested by panning. Incidentally, a spoon is one of the most useful tools that a placer-gold hunter can take along with him if the sand in bedrock crevices and beneath boulders is to be panned. Fig. 7.2 shows some favorable locations for the deposition of gold which can be recovered in a meandering stream without diving, that is, by panning, etc., in the usual manner. The rockhound should also always investigate such things as ant hills and gopher holes (see Chapter 6) in a placer gold region and test the excavated material for gold.

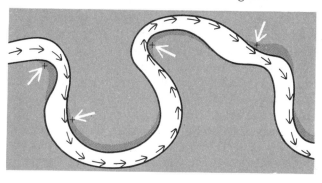

Fig. 7.2: Diagram of part of a meandering river. Arrows indicate where gold particles are most likely to concentrate. (Courtesy of Mineral Information Service, California Division of Mines and Geology)

Equipment for "Mining" Placer Gold. From what has already been said, it is probably apparent that the amount of equipment used for extracting placer gold depends upon the amount of effort which the gold hunter wants to put into the search. No matter the amount of effort, however, gravel is going to have to be dug, sorted to at least some extent, and carried for at least some distance. Many rockhounds consider a shovel, a pick, a simple screen, and one or two pails as basic working tools for moving and sorting stream gravel. Whether a sluice box or a gold pan is used, a pair of tweezers to use in picking out the smaller pieces of gold is a "must." The pocket magnifying glass will be found to be extremely helpful in examining and testing particles, and a small transparent bottle partially filled with water makes a good combination carrying and display case for the gold you find. Some rockhounds, no matter where they go, always bring along, in the car, a shovel and either a gold pan or sluice box just in case they find an interesting-looking stream.

How to Pan for Gold

The pan used for gold panning should be one with sloping sides. A frying pan makes a fairly efficient gold pan but most gold seekers finally buy a regular gold pan for a few dollars. To pan, fill the pan from about one-half to two-thirds of its capacity with material of as nearly the same size as possible and then submerge the pan in water. Stir up the material by hand, making sure that it all gets wet. Be sure to break up any clay balls, etc. With the pan still submerged, partially rotate the pan quickly back and forth a few times. This helps to size the material (preliminary sizing could have been done by screening or by hand) and also helps to float off some of the organic material. In addition, any particles of gold start their journey toward the bottom of the pan.

Next, lift the pan out of the water, remove the larger particles of gravel, and get the water swirling by using a circular motion. Every now and then, dip the pan slightly away from you with a somewhat jerky movement so that some water and some of the lighter rock material goes over the lip of the pan. Continue doing this until there is not enough water left in the pan to correctly float material over the edge, stop the circular motion, and submerge the pan again. The pan is then raised above the water again, the larger particles of gravel thrown out, and the panning process is thus continued through its several operations until practically all that seems to be left in the pan is a relatively thin layer of black sand. Most of this is a black iron sand which is magnetic.

Theoretically, it is possible to continue panning and separating any gold which happens to be there from the iron sand. Practically, this is difficult to do without losing some gold unless one has had considerable experience in panning. What the beginner should now do is to pick out whatever gold particles are visible, using the tweezers, and then put enough water into the pan so that the black sand can be strung out as thinly as possible when the pan is tipped. This procedure, repeated several times, will reveal any gold particles. Any particles of doubtful identity may be tested as previously described in this chapter. If there is quite a bit of black sand in the pan it is important that the black sand be spread out as thinly as possible in order that the thinner and smaller flakes of gold are not hidden during the process.

How to Make and Use a Sluice Box

A simple but very effective wooden sluice box which can be easily carried in an automobile can be made by first nailing two sides onto a bottom piece of wood so that a channel about three feet long, six inches high, and twelve inches wide is formed. The wood used should be approximately one inch thick. The bottom of the box should then be covered by either canvas or thin carpeting over which is laid heavy (no. 13 or no. 14) wire screen of quarter-inch mesh. Cleats are recommended for securing the screen and the canvas, the cleats being placed along the sides of the box, above the screen.

The sluice box may be placed directly in the stream so that a *shallow* depth of water flows through it at a fairly rapid rate. If the part of the stream where it is desired to use the sluice box is flowing sluggishly, a partial dam may be built from mud and rock and the sluice box set up just below the "spillway" (see Fig. 7.3). The operation of the sluice box is simple and consists only of supplying sized gravel and sand to the upper part of the sluice box and making sure that the flow of water is such that the heavier particles are remaining in the box, trapped in the screen, and the lighter particles are being discharged over the lower end. Any correction necessary is usually easily accomplished by slightly changing the slope and depth of immersion of the box. As in panning, the larger pieces of gravel can be thrown out, but care should be taken not to throw away garnets and other gemstones which are commonly found in stream gravels. It is of course also possible to operate a sluice box on land, either dipping the water needed from the stream or running a length of garden hose upstream to furnish a constant supply of water.

It is often possible to pick out some particles of gold directly from the sluice box, but iron sand commonly hides

Fig. 7.3: Gold sluices vary in size from those like this one in Alaska in boom days to portable sluice boxes which can be carried in a rockhound's car. (Photo by F. C. Schrader, U.S. Geological Survey)

many of the gold flakes and will sometimes even cover small nuggets. From time to time, therefore, the screen and canvas (or carpeting) should be carefully removed (this is why cleats were recommended) and their contents just as carefully washed into a container of some kind, to be later panned.

The sluice box method is usually much more satisfactory than the panning method as far as both effort and results are concerned. Panning is hard work and those who have tried both methods almost always use the gold pan only for the final separation as outlined above. Even where much traveling on foot is involved, many knowledgeable rockhounds still use the sluice box. For one thing, excellent results can be obtained with a sluice box only two feet long; also, lightweight sluice boxes made of material such as Fiberglas are now on the market.

Other Methods of Recovering Gold

Dry Washers. *Dry washers* may sometimes be used for the extraction of placer gold in some areas where lack of water makes other methods impossible. In effect, a dry washer blows screened material over a set of riffles, and thus its principle is that of the sluice box. Just as the operation of the sluice box depends upon the presence of water, the efficiency of the dry washing method depends upon the almost absolute lack of water. As almost all soil contains enough moisture to keep particles of varying sizes from separating, even under a blast of air, true dry-washing areas are rare.

Fig. 7.4 shows a dry washer. Gravel is shoveled onto screen (A) and the finer material falls into the hopper (B). The finer material then falls from the lower end of the

Fig. 7.4: Dry washers can sometimes be effectively used to separate gold from sand where water is not available. Many dry washers are run by small engines which replace the crank shown. (Courtesy of Mineral Information Service, California Division of Mines and Geology)

hopper onto the riffles (C). The lighter particles are lifted over the riffles by air from the bellows (D) and finally go over the lower end of the riffles and onto the ground. The particles of gold and black sand remain caught by the riffles.

Turning the crank (E) operates the washer. Some washers are run by gasoline engines but, in either case, the screen (A) is vibrated by a cam on the crankshaft, in this particular type of washer. In the type of washer shown, an eccentric operates the bellows. The shape of the screen (A) can be adjusted so that the larger material slides off.

The Long Tom and the Rocker. The *long tom* is a combination of sluice and riffle box, the gravel being roughly sorted in the sluice box, and the gold and black sand being caught in the riffle box. The length of the usual long tom may be anywhere between ten and twenty feet.

The *rocker* is essentially a sluice box which is rocked back and forth like a cradle, on a rounded base of two rockers. The typical rocker is about four feet long and about fifteen inches wide. Both the long tom and the rocker were used extensively in gold rush days and are still used to some extent. Obviously, however, the average rockhound will elect to use a portable sluice box and a pan—at least until he strikes it much richer than most rockhounds do!

Gold Discoveries in the United States

Gold has been found in many areas of the United States but the term "found" does not necessarily mean that the gold was always found in quantity, nor does it necessarily mean that gold can be found in a particular, named locality now. In general, however, the rockhound has from a good to excellent chance of finding at least a little gold today in most of the regions listed in the following table.

Where Gold Has Been Found in the United States
(A Partial List)

State	County
Alabama	Chilton, Clay, Cleburne, Colbert, Randolph, Talladega, Tallapoosa.
Alaska	Alaska does not have counties. Some of the

State	County

	regions where gold is found are: SE Alaska, Prince William Sound, Kenai Peninsula, SW Alaska, eastern part of Kushkokwim Valley, Yukon Basin, Seward Peninsula, Kobuk River.
Arizona	Apache, Coconino, Gila, Graham, Maricopa, Mojave, Pima, Pinal, Santa Cruz, Yavapai, Yuma.
Arkansas	Garland, Saline.
California	Amador, Butte, Calaveras, Colusa, Contra Costa, Eldorado, Fresno, Imperial, Inyo, Los Angeles, Madera, Mariposa, Mendocino, Mono, Napa, Nevada, Placer, San Bernardino, San Diego, Siskiyou, Trinity, Tuolumne, Ventura.
Colorado	Adams, Alamosa, Arapahoe, Baca, Boulder, Chaffee, Clear Creek, Conejos, Costilla, Custer, Denver, Dolores, Douglas, Eagle, Elbert, El Paso, Fremont, Garfield, Gilpin, Grand, Gunnison, Hinsdale, Huertano, Jackson, Jefferson, Lake, La Plata, Mineral, Moffat, Montezuma, Montrose, Ouray, Park, Pitkin, Rio Grande, Routt, Saguache, San Juan, San Miguel, Summit.
Georgia	Cherokee, Forsyth, Gordon, Hall, Lumpkin, McDuffie, Paulding, White, Wilkes.
Idaho	Adams, Blaine, Boise, Boundary, Cassia, Clearwater, Custer, Elmore, Gem, Idaho, Kootenai, Lemhi, Owyhee, Shoshone, Valley.
Illinois	Hardin.
Indiana	Brown, Franklin, Jennings, Monroe, Morgan, Northington, Warren.
Iowa	Jackson.
Kansas	Ellis, Gove, Trego.
Maine	Cumberland, Franklin, Hancock, Knox, Oxford, Penobscot, Somerset, Waldo, Washington.

State	*County*
Maryland	Baltimore, Montgomery, Prince George.
Massachusetts	Essex, Hampden, Hampshire, Worcester.
Michigan	Marquette.
Minnesota	Benton, Fillmore, Itasca, Kandiyohi, Olmsted, St. Louis, Wabasha.
Mississippi	Jackson.
Missouri	Adair, Macon.
Montana	Beaverhead, Broadwater, Cascade, Chouteau, Deer Lodge, Fergus, Granite, Jefferson, Lewis and Clark, Madison, Mineral, Missoula, Park, Phillips, Powell, Ravalli, Silver Bow.
Nebraska	Franklin, Harlan, Seward, Stanton.
Nevada	Churchill, Clark, Douglas, Elko, Esmeralda, Eureka, Humboldt, Lander, Lincoln, Lyon, Mineral, Nye, Ormsby, Pershing, Storey, Washoe, White Pine.
New Hampshire	Carroll, Coos, Grafton.
New Mexico	Colfax, Grant, Lincoln, Rio Arriba, Sandoval, Santa Fe, Sierra, Socorro.
New York	Allegany, Dutchess, Erie, Fulton, Hamilton, Herkimer, Rockland, Saratoga, Washington, Westchester.
North Carolina	Burke, Cabarrus, Cherokee, Clay, Cleveland, Caldwell, Catawba, Davidson, Franklin, Gaston, Granville, Guilford, Henderson, Jackson, Lincoln, McDowell, Mecklenburg, Moore, Montgomery, Nash, Person, Polk, Randolph, Rowan, Rutherford, Stanly, Transylvania, Union, Watauga, Wilkes, Yadkin.
Oregon	Baker, Clackamas, Coos, Crook, Curry, Douglas, Grant, Harney, Jackson, Josephine, Lane, Lincoln, Malheur, Marion, Wheeler.
Pennsylvania	Chester, Lebanon.

State	*County*
South Carolina	Abbeville, Cherokee, Chesterfield, Edgefield, Greenville, Kershaw, Lancaster, Laurens, Oconee, Pickens, Saluda, Union, York.
South Dakota	Custer, Lawrence, Pennington.
Tennessee	Blount, Monroe, Polk.
Texas	Brewster, El Paso.
Utah	Beaver, Box Elder, Grand, Iron, Juab, Kane, Piute, Salt Lake, San Juan, Tooele, Uinta, Utah, Wasatch.
Vermont	Bennington, Windsor.
Virginia	Buckingham, Culpeper, Floyd, Fluvanna, Goochland, Montgomery, Orange, Prince William, Spotsylvania, Stafford.
Washington	Asotin, Chelan, Clallam, Clark, Douglas, Ferry, King, Kittitas, Lincoln, Okanogan, Snohomish, Stevens, Thurston, Whatcom, Yakima.
Wisconsin	Clark, Douglas, Polk.
Wyoming	Big Horn, Crook, Fremont, Hot Springs, Johnson, Laramie, Sheridan.

Chapter 8

Gemstones and Gems: Diamond, Ruby, and Sapphire

The current chapter and Chapters 9, 10, and 11 explain how to find and identify what are generally considered to be the most important gemstones found in the United States. This brings up the point that much of the material found by the rockhound will not be of true gem quality. Suppose, for example, that we find some crystals of corundum which appear to be of the variety known as ruby, but that the crystals are far from being of what is usually considered gem quality. What have we found—ruby, red corundum, or what? In such a case—and there will be many of them—label the find as "Corundum, variety ruby," or "Quartz, variety amethyst," whatever it may be, add it to your collection and enjoy it.

Gemstones, Gems, and the Great American Diamond Field

Why are some minerals and mineral varieties gemstones while others are not? If we think of the gems which we have seen, we would probably say that most gemstones: (1) have attractive colors and lusters, (2) are transparent or translucent, (3) are hard, and (4) are rare. There are many exceptions to this assessment, however, either in part or in whole, and some gemstones would be hard to identify as such by checking their characteristics against those given above. As a matter of fact, some independent thinking rockhounds believe that a gemstone should be defined as any material out of which something attractive can be made by cutting and polishing. One such California rockhound suddenly started wearing a ring whose extremely black, dull stone evoked much curiosity from fellow rockhounds, and many guesses as to the identity of the material. Finally, after a few months, after most of his friends had admitted that it was an unusual and somehow attractive stone, the rockhound admitted that he had shaped the "stone" out of hard licorice.

Although substances like licorice will probably never attain the stature of being called gemstones, it is true that gemstones do not necessarily have to be minerals. Amber, for example, is a fossil tree resin and is a gemstone. Jet and pearl, also organic in origin, are also gemstones.

The question often arises as to the difference between "gemstone" and "gem." The two words are often used interchangeably but in this book we will consider in general that a "gem" is the final product, after any cutting and polishing to increase attractiveness. Thus we find *gemstones* in the field and from them we shape *gems*, a contextual relationship which usually will govern the usages of the two words in this particular book and make it clear just what we are talking about.

The boundary line between two other terms, "precious" and "semiprecious," as applied to gemstones, is also somewhat arbitrary. Usually, however, diamond, ruby, sapphire, and emerald are regarded as the precious stones, a distinction which they have held throughout much of historic time. Interestingly enough, one of the strangest dramas involving man's search for these four precious stones unfolded, not in a mysterious Eastern land, but right here in the United States, in 1871.

In that year, two prospectors told a small group of San Francisco's leading businessmen that they, the prospectors, had found a diamond field in the desert. They not only showed the businessmen a number of diamonds, but also some rubies, sapphires, and emeralds which they said had been found in the same "diggings." Three of the San Franciscans and a mining engineer made a highly secret trip to the gem fields—somewhere in Wyoming, apparently—with the prospectors and everyone found more diamonds, rubies, sapphires, and emeralds. Most of the gemstones were found just below the surface of the ground. Another businessman then brought samples of the stones to New York where he was assured by experts that the samples were of good gem quality.

Everything, including a glowing report from the mining engineer who had examined the property, now seemed to add up to instant wealth. A mining company was quickly formed by the excited little group of businessmen, the prospectors received $660,000 on account, and the law which now covers the mining of gemstones in the United States was pushed through Congress. Just as worldwide excitement concerning the fabulous field was at its peak, however, a government engineer who had "just happened" to visit the area at that time sent a fateful telegram to San Francisco. According to the wire and a subsequent full report, this was one of the geologically most unusual gem fields the world had ever seen. Other than the fact that neither diamond or emerald would normally occur in quantity with ruby and sapphire, to say nothing of occurring together, the gem field showed other major deviations from geologic principles. Some stones which he had found, the engineer reported, were in "ant hills" which no normal ant would have built in the first place. The engineer reported that he had also found gemstones in rock crevices and beneath depressions in the soil which were apparently the imprints of boot heels. There was much more and, of course, the bubble was pricked but not before financial markets in America and Europe had been considerably affected by the great American gem field.

The whole truth of just how many people were in on the attempted swindle will probably never be known, but it is now known that the two prospectors obtained the gemstones in Europe where they payed a total price for them which was far less than the sum of $660,000 which they received from the eager San Franciscans. As a matter of fact, the gemstones were "rejects," another baffling factor in this strange story.

It is believed by many who have studied this bit of Americana that the "salted" field was somewhere near Rawlins, Wyoming. Today, that general area happens to be a favorite jade-hunting region and it may be that, someday, some jade seeker will find one of these diamonds, rubies, sapphires, or emeralds and wonder where the precious stone came from and just what its story is.

Three of the precious stones—diamond, ruby, and sapphire—are dealt with in this chapter. The fourth precious stone, emerald, is discussed, with some other gemstones, in the next chapter, Chapter 9.

Diamond

Chemical composition: carbon.
Chemical formula: C
Color: various.
Luster: adamantine when cut, often greasy or dull when found.
Diaphaneity: transparent to opaque.
Hardness: 10
Specific gravity: 3.5
Cleavage: perfect octahedral.
Fracture: conchoidal.
Crystal system: isometric.

Diamonds (see Plate 3.D) were discovered in the river gravels of India many centuries before their discovery in Brazil in 1728. Just as India's production of diamonds dwindled as that of Brazil mounted, so the Brazilian production of diamonds ultimately dwindled and became relatively minor compared to that of South Africa. It was in South Africa, in 1866, that the son of a Boer farmer picked up a "pebble" which was soon identified as a large diamond. Thus began the diamond rush of South Africa. At the present time, South Africa supplies over 90 percent of the world's diamonds, for jewelry and for industrial uses as cutting agents, etc.

Diamonds in the United States. Other than those diamonds "found" in the suddenly generated gem field in Wyoming (?) a century ago, many diamonds have been found in the United States, one of the most interesting areas of discovery being near Murfreesboro, Arkansas (see Fig. 8.1). More than 50,000 diamonds have been found in that region, in *kimberlite*, a rare form of peridotite (see Chapter 6). In

South Africa, the kimberlite (named after Kimberley) weathers to the famous diamond-bearing "blue ground" (clay) of that country. In Arkansas, the kimberlite has weathered to a soft yellowish or greenish clay and dark soil. The majority of the Arkansas diamonds found have been found in this clay and dark soil.

The Murfreesboro area contains four known exposures of kimberlite, at least one of which is apparently part of the solidified conduit of a former volcano. It is in such volcanic

Fig. 8.1: Searching for diamonds at the Crater of Diamonds, Murfreesboro, Arkansas. For a nominal fee, visitors may search all day and they keep what they find. Over 55,000 diamonds have been found in this area, many of the stones having been over 20 carats in weight. (Photo by Donnie Kizza)

pipes, it is believed, that sufficient pressure was created by the cooling magma far below the then-surface to form diamonds.

Diamonds have also been found in the sands and gravels of present and former stream beds in North Carolina, South Carolina, Virginia, Georgia, Alabama, West Virginia, Texas,

Idaho, Montana, California, and Oregon, many of these discoveries having been made in conjunction with placer gold mining operations.

One of the most interesting occurrences of diamonds in the United States involves the Great Lakes region. Thousands of years ago, glaciers, moving from what is now Canada, apparently plowed through one or more diamond-bearing formations and finally deposited some of the diamonds in the Great Lakes area. These diamonds have been found in Wisconsin, Michigan, Indiana, and Ohio. Diamonds possibly from the same source have also been found in Kentucky and Tennessee. Not many discoveries of diamonds have been made in the Great Lakes region in recent years, but the rockhounds there keep hoping.

How to Recognize Diamonds. First of all, if you do find something which you think may be a diamond don't test it by hitting it hard. Diamond is the hardest known natural substance but it is also brittle and it will break fairly easily beneath a blow.

If you find a diamond which has weathered out "in place" from the parent rock, such as the diamonds found near Murfreesboro, the cleaned diamond will commonly sparkle in sunlight and will also reveal whether it is transparent, etc. On the other hand, a diamond found in stream gravel or in glacial material usually looks like a greasy, rounded and somewhat cloudy-appearing piece of quartz. The feature of rounding, by the way, is due to the fact that diamond is isometric and commonly crystallizes in shapes (see Fig. 8.2) which are easily rounded by stream action, etc., and it is this tendency toward rounding which helps to distinguish a stream diamond from a piece of stream quartz. The test for hardness should, of course, always be made on any material found, even if it appears to be a piece of rounded glass.

Contrary to popular belief, very few, if any, diamonds are absolutely colorless, and diamonds come in almost all colors. Some diamonds are black. Remember also that uncut diamonds do not flash and gleam as do cut diamonds, television and newspaper cartoons notwithstanding. Also, although most people seem to hopefully visualize a discovered dia-

mond as approximately the size of a marble, most diamonds
are probably so small that they will never be recovered. Do
not, however, throw away anything just because it happens
to be fairly large. Many of the diamonds found in stream
gravels in the United States have approached 5 carats in
weight, a carat being one fifth of a gram. Some diamonds
found in the Great Lakes area have weighed in the neighbor-
hood of 20 carats, and a considerable number of diamonds
ranging in weight from 4 to more than 30 carats have been
found in Arkansas, at the Crater of Diamonds.

Fig. 8.2: Diamond crystal

Where and How to Look for Diamonds. Diamonds are mined
from kimberlite in only a few places in the world, two of
these being Arkansas and the diamond fields of South Africa.
As outcrops of diamond-bearing peridotite are obviously very
rare, there seems to be a discrepancy between the lack of
this host rock and the wide dissemination of diamonds
throughout the stream gravels of much of the world. The
point, of course, is that someday someone may discover that
diamonds can form in a type of rock different than peridotite
and under conditions different than those existing in a cooling volcanic conduit.

It has been estimated that for every diamond recovered
from stream gravels and sands in the United States, and
from glacial material, there are at least one thousand more
which have not yet been discovered, and streams and stream
gravels should be regarded as prime hunting grounds by the
diamond seeker. Being heavier than the average crustal rock,
diamonds tend to concentrate in much the same places that

gold concentrates, that is, in places where the forward velocity of the stream is reduced. Also, as when searching for gold, don't forget the places where the stream formerly ran but which may now be literally high and dry. Included, of course, are those valleys, large or small, where streams once ran but which do not now contain streams.

How to Work Over Stream Gravels for Diamonds. As the typical diamond found in stream gravels in the United States is small, the first thing to do is to screen the gravel to be processed through a, say, ¼-inch mesh screen first and then through a, say, ⅛-inch mesh screen. The "no go" material on the ¼-inch mesh screen and the "go" material which passed through the ⅛-inch mesh should be saved for subsequent examination for both gemstones and gold. If the material to be screened is muddy or clayey, it is extremely important that it be thoroughly cleaned with water and rolled back and forth by hand on the screen to make sure that all mud and clay are broken up. If a nest of small screens is used, this process may be carried out with the screens submerged in water, otherwise the water will usually have to be poured or hosed onto the material.

After the material to be processed is further sized carefully, this time by hand, the procedure to be followed is largely a matter of choice. The cone sieve (see Chapter 2) can be very effectively used for diamond recovery. Stream diamonds are, as previously mentioned, roughly spherical in shape and, as can be shown mathematically, the cone sieve is especially efficient in the recovery of rounded material.

Some rockhounds make it a practice to first run such sized material through a sluice box while others prefer the gold pan for gemstone recovery. A variation of the gold pan is the *batea*, a cone-shaped receptacle of the same general dimensions as those of a cone screen. A *batea*, however, is not made of screen but is made of sheet metal or wood. *Bateas* are used in Mexico, Central America, and South America for the recovery of gemstones and gold. A similar device is used in Asia, in some places. For those who would like to try the *batea* method, a wooden chopping bowl makes a very good *batea*. *Bateas* are especially effective in concentrating heavier material if the swirling, eccentric motion used with the gold pan is combined with a jiggling, sidewise action.

Ruby and Sapphire

Chemical composition: aluminum oxide.
Chemical formula: Al_2O_3
Color: sapphire is commonly blue, but may be any color except red. Ruby is always red.
Luster: adamantine to subadamantine.
Diaphaneity: transparent to translucent.
Hardness: 9.0
Specific gravity: 3.9–4.1
Cleavage: no actual cleavage, but usually parts fairly readily.
Fracture: conchoidal to uneven.
Crystal system: hexagonal.

Ruby and sapphire (see Plate 3.E) are varieties of corundum, the same material which is part of the naturally occurring abrasive known as *emery,* the other mineral in emery being *magnetite.* The red color of ruby results from a small quantity of chromium in the corundum while the typical blue of sapphire is probably due to inclusion of elements such as titanium.

Corundum is somewhat unique in that it is not usual (as does happen in the case of corundum) for an oxide of a metal to be heavier than the metal itself. The specific gravity of corundum (about 4) is high for a nonmetallic and this brings up the fact that a two-carat sapphire or ruby is smaller than a two-carat diamond. The reason, of course, is that the carat is a unit of weight and diamond has a lesser specific gravity than that of corundum.

The most valuable rubies have the color of red known as "pigeon's-blood red," a term which has been handed down through the ages. Strangely enough, the dark red color of a ruby turns to green when a ruby is heated sufficiently, but the red color returns when the ruby has cooled enough. Corundum of gem quality which has a natural yellow color is often sold as "Oriental topaz" while that of a deep purple color is often sold as "Oriental amethyst." Incidentally, the correct and incorrect names of a number of gemstones which are sold under their incorrect names in the United States are listed at the end of Chapter 14.

The effect of *asterism* is seen in some rubies and sapphires, due to a number of inclusions or small, hollow tubes which, because of the hexagonal symmetry of corundum, are arranged 60 degrees apart. If such a stone is cut in deep cabochon, light is reflected from the interior in the form of a six-sided star. Thus we have *star rubies* and *star sapphires*.

Ruby and Sapphire in the United States. Rubies and sapphires have been mined for centuries in such places as Burma, Thailand, India, Afghanistan, and China, mostly by primitive methods. In the United States, rubies have been commercially mined in North Carolina and have been found in Colorado, Wyoming, and Montana. Sapphires have been commercially mined in Montana and have also been found in California, Colorado, Idaho, Indiana, and North Carolina. Approximately 30 million dollars worth of sapphires have been mined in the Yogo Gulch area of Montana, in Judith Basin County.

Where and How to Look for Ruby and Sapphire. Ruby and sapphire form in metamorphic rocks such as marble, schist, and gneiss, and in igneous rocks, especially those which have a relatively low content of silica. In general, therefore, it would probably be a waste of time to look for ruby and sapphire in igneous rocks which contain a considerable amount of quartz, but this does not mean that dark-colored igneous rocks should be favored as likely host material. As a matter of fact, rubies and sapphires are often found—when they are found—in pegmatites and other igneous rocks of generally light color.

At Yogo Gulch, in Montana, sapphires of excellent quality are found in an igneous dike which intrudes into beds of limestone. In this region, much of the dike material has weathered to clay at the surface, a fact which is worth remembering in searching for likely outcrops, especially in humid regions. In other words, a yellow, green, gray or blue clay on the surface may signify the presence of an igneous or metamorphic rock below the clay, and the clay or rock, or both, may contain gemstones.

It must not be inferred, however that clay always lies above the rock from which the clay was formed, or that clay-forming rock has an exceptionally good chance of containing gemstones. In the first place, much clay has been transported from its site of formation to positions which may be many miles distant, by streams, glaciers, etc. Secondly, clay is common in humid regions where the underlying rock from which the clay was derived is limestone or a similar rock.

Investigation of any clay, however, is recommended. The Spruce Pine district of North Carolina, for example, is one of the major clay-mineral mining regions in the world. It is also one of the very few regions where sapphires, rubies, and emeralds have been found occurring together in the same general area, one exception being the "salted" gem field of the last century, in Wyoming. Thus a clay deposit—and a good deposit of clay is extremely valuable—is worth investigating for two good reasons, in many instances.

How to Recognize Ruby and Sapphire. The extreme hardness of corundum (9.0) is, of course, the great distinguishing characteristic of corundum. Ruby is always of red color while sapphire, although usually blue, may be almost any color except red. Some sapphire also exhibits several colors within a particular stone. If the gemstone is not too water-worn, its often barrel-shaped crystals (see Fig. 8.3) constitute another easily recognized characteristic.

Although hard, corundum, like diamond, is brittle and if

Fig. 8.3: Corundum crystal

you think that you may have found some variety of corundum, don't try to prove it by a blow, especially if the color is blue or red. Corundum does not have true cleavage but it does break rather easily under impact, into a number of somewhat cube-shaped particles and pieces. Such tests involving impact, incidentally, have often resulted in rockhounds thus becoming much more informed than they wanted to be.

How to "Mine" Ruby and Sapphire. As in the case of diamonds, the average rockhound in the average area is more likely to find rubies and sapphires in stream gravels, etc., than in weathered or solid rock, and the same methods used in recovering diamonds from stream gravels can be used for the recovery of rubies and sapphires. Thus, the sluice box, the gold pan, the cone sieve, and the *batea* can all be used to recover the corundum gemstones.

The material should, of course first be screened and washed, and then sorted by hand, at least to some extent, before using the sluice box, gold pan, cone sieve, or *batea*. Just as when looking for gold or diamonds, look in the old stream gravel, too, in places where the velocity of the stream slackened for some reason. For example, you might find an exposure of stream gravel in which there is a large buried boulder. In such a case, the gravel on the upstream face of the boulder should be dug out, washed, and screened. Then, after some sorting by hand, they can be processed with sluice box or gold pan, etc. In some places such as the Cowee Ruby Mines area of North Carolina, rockhounds can take their gravel to flumes in which the gravel can be washed, screened, sorted, and inspected for gemstones.

Possible Future Discoveries of Gemstones and Minerals

Will diamonds, rubies, and sapphires ever be found in new areas in the United States? We could, for that matter, ask the same question concerning any mineral or gemstone, and perhaps the best attempt at an answer would be the recounting of an important geological truth: the natural intersection of the ground surface with mineral-bearing rock is essentially a matter of chance. Who knows, for example, what minerals lie buried beneath our feet as we walk in the field, minerals which will certainly be exposed some day, possibly after the next rain or perhaps not for thousands of years? Who knows what rocks were exposed by weathering last year, and who knows what kinds of minerals will be found in the stream valleys below these new outcrops, some day?

One of the most important things that any rockhound can learn is the fact that Nature's lottery alone determines what mineral specimens will be naturally exposed, and when, and where, and how. Another fact, just as important, is that the discovery of these minerals depends upon being in the right place at the right time, and doing the right thing. In other words, although we certainly cannot predict what minerals will someday be found and where, we can say with some sense of expectation that yesterday's apparently barren hillside or stream channel or stream gravel may be the scene of tomorrow's discovery.

Chapter 9

Tourmaline, Topaz, the Beryllium Gemstones, and Spodumene

Tourmaline, topaz, most of the beryllium gemstones, and spodumene are silicates, their one common hunting ground being pegmatites. These minerals occur together so frequently in pegmatites that the discovery of one in a pegmatite should be taken as an indication that some and possibly all of the other minerals are close by.

Tourmaline

Chemical composition: complex sodium-aluminum or calcium-aluminum borosilicate.
Chemical formula: varies with kind of tourmaline.
Color: red, green, purple, blue, black, brown, colorless.
Luster: vitreous.
Diaphaneity: transparent to opaque.
Hardness: 7.0–7.5
Specific gravity: 3.0–3.2
Cleavage: none to poor.
Fracture: conchoidal to uneven.
Crystal system: hexagonal.

Tourmalines (see Plate 3.F) contain varying amounts of sodium, magnesium, calcium, iron, lithium, fluorine, and hydrogen, and thus can be divided into three main classes: (1) the alkali-rich tourmalines, (2) the magnesium-rich tourmalines, and (3) the iron-rich tourmalines. The alkali-rich tourmalines, containing sodium and lithium, among other elements, furnish most of the best tourmaline gemstones.

Color is one of the most notable features of the lithiatourmalines. The colors of these tourmalines cover a wide range from crystal to crystal, and a given crystal commonly exhibits two and sometimes more than two colors within the crystal.

In addition to being a popular gemstone, tourmaline finds several important applications in instrumentation. Tourmaline is both pyroelectric and piezoelectric in that either heat or pressure, properly applied, will cause the ends of a tourmaline crystal to become oppositely charged, electrically. Thus, thanks to tourmaline and a few other minerals which exhibit similar properties, we can measure pressure generated by underwater and above ground blasts, a submarine can determine its depth, and so on. Along these lines, it is interesting to note that specimens of tourmaline in a collection often get dustier than other specimens since, with changes in temperature, more and more dust and dirt particles are attracted to the electrically active tourmaline, much as a television set collects dust.

Varieties of Tourmaline. Pink or rose-red tourmaline is called *rubellite,* violet-red to purple tourmaline is called *siberite,* dark blue tourmaline is known as *indicolite,* and black tourmaline is *schorl.* Colorless tourmaline is very rare and is known as *achroite.* Magnesium-rich tourmalines are usually brown in color.

Tourmaline in the United States. Tourmaline of fair to excellent gem quality has been found in California, Maine, Colorado, Connecticut, Arizona, Massachusetts, New York State, and Pennsylvania. Actually, tourmaline in one form or another can be found in practically every state of the Union as it is a common accessory mineral in several kinds of rock. Its known occurrences of gem quality in the United States, however, are limited.

How to Recognize Tourmaline. Crystals of tourmaline in which there are several colors within a single crystal are easy to recognize as tourmaline because the colors will almost always contrast sharply in hue (red and green, for example). Furthermore, the colors within a crystal commonly terminate against each other suddenly, without any noticeable blending. Many such tourmaline crystals therefore give the appearance of having been made from two crystals of the same size but of different color which were each broken into two pieces, the top piece of one crystal then having been cemented onto the bottom piece of the other crystal.

Even though a crystal of tourmaline may not show any telltale colors or color patterns—much of the tourmaline which will be found will be black, for instance—tourmaline can be easily identified by an outstanding characteristic: in cross section, viewed along the long axis, tourmaline crystals usually approximate the shape of a triangle whose sides are bulging outward. Tourmaline crystals are also very often striated in a direction parallel to the long axis of the crystal, to the extent that the striations are sometimes actually groovy, in the older sense of that word. All in all, tourmaline is an extremely easy mineral to identify.

Where and How to Look for Tourmaline. Tourmaline as such is found in granites, pegmatites, schists, and metamorphosed limestones. The gem varieties of tourmaline, however, are associated chiefly with pegmatites, and thus the matrix of a typical collection specimen of tourmaline is a pegmatite of some kind. Although tourmaline "float" may be found in streams and stream deposits, tourmaline crystals (see Fig. 9.1) commonly contain fractures. Furthermore, quite a bit of tourmaline is not much harder than quartz, and the result is that, due to fractures and relative softness, pieces of tourmaline found in streams and stream gravel are usually fragmental and at least somewhat rounded.

As previously indicated, the best places to look for tourmaline are pegmatite dikes, especially near the "cores" of

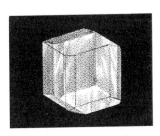

Fig. 9.1: Tourmaline crystal

the dikes. Having said that, it must also be said that finding the core of a pegmatite dike is much more easily said than done, especially if the dike is strongly weathered and is perhaps partly covered over by soil. In many exposed pegmatite dikes, however, a sequence of light-colored mica abutting pegmatite which in turn abuts quartz frequently solves the mystery, as the quartz in such a sequence is usually at the core of the dike. Cores often contain pockets, and it is in these pockets that many of the most striking specimens of tourmaline are found. It was in such a pocket that two boys in Maine, in 1820, found the glittering deposit of gem tourmaline which was to launch the commercial mining of gem tourmaline in that state. Incidentally, the boys found the tourmaline near the base of a tree, and this brings up the point that tree roots tend to follow joints and cracks and therefore sometimes lead directly into a pocket. There have been instances when large trees have fallen over and have exposed pockets of tourmaline and other gemstones in pegmatite, in areas where even the existence of pegmatite had not been before suspected.

Topaz

Chemical composition: aluminum fluosilicate.
Chemical formula: $Al_2SiO_4(F,OH)_2$
Color: colorless, brown, light blue, pink, yellow.
Luster: vitreous.
Diaphaneity: transparent to translucent.
Hardness: 8.0
Specific gravity: 3.4–3.6
Cleavage: one perfect, parallel to base.
Fracture: conchoidal.
Crystal system: orthorhombic.

Topaz is an aluminum silicate containing fluorine, the most valuable kinds of topaz being the wine-yellow and dark-pink varieties. The idea that topaz is always yellow seems to be prevalent although topaz is found in several colors, including light blue. Brown topaz from Brazil can often be heated to bring about a lasting pink color which, of course, means that it can then be sold for a higher price. Due to its perfect cleavage, topaz is somewhat hard to work with as many an amateur lapidary has discovered. It is not uncommon for a lapidary to start out with one piece of topaz to be shaped for a ring, and end up with two smaller pieces of topaz and two rings. Topaz might be regarded as one of Nature's seltzer bottles in that topaz very often contains tiny inclusions of liquid carbon dioxide.

How to Recognize Topaz. Although topaz commonly occurs in prisms (see Fig. 9.2) of one kind or another, its hardness and specific gravity (both higher than those of beryl and tourmaline) distinguish topaz from the two other minerals, beryl being the most common beryllium gemstone.

Where and How to Look for Topaz. Topaz, like tourmaline, occurs in pegmatite dikes but topaz is also found in some miarolitic cavities in granites. When in pegmatite country the rockhound should, as in the case of searching for tourmaline (and beryl, to be discussed later), look for the white mica-pegmatite-quartz sequence as good topaz is also associated with the quartzitic cores of pegmatite dikes. In granitic rock territory, the rockhound should always keep in mind the possibility of miarolitic cavities. Such cavities may actually be visible or, as explained in Chapter 6, they can sometimes be found by a distinctive pattern in what appears to be solid rock.

Although fragmental and rounded pieces of topaz are found in some streams and stream deposits, the fact that topaz, although hard, cleaves easily means that the occurrence of good crystals of topaz in streams and stream gravel is, in general, unlikely. Light-colored rhyolite flows some-

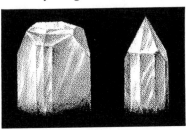

Fig. 9.2: Topaz crystals

times contain gas cavities (amygdaloidal cavities) in which topaz is found. Cracks usually form around these cavities as the lava cools, and these cracks are often the only visible indication that there is a cavity in the rock. A few minutes of widening such cracks with hammer and prybar, and removing some rock, have often paid off handsomely in the form of revealing a cavity lined with crystals. Topaz of gem quality has been found in California, Utah, New Hampshire, Colorado, Texas, and Maine.

Beryl

Chemical composition: beryllium aluminum silicate.
Chemical formula: $Be_3Al_2(SiO_3)_6$
Color: green, blue, yellow, pink, colorless.
Luster: vitreous.
Diaphaneity: transparent to translucent.
Hardness: 7.5–8.0
Specific gravity: 2.6–2.8
Cleavage: indistinct.
Fracture: conchoidal.
Crystal system: hexagonal.

Beryl (see Fig. 9.3) is beryllium aluminum silicate and its gem varieties include *emerald, aquamarine, golden beryl,* and *morganite.* Emerald is one of the long established "big four" precious stones, the other three—diamond, sapphire, and ruby—having been discussed in Chapter 8. Emerald is slightly softer than the other varieties of beryl but other than that, the only difference between the beryl gemstones is one of color. Emerald is grass green in color, aquamarine ranges from green blue to blue green, golden beryl is, of course, golden yellow, and morganite is anywhere between pink and rose red in color. A pure, colorless variety of beryl is known as *goshenite* (named after Goshen, Massachusetts, where this variety was apparently first found and identified). A beryllium silicate called *euclase* is rare and costly but it also happens to look much like aquamarine, the result of this being that any potential market for euclase is more than satisfied by the relatively ubiquitous and less costly aquamarine, and by blue topaz.

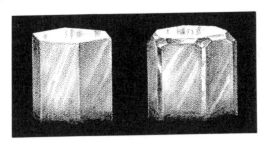

Fig. 9.3: Beryl crystals

Beryl also furnishes us with most of our supply of *beryllium*, a metallic element and the lightest of the rigid metals. Beryllium has many important applications, most of it being used as an alloying element to harden copper, zinc, nickel, and other metals. Beryllium-copper alloys are nonsparking and tools made of this alloy are used where the use of steel tools might be dangerous. Beryllium is also used in high-temperature ceramics. *Beryllium fumes and dust are highly toxic* and the lapidary who works with beryllium minerals should always observe the necessary precautions when cutting, grinding, or polishing a beryllium mineral.

Emerald

Almost four thousand years ago, a mine near the Red Sea supplied Queen Cleopatra of Egypt with emeralds of great size. Emeralds have been mined in many countries throughout the world but the best emeralds have come from Colombia, South America, from old Inca mines which were active long before the Spanish conquest. During the Conquest, the Spaniards found many emeralds in the jewelry and ornaments of the natives and in temples, where many of the emeralds were of almost unbelievable size, one of them being of the approximate dimensions of an ostrich egg. Despite the far from gentle blandishments of the Spaniards, the Indians never did reveal the locations of the emerald mines which they had caved in and covered over so the Spaniards could not find them. One of the mines was discovered by accident in the sixteenth century and a second mine was found approximately fifty years ago.

Emerald in the United States. Emeralds have been mined commercially in North Carolina, and emerald discoveries have been reported in South Carolina. As the known occurrences of emerald in the United States are very limited, the Big Crabtree Mine near Little Switzerland, North Carolina, is a kind of Mecca for the emerald-seeking rockhound in the United States. That particular mine has produced emeralds of good quality in the past, and the area is now open to rockhounds on a "pay to dig" basis.

How to Recognize Emerald. Beryl of all kinds is brittle and easily fractured. Any test for hardness should therefore be very carefully made, especially if the specimen has the color of emerald. Most emeralds have flaws, and some particular kinds of flaws contribute to the overall brittleness of a particular specimen. Once the hardness has been determined as that of beryl—intermediate between the hardnesses of quartz and topaz—this fact and the grass green color will be sufficient to identify the gemstone as emerald.

Where and How to Look for Emerald. As brought out in Chapter 8, the known geographic occurrences of a particular mineral are largely matters of chance; thus, it seems very probable that at least some minerals and gemstones will someday be found in regions where they are not now known to occur. Interestingly enough, one of the most likely candidates for such future discovery seems to be emerald, considered by some to be more valuable than diamond.

The geological reasons for this assessment are simple. Emerald typically occurs in highly metamorphosed schists, in gneiss, in calcite veins, in marble, and in metamorphosed limestone which cannot be properly called marble. These are all common rocks, and it seems very improbable that emerald occurrence in the United States would be restricted to the Carolinas. But, some will say, emerald has never been found in any place in the United States other than the Carolinas. Perhaps that particular variety of beryl does occur in the Carolinas, only, due to some unique locally present geological factor which makes one variety of beryl have a grass green color and a slightly lesser hardness than that of other varieties. Perhaps—except that *U.S. Geological Survey Bul-*

letin 1042-*G* lists emerald as having also been found, some years ago, in Massachusetts, in Chesterfield, and the geology of that part of Massachusetts is much like the geology of many New England regions, and so on. This statement is not meant to level the New England or any other hills and mountains with an emerald rush, but only to again emphasize that many minerals and varieties of minerals, like gold, "are where you find them."

This does not mean, of course, that emerald or any other gemstone is just as liable to be found in one type of rock as another. Regions of metamorphic rocks would obviously be logical areas in which to search for emerald as would be high-silica pegmatites. Also, be on the lookout for black tourmaline and colored tourmaline, on the slopes of hills and in stream channels and valleys. Black tourmaline is often an indicator mineral of the presence of gneiss or schist while colored tourmaline often indicates that a pegmatite dike is somewhere in the general area. Black tourmaline is also found in some pegmatite dikes.

Aquamarine, Golden Beryl, and Morganite

Aquamarine. Aquamarine (see Plate 4.A), varying from blue green to green blue in color, is the most common variety of semiprecious beryl found in the United States, and its occurrence is virtually restricted to granite pegmatites. Some years ago, a giant crystal of beryl, measuring 18 feet by 4 feet and weighing approximately 18 tons, was found in Maine. The crystal was opaque to transparent throughout its length but a considerable portion of it was blue-green aquamarine. A 243-pound crystal of aquamarine, transparent throughout its length and of gem quality, was found in Brazil. Lest the beginner gain the idea, however, that block and tackle should be brought along when hunting for aquamarine, a good aquamarine about one inch long is considered by many rockhounds to verge on the fabulous.

Aquamarine is much less valuable than emerald but to the rockhound this is more than made up for by the facts that aquamarine crystals are larger, have more uniform transparency, and the chances of finding aquamarine are much greater than are those of finding emerald. For example, aquamarine has been commercially mined in California, Colorado, Connecticut, Georgia, Maine, Montana, New Hampshire, and North Carolina. Aquamarine has also been found in Alabama, Idaho, Maryland, Massachusetts, Pennsylvania, South Carolina, South Dakota, and Utah. The almost unbelievable deep blue of some aquamarines sold by jewelers is just that—unbelievable, as far as any natural color of aquamarine is concerned. These aquamarines are varieties of beryl which have been heated by someone to a deep blue color. The color is permanent, unlike some colors imparted to some other gemstones in the same way.

Golden Beryl. Golden beryl, golden yellow in color, like aquamarine, is found almost exclusively in pegmatite dikes. Like aquamarine, crystals of golden beryl are in general larger than crystals of emerald and have more uniform transparency. Golden beryl has been found in California, Connecticut, Maine, Maryland, New Hampshire, New York, and North Carolina.

Morganite. Morganite, named after the late J. P. Morgan, financier and rockhound, ranges in color from pink to rose red. Morganite has been found in only a few states such as California, Maine, and Utah. It is found in pegmatites.

Chrysoberyl

Chemical composition: beryllium aluminum oxide.
Chemical formula: $BeAl_2O_4$
Color: Greenish, yellowish, yellow, gray, blue green, brown.
Luster: vitreous.
Diaphaneity: transparent.
Hardness: 8.5
Specific gravity: 3.5–3.8
Cleavage: one good, parallel to crystal faces.
Fracture: conchoidal to uneven.
Crystal system: orthorhombic.

Chrysoberyl is a double oxide of beryllium and aluminum and is intermediate in hardness between topaz and corundum. Being extremely rare, it is a much sought-after gem-

Fig. 9.4 : Chrysoberyl twin

stone and chrysoberyl of gem quality commands a high price. Due to twinning, crystals of chrysoberyl are often heart shaped or pseudohexagonal (see Fig. 9.4).

Alexandrite, a variety of chrysoberyl, was discovered in Russia at about the same time that Czar Alexander II reached his majority and the gemstone was named in his honor. Three colors, emerald green, orange yellow, and columbine red, can be seen in alexandrite. The overall color of the stone in daylight is emerald green, but under artificial light the color of alexandrite is violet red.

Cat's eye, another variety of chrysoberyl, has a greenish color, is opalescent, and has fine fibrous inclusions. If cat's eye is cut in cabochon on the correct face, a slit of light seems to change position on the rounded surface as the stone is turned, hence the name "cat's eye." The effect is called *chatoyancy.*

Most specimens of gem chrysoberyl come from foreign countries but some large specimens have been found in Colorado, some larger than seven inches. Chrysoberyl has also been found in Connecticut, Maine, and New York. Discoveries of chrysoberyl in the latter named state were made while excavating for buildings in New York City.

How to Recognize Chrysoberyl. Chrysoberyl is usually easy to recognize as, much more often than not, chrysoberyl crystals are twinned into what could be called either heart-shaped or arrowhead-shaped pairs, depending upon the whim or mood of the rockhound who finds chrysoberyl. The twinning sometimes produces a hexagonal-appearing specimen. In any event, chrysoberyl specimens are also usually strongly striated; thus its hardness (8.5), luster, twinning, and striations make chrysoberyl one of our most easily recognizable gemstones.

Where to Look for Chrysoberyl. In the United States, chrysoberyl should be looked for in high-silica pegmatites, mica schists, gneisses, and light-colored igneous rocks in all of which chrysoberyl may appear as a yellow-green "arrowhead" stuck into the rock. Look for chrysoberyl wherever beryl, tourmaline, and apatite are found. Stream valleys and stream gravel are excellent places in which to look for chrysoberyl as, for one practical thing, most of the gem quality chrysoberyl is found in stream deposits. Chrysoberyl is therefore added to the list of minerals and gemstones which are most easily found by sluicing, panning, etc., and the operations such as screening and sizing are carried out just as they are for other gemstones.

Spodumene

Chemical composition: lithium aluminum silicate.
Chemical formula: $LiAlSi_2O_6$
Color: white, lavender, buff, yellow, green, pink.
Luster: glassy to silky.
Diaphaneity: opaque to transparent.
Hardness: 6.5–7.0
Specific gravity: 3.1–3.2
Cleavage: two perfect prismatic cleavages.
Crystal system: monoclinic.

Like tourmaline, topaz, and most of the beryllium gemstones, the spodumene gemstones are also found in pegmatites. Spodumene is an ore mineral of lithium and commonly occurs in the form of striated prisms. These prisms are sometimes larger than the usual prism-shaped crystal found in the field, as shown by some 40-foot crystals of spodumene found in South Dakota a number of years ago.

Kunzite, one gem form of spodumene, is transparent and may vary in color from bluish pink to lilac pink. *Hiddenite,* the other gem variety of spodumene, is also transparent and may be anywhere from yellowish green to emerald green in color. Both hiddenite and kunzite typically have scarred and etched crystal faces when found and there have possibly been instances where rockhounds have thrown away some battered-appearing crystals without realizing that they were discarding specimens of a very rare and valuable gemstone.

Lithia-rich pegmatite dikes are, of course, the homes of the spodumene gemstones. Such dikes are more or less well known in areas in Maine, Connecticut, Massachusetts, North Carolina, South Dakota, New Mexico, and California. Good kunzite has been found in California, North Carolina, Connecticut, and Maine. Good hiddenite has been found in North Carolina and South Dakota.

Chapter 10

Quartz, Opal, and Petrified Wood

Most rockhounds never experience the thrill of discovering a rare and valuable gemstone like emerald but, given the right locality, anyone can easily find good specimens of quartz, opal, and petrified wood. Despite the prevalence of the silica gemstones, their varieties are so attractive that they have all enjoyed a well-deserved popularity down through the ages. Pliny the Elder (23–79 A.D.), for example, described many quartz gemstones in his voluminous writings. It was, incidentally, Pliny's curiosity concerning geological phenomena which caused this philosopher and admiral of the Roman navy to become the Roman equivalent of a rockhound. It was also this same curiosity which led him too close to the roaring, exploding Vesuvius in 79 A.D. and to concurrent martyrdom in science.

Quartz is silica (SiO_2) in crystallized form, that is, quartz has a definite and unique arrangement of its component elements, silicon and oxygen. Opal, on the other hand, is an amorphous silica which contains water, the formula for opal being $SiO_2 \cdot n\ H_2O$. Opal does not therefore have crystalline structure and, as the "n" in its formula indicates, opal contains varying amounts of water. Technically, opal is not a mineral since it is not crystallized.

Silica of some kind is usually the replacement material in petrified wood, but other kinds of replacement substances such as native copper and pyrite at times also "petrify" wood. One of the most interesting petrifactions of wood occurred in what is now Arizona when the buried wood was replaced by a substance containing a high percentage of uranium. Some of these stone logs sold for approximately $100,000 each, as they were virtual concentration bins of uranium.

Quartz

Chemical composition: silicon dioxide.
Chemical formula: SiO_2
Color: can be almost any color.
Luster: vitreous.
Diaphaneity: transparent to opaque, depending upon type and impurities.
Hardness: 7.0
Specific gravity: 2.58–2.65
Cleavage: none usually observable.
Fracture: conchoidal.
Crystal system: hexagonal.

Quartz is the most common mineral in the earth's crust. In ancient times, colorless quartz was believed by some peoples to be permanently frozen ice while other cultures believed that some varieties of quartz had powers to ward off evil. Death by thirst was included, some Oriental people believing that a quartz pebble held in the mouth would prevent thirst, an idea which seems not to have been confined to ancient cultures. For example, Boy Scout handbooks of some fifty years ago advocated much the same procedure, one result being that many small hikers ultimately and suddenly found themselves with a pebble in their stomachs, and just as thirsty as ever.

Varieties of quartz such as flint have of course long been used throughout the world for arrowheads and spearheads, etc., while rock crystal has been long used to make a large variety of objects, from goblets and carved figures to crystal balls, the latter use again reminding us of the ancient beliefs that quartz had magical powers. Many varieties of quartz have held age-old rank throughout the world as prized gemstones and today the demand for quartz gemstones is at an all time high. A deposit of gem quality quartz is worth considerable money but of more interest to most rockhounds is the fact that good quartz specimens can be found in virtually every one of the fifty states.

Quartz is either crystalline or *cryptocrystalline* which means that the crystalline structure is so fine that it cannot be seen with ordinary microscopes. Clear quartz crystal has been used for many years in optical instruments but the principal use of quartz crystal today is in radio, radar, television, ultrasonics, and similar fields. Every time a long distance telephone call is made by direct dialing, for instance, the call is made possible by the use of components made of quartz. Some "electronic" quartz is now made synthetically in the United States but a considerable amount is still imported from Brazil, from which country radio-quality quartz was flown to the United States and England, during World War II.

Much quartz in the form of quartz sand is used in the manufacture of all kinds of glass, including fused quartz glass which allows the passage of ultraviolet light. For example, mercury vapor sun lamps, and ultraviolet lights used in prospecting, have fused quartz glass.

Crystalline Quartz

In speaking of "crystalline" quartz, we will be talking about those varieties of quartz which are obviously crystalline and which therefore, in general, are often found in crystal form. The crystal form of quartz is often far from being a textbook example, however. Although quartz crystallizes in the hexagonal system, its prisms are commonly terminated in manners which seem to make the entire crystal look anything but symmetrical about any axis, as shown in Fig. 10.1, and the rockhound should become familiar with this peculiarity of quartz. At times, however, quartz crystals are found which are perfectly symmetrical, looking like glass prisms which have been sharpened at one end.

Amethyst. One of the consistently most popular gemstones, *amethyst* (see Plate 4.B) is purple to violet in color and is transparent. *Siberian amethyst* is reddish violet in color and is considered to be the most valuable form of amethyst. Amethyst localities in the United States include areas in Georgia, Arizona, Virginia, North Carolina, Michigan, Montana, Colorado, Pennsylvania, Maine, Indiana, South Carolina, Maryland, Texas, and New Hampshire.

Tiger's eye. *Tiger's eye* is golden-brown quartz with a fibrous structure resulting from the fact that this variety of quartz is pseudomorphic after a type of asbestos. Tiger's eye is rare in the United States.

Citrine. *Citrine*, the golden-yellow and transparent variety of quartz is very similar to topaz in appearance. Citrine is rare in the United States but it has been found in North Carolina, Nevada, and California. Despite its rarity, a considerable amount of United States produced citrine is sold in this country, the apparent anomaly being explained by the fact that heat treatment can change several varieties of quartz into what, technically, is citrine. The saga of citrine does not stop there, however. The synthetically produced citrine is often so attractive that the citrine label is completely bypassed, and the mineral is thereupon sold as topaz, which it is not (see the list of incorrect and correct names of gemstones, at the end of Chapter 14).

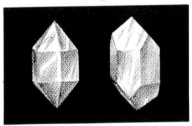

Fig. 10.1: Quartz crystals

Milky Quartz. The quartz veins cutting through igneous and metamorphic rocks are often composed of *milky quartz*. This variety of quartz contains microscopic inclusions of carbon dioxide and water, and the "milky" effect is apparently due to these inclusions. Crystals of milky quartz are rare, but some form of milky quartz, varying from being translucent to almost opaque, can be found in virtually every one of the United States.

Rose Quartz. *Rose quartz*, a specimen of which is shown in Plate 4.C, varies from pink to rose red in color and ranges from being transparent to translucent. Crystals of rose quartz are extremely rare but the massive form is found in several states, including Maine, Michigan, South Dakota, Connecticut, New York, Colorado, Nevada, North Carolina, and California.

Quartz Crystal. Quartz crystal, or *rock crystal,* is the colorless, transparent variety of crystal quartz. Beautiful specimens of quartz crystal are found in Arkansas, while New York State furnished the famous "Herkimer diamond." Good quartz crystal (see Plate 4.D) can be found in almost every state, some of the more famous collecting localities being in Arkansas, New York State, Maine, Rhode Island, North Carolina, Georgia, Texas, and Vermont.

Sagenite. Some of the world's most spectacular mineral specimens are quartz crystals which seem to have been pierced by rodlike or hairlike inclusions of some kind (see Plate 4.E). Such quartz specimens are called *sagenite.* The inclusions can be any of several minerals. If the inclusions are of rutile, the specimen is "rutilated quartz." If the inclusions are tourmaline, the specimen is "tourmalinated quartz." Excellent specimens of sagenite have been found in Colorado, New Hampshire, North Carolina, California, Virginia, Pennsylvania, Rhode Island, and Maine. Sagenite of varying quality has been found in many of the fifty states.

Smoky Quartz. *Smoky quartz* (see Plate 4.F) is smoky yellow to dark brown in color, sometimes approaching black. It is an extremely popular gemstone, particularly in Scotland where it is known as "cairngorm." Excellent crystals of smoky quartz have been found in Colorado, North Carolina, Montana, New York State, Massachusetts, Pennsylvania, South Carolina, Maine, Arkansas, Missouri, and California.

Aventurine. *Aventurine* is crystal quartz which contains spangled inclusions of minerals such as mica and hematite. Aventurine is rarely found in the United States but the resulting gap between supply and demand is partly closed, in a fashion, by imitation aventurine, used in some jewelry and made of glass containing inclusions of metal particles.

How to Recognize Crystalline Quartz. The glassy appearance of crystalline quartz and the hardness of 7.0 will usually distinguish quartz from most other minerals with which it might be confused. Another distinguishing trait is the decidedly conchoidal fracture of quartz. If crystals can be seen, their hexagonal form along with the characteristic crystal terminations will usually alone identify quartz. The majority of the varieties of crystalline quartz often occur in good crystals, the only major exception, as pointed out before, being rose quartz.

Where to Look for Quartz Crystals. Quartz can be found in almost any stream, in one form or another, but finding a good quartz crystal in stream channels or stream deposits is somewhat rare. Quartz occurs in virtually all types of rocks as a constituent mineral, and is also a very common vein mineral. The largest quartz crystals are found in cavities where, supposedly, the crystals were thus allowed to grow to some size. In searching for quartz crystals, the rockhound should look for miarolitic and other types of cavities, including vein cavities. Quartz is often found in *geodes* (see Chapter 12). Inspection of the chalcedony wall of a geode, once the geode is opened, often reveals planes of weakness along which crystals and matrix material can be safely removed without damage to the crystals. Often, however, a good, crystal-lined geode makes an unusual specimen in itself and is therefore left intact.

Cryptocrystalline Quartz

As stated previously, the crystalline structure in cryptocrystalline quartz cannot be seen with ordinary microscopes, this being the reason why cryptocrystalline quartz usually has a dense appearance when found under normal conditions. Seen under an electron microscope, however, cryptocrystalline quartz usually shows either a fibrous pattern or a granular pattern. To the naked eye, the fibrous form has a higher luster and a more waxy appearance than does the granular type. The fibrous form is *chalcedony*, a term, unfortunately, which is applied with several different meanings to crystocrystalline varieties of quartz. In general, however, agate, onyx, carnelian, chrysoprase, and heliotrope are considered as forms of chalcedony. Jasper, chert, and flint show granular structures under the electron microscope and are considered not to be chalcedony.

Agate. *Agate* (see Plate 5.A) is a popular gemstone and is a form of chalcedony in which the colors are distributed either seemingly haphazardly or in curved bands. Varieties of agate include *banded agate, clouded agate,* and *moss agate.* Moss agate, contrary to fairly prevalent belief, does not contain moss, the "moss" actually being manganese oxide.

Another kind of agate, *landscape agate,* seems to picture landscapes complete with trees and bushes. The "vegetation" is actually mineral matter, as in the case of moss agates, but the origin of landscape agates was a subject for heated argument in past generations. One hypothesis maintained that a given agate, before it became a landscape agate, resting on the surface of the earth, somewhere, had been somehow coated with a light-sensitive salt of some kind. Then, the hypothesis continued, a lightning flash somehow imprinted the outline of a nearby landscape onto and throughout much of the agate. Some supporters of this hypothesis even claimed that they could see a few animals lurking in the bushes, in some agates. The known occurrences of agate such as moss agate and landscape agate are rather limited, but at least some form of agate has been found in practically every state in the United States.

Onyx. The chief difference between agate and *onyx* is that whereas the colored bands in agate are curved and may be of different thicknesses, the bands in onyx are nearly straight, parallel, and of uniform thickness. The bands in onyx are usually black and white, alternating. Onyx is found in most states. *Mexican onyx* is not true onyx at all but is banded limestone or banded marble.

Carnelian. *Carnelian,* sometimes called *sard,* is a clear chalcedony whose color may range from yellow to red. In the United States, carnelian has been found in California, Washington, Oregon, Utah, Arizona, Nevada, North Dakota, South Dakota, Minnesota, Iowa, Wisconsin, Illinois, Michigan, Indiana, and Ohio.

Chrysoprase. The form of chalcedony called *chrysoprase* is apple green in color and is translucent. The green color is due to nickel, and chrysoprase is therefore an indicator mineral used in the search for nickel deposits. In the United States, chrysoprase has been found in California, Oregon, Pennsylvania, North Carolina, Colorado, New York State, and Arizona.

Heliotrope. *Heliotrope,* or *bloodstone,* is dark green chalcedony with spots of bright-red jasper throughout it. According to legend, bloodstone first came into being when drops of blood from the crucified Christ fell onto a green stone at the base of the Cross. In the United States, heliotrope has been found in Georgia, Oregon, Colorado, and New York State.

Jasper. *Jasper* (see Plate 5.B), a nonchalcedony, is opaque and may be just about any color. The popular picture of jasper is of a red or reddish mineral, but it can be black, bluish, yellow, brown, or even green. There are few states in the United States in which jasper is not found.

Chert. *Chert,* like jasper (cryptocrystalline but not a chalcedony), usually contains many impurities. Chert has a dull luster and is extremely resistant to wear. The color of chert can be gray, white, yellow, brown, and reddish.

Flint. *Flint* is sometimes considered to be a form of chert. Flint, however, is usually darker in color than chert and sometimes even has a vitreous luster. Thin pieces of flint may be transparent to translucent. Both flint and chert were used by various peoples for tools, spearheads, and arrowheads, and flint and chert are widespread throughout the United States (Hawaii excepted) and much of the rest of the world. As the reader has no doubt already gathered, it is often very difficult to say with certainty whether a given specimen is jasper, chert, or flint.

How to Recognize Cryptocrystalline Quartz. The chalcedonies are typically fairly smooth and translucent. Chert, flint, and jasper, however, usually look rougher in appearance than the chalcedonies and they lack the usual translucency of chalcedony. Separating the chalcedonies from the varieties of chert, flint, and jasper is usually a simple task, but as already pointed out, it is often difficult to distinguish between chert, flint, and jasper.

In addition to translucency and a rather waxy appearance, chalcedony often tends to form in more or less botryoidal form, another distinguishing feature. Once a chalcedony is identified as such, details such as banding, type of banding, color, etc., will then quickly identify the type of chalcedony.

How to Find Cryptocrystalline Quartz. Jasper, chert, and flint are the kinds of minerals which are hard to find, and they are usually collected on trips when the rockhound is really looking for something else. Chalcedony, however, is another story, and the type of chalcedony most commonly sought in the United States is agate of one kind or another.

Some of the best, if not the best, agate occurs as nodules in igneous rocks such as basalts. The fact that many basalts are of relatively recent origin also means that many hills are capped by basalt now, or entirely made up of basaltic flows. In many regions in the United States, therefore, agate is weathering out of the rocks and is moving downhill. One of the best places to look for agate, then, would be on such a hillside where tools such as rakes, screens, and shovels are often the order of the day. Agates are also found in stream gravel, in the glacial drift (glacier-deposited material) in and around the Great Lakes States, and in both lake-beach placers and ocean-beach placers. Ocean-beach placers on both coasts of the United States have furnished a considerable amount of good chalcedony of various kinds.

The rockhound who lives in an interior region should certainly prospect likely looking hills for chalcedony, and should also investigate places such as those where streams empty into lakes or other streams. Some excellent chalcedony has been found in this way and, incidentally, this is a good way of quickly getting some idea as to what kinds of rocks and minerals are in a particular area. As much chalcedony is found in stream gravel, it follows that a good hunting ground for chalcedony—and an easily worked one—would be a gravel pit.

Opal

Chemical composition: silicon dioxide, with water.
Chemical formula: $SiO_2 \cdot n\ H_2O$
Color: Practically all tints.
Luster: glassy to waxy.
Diaphaneity: transparent to translucent.
Hardness: 5.2–6.5

Specific gravity: 1.9–2.2
Cleavage: none.
Fracture: conchoidal.
Crystal system: not applicable (opal is amorphous).

Most opal is semiprecious although some is classed as "precious opal." Opal (see Plate 5.C) may be colorless or almost any color, or almost any color combination, and opal is sometimes black. In some varieties of opal, interference of light causes a striking play of colors called *opalescence* (see Chapter 4). There are many varieties of opal, the black opals which show opalescence being the most valuable.

Opal is porous and is therefore easily stained, and care should be taken not to let opal stand near dirty water or colored fluids, etc. Some people, however, bring opal and colored fluids together by design. Almost all of the brilliantly colored opal sold has been artificially colored as have many of the more sedate-appearing opals for that matter. Opal loses water fairly readily and for that reason a naturally-colored opal should be placed in clean water from time to time, to prevent cracking. Opal should not be exposed to sudden changes in temperature since even small temperature changes can cause internal stresses capable of fracturing a specimen of opal. *Precious opal* has been found, in the United States, in Washington, Idaho, Oregon, and Nevada. Common opal is widely distributed throughout the United States. *Hyalite* opal, a transparent and colorless variety, has been found in Florida, Oregon, Georgia, New Jersey, North Carolina, and New York State.

How to Recognize Opal. The only mineral that opal is likely to be confused with is quartz, and in this case the hardness of opal (less than that of quartz) will identify the specimen as opal. The rockhound should also remember that opal, as it is not crystalline, never forms crystals except, sometimes, as pseudomorphs.

Where to Look for Opal. Opal is found in cavities in volcanic rock and is also found in sedimentary rock. It is often found in hot spring deposits and sometimes is the replacement material in petrified wood. Great care must often be exercised both in extracting a specimen of opal and transporting it because of opal's tendency to fracture for, seemingly, no valid reason.

Petrified Wood

It seems to be popularly believed that wood becomes "petrified" by remaining on the surface for thousands of years in a hot dry climate whereupon, somehow, the wood is finally petrified. Much the reverse is actually true. Wood which becomes petrified must somehow be first buried. Then, water containing dissolved mineral matter enters and interacts with the cellular structure of the wood until the wood has been replaced by mineral matter, actually a process which is much more complicated than it was thought to be only a few years ago. Finally, with erosion, the "wood" once more becomes exposed at the earth's surface where we find it today (see Fig. 10.2).

Fig. 10.2: Petrified tree stumps in the North Dakota Badlands. In order for wood to become petrified, it must be buried by sediments or volcanic ash. Then, underground water, carrying material in solution, replaces the wood with mineral matter. After a period of erosion, the "wood" is again exposed on the surface. (Courtesy of North Dakota Travel Department)

The burial of the wood before it becomes petrified can occur in several ways including burial in place by volcanic ash, by river sediments burying wood in place during a flood, and burial of river-transported logs in lake sediments. Incidentally, the first two types of burial would largely result in petrified tree trunks with branches still on them, while burial of river-transported logs would involve the burial of logs which had many if not most of their branches stripped away as the tree trunks careened down flood-swollen rivers. In any case, if the substance which replaces the wood is silica, as is generally the case, the wood is commonly *jasperized, opalized,* or *agatized.* Petrified wood is found in many places in the United States including well-known localities in New Jersey, New York State, Connecticut, Delaware, Kansas, Nebraska, Ohio, Illinois, Michigan, Indiana, South Dakota, North Dakota, Missouri, Nevada, Wyoming, Texas, California, Utah, Idaho, Oregon, Arizona, and Washington.

How to Recognize Petrified Wood. Petrified wood is easily recognized by the cell structure of the original wood, often including that of the bark of the tree. Growth rings are also often faithfully preserved. A specimen of petrified wood is shown in Plate 5.D.

Where to Look for Petrified Wood. Most petrified wood is of course found in sedimentary rock regions, and good specimens of petrified wood are often found in stream gravel. This means, as already mentioned in Chapter 6, that gravel pits are often prime places in which to hunt for petrified wood.

Petrified Wood on Public Lands. When rockhounding on public land administered by the Bureau of Land Management (and remember that you *cannot* collect specimens in national parks or national monuments) the maximum quantity of petrified wood that one person is allowed to remove without charge, per day, is 25 pounds in weight plus one piece. Not more than 250 pounds of petrified wood may be removed without charge by one person in one calendar year, and a special permit for free use of petrified wood must be obtained for any specimen which weighs over 250 pounds. Except for removal of museum pieces—and that requires a special permit—the use of explosives and power equipment is forbidden. Light trucks up to one-ton capacity, used in connection with campers or trailers, or as a principle means of transportation, may be used for hauling purposes.

Petrified wood obtained under "free use" must be for personal use and may not be bartered or sold to commercial dealers. The law also stipulates that petrified wood must be removed in a manner that avoids unnecessary soil erosion or needless damage to the land or resources.

PLATES

Plate 1

A. Granite from Yosemite Valley, California. Granite like this is approximately 70 percent feldspar, 20 percent quartz, and 10 percent dark (iron and magnesium) minerals.

B. Alkaline basalt with peridotite nodule from California. Basalts are the most prevalent types of lavas.

C. Diorite from California. Diorite is an intrusive igneous rock.

D. Graphic granite, a form of pegmatite. Pegmatite dikes of the complex variety are hosts for many gemstones. Specimen from California.

E. Obsidian, or "volcanic glass." Technically, obsidian is really a glass and is therefore neither a rock nor a mineral.

F. Sandstone, a sedimentary rock. The red sandstone shown is nonmarine. The yellowish sandstone is of marine origin and contains fossils. Both specimens from California.

Plate 2

A. Shale (sandy). Shale is a sedimentary rock which is typically formed in shallow seas; thus it commonly contains both marine and land-derived fossils. Specimen from California, from the author's collection.

B. Algal limestone of Lower Cambrian age from California.

C. Slate from California. As is evident from the photograph, slate may be produced by the metamorphism of shale.

D. Mica schist from South Dakota. Schists are of metamorphic origin and are associated with the occurrences of several gemstones.

E. Gneiss from Massachusetts. Gneiss is a metamorphic rock.

F. Native gold. The nugget at the left is approximately two inches long, and it weighs just over five ounces. The specimen of wire gold on the right was found in Oregon.

Plate 3

A. Pyrite. A sulfide of iron, pyrite is often mistaken for gold and is one form of "fool's gold." Specimen from Colorado.

B. *Left,* chalcopyrite with magnetite from Pennsylvania; *right,* chalcopyrite with sphalerite, galena, and quartz from New Mexico. Chalcopyrite, a form of "fool's gold," is an ore of copper and it tarnishes fairly quickly.

C. Mica. *Left,* phlogopite from North Carolina; *center,* muscovite from New Hampshire; *right,* biotite, from Ontario, Can-

Plate 3 (*cont.*)

ada. Various micas are often mistaken for gold in stream beds.

D.   Diamond crystals from Africa. The top left and the lower right specimens are twinned.

E.   *Top left*, ruby from Norway; *lower left*, ruby crystal from Madagascar; *top right*, sapphire from Montana; *lower right*, stream gravel sapphires from Ceylon. Ruby and sapphire are gemstone varieties of corundum.

F.   Tourmaline crystals, with quartz, from California.

Plate 4

A.   Aquamarine, a variety of beryl. The crystal on the left is from Minas Gerais, Brazil; the one on the right is from New Hampshire.

B.   Amethyst. *Left*, section of geode from Uruguay; *center*, single crystal from Minas Gerais, Brazil; *right*, with calcite, from Mexico. Amethyst is a gemstone variety of quartz.

C.   Rose quartz. The crystals on the left are from Minas Gerais, Brazil; the specimen on the right is from Colorado. Crystals of rose quartz are rarely found.

D.   Quartz crystals from Arkansas.

E.   Sagenite. *Left*, rutilated quartz from Minas Gerais, Brazil; *right*, rutilated quartz from New Hampshire.

F.   Smoky quartz from California.

Plate 5

A.   Polished section of agate from Brazil.

B.   Jasper, a form of cryptocrystalline quartz. Specimen from California.

C.   Common opal from Nevada. Technically, opal is not a mineral as it is noncrystalline.

D.   Petrified wood from Arizona.

E.   Orthoclase feldspar. The large light-colored crystals are from Pike's Peak, Colorado. The yellow crystal is of gem quality and is from Madagascar.

F.   *Left*, amazonite (green), with cleavelandite (light colored), and smoky quartz. Amazonite and cleavelandite are feldspar varieties; *right*, amazonite from Virginia.

Plate 6

A.   Moonstone. This specimen is a variety of albite (feldspar). The effect at the top is called "opalescence." Specimen from New York State.

Plate 6 (*cont.*)

B. Garnet. *Center*, essonite from Canada; *front row, left to right*: brown garnet from California, pink garnet from Mexico, green garnet (*demantoid*) from Italy, red garnet from California, dark-green garnet (*uvarovite*) on chromite from California.

C. Jade, variety *nephrite*. The pebble came from Jade Cove, California. The polished slab is of jade from Wyoming.

D. Serpentine (green) from California. *Bowenite*, a form of serpentine, resembles nephrite jade and is the state mineral of Rhode Island.

E. Turquoise of good gem quality from Arizona. Turquoise is a copper gemstone.

F. Azurite is partially replaced by malachite in the specimen on the left; the specimen on the right is "velvet" malachite. Azurite and malachite are copper gemstones; both these specimens came from South Africa.

Plate 7

A. *Left*, azurite on botryoidal malachite; *center*, azurite crystals with malachite; *right*, "velvet" malachite. All of these specimens came from Bisbee, Arizona.

B. Quartz crystals coating chrysocolla (a copper gemstone) from Arizona.

C. Malachite coated with calcite from Arizona. Malachite is a copper carbonate.

D. A somewhat unusual and beautiful form of azurite from Arizona. Azurite is a copper gemstone and is sometimes an ore of copper.

E. Quartz geode from Keokuk, Iowa.

F. Twins and individual crystals of staurolite from Georgia and South Carolina.

Plate 8

A. Petrified whalebone from California. Such material usually takes a good polish and is sought by rockhounds who are also lapidaries. Specimen from the author's collection.

B. Tree gum from Australia. Such gum is often sold as *amber*, which is a fossil tree resin and is relatively rare.

C. Native copper from Michigan.

D. Bornite and chalcopyrite, ores of copper. Bornite is also known as "peacock ore." Specimen from Arizona.

E. Galena on chert. The entire specimen is "sprinkled" with chalcopyrite and sphalerite.

F. Rhodonite (red) in calcite, with franklinite (black). Specimen from Franklin, New Jersey.

A. GRANITE

B. BASALT

C. DIORITE

D. PEGMATITE

E. OBSIDIAN

F. SANDSTONE

PLATE 1

A. SHALE

PLATE 2

B. LIMESTONE

C. SLATE

D. MICA SCHIST

E. GNEISS

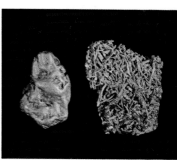

F. GOLD

PLATE 3

A. PYRITE

B. CHALCOPYRITE

C. MICA

D. DIAMONDS

E. RUBY AND SAPPHIRE

F. TOURMALINE

PLATE 4

A. AQUAMARINE

B. AMETHYST

C. ROSE QUARTZ

D. QUARTZ

E. SAGENITE

F. SMOKY QUARTZ

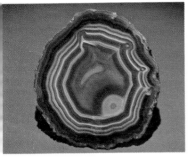

A. AGATE

PLATE 5

B. JASPER

C. OPAL

D. PETRIFIED WOOD

E. FELDSPAR

F. AMAZONITE

PLATE 6

A. MOONSTONE

B. GARNET

C. NEPHRITE JADE

D. SERPENTINE

E. TURQUOISE

F. AZURITE AND MALACHITE

A. AZURITE AND MALACHITE

B. CHRYSOCOLLA

C. MALACHITE

D. AZURITE

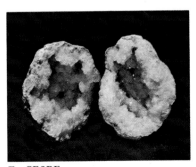

E. GEODE

F. STAUROLITE

PLATE 7

PLATE 8

A. PETRIFIED WHALEBONE

B. AMBER

C. NATIVE COPPER

D. BORNITE AND
   CHALCOPYRITE

E. GALENA

F. RHODONITE

Chapter 11

Feldspar, Garnet, Jade, and the Copper Gemstones

Feldspar and garnet are found in many places throughout the United States and both groups of minerals rank high in the list of rock and gemstone material which is likely to be found by the rockhound. Feldspars are silicates containing aluminum and are the most common minerals in igneous rocks. Thus, feldspars as a group are also the most abundant minerals in the earth's crust, quartz being the *one* most abundant mineral in the crust. There several feldspar gemstones.

Garnet is also an extremely common and ubiquitous family of minerals, and it occurs in metamorphic and igneous rocks, in grains and crystals ranging from microscopic in size to the size of a baseball, and sometimes larger. Probably at least ninety times out of one hundred, any red grains seen in igneous or metamorphic rocks or found in a gold pan, etc., or any reddish crystals in or protruding from metamorphic rocks, are garnets. Garnet supplies a number of gemstones, some of the most easily worked "garnet fields" being in Utah. There, in several areas, according to the *Utah Fact Book* (see list of free rockhound material in Chapter 1), ants often obligingly haul garnets to the surface where they leave them on or near ant hills.

Jade, another gemstone discussed in this chapter, is rare, especially when its known occurrences are compared with those of the feldspar and garnet gemstones. The other gemstones discussed in this chapter, the copper gemstones, contribute some of our most beautiful mineral specimens.

The Feldspars and Their Gemstones

Chemical composition: aluminosilicates.
Chemical formula: see description of each feldspar.

Color: white, pink, gray, flesh, brown, yellow, colorless.
Luster: vitreous; pearly at times.
Diaphaneity: transparent to translucent to opaque.
Hardness: 6
Specific gravity: 2.5–2.8
Cleavage: Good, in two directions at about 90 degrees.
Fracture: conchoidal.
Crystal system: orthoclase is monoclinic; all other feldspars
   are triclinic.

Not only do the feldspars furnish several attractive gemstones (see Plates 5.E, 5.F, 6.A), they are also key minerals
in the ceramics and glass-making industries. In the ceramics
industry, ground fused feldspar forms the glass in china, in
the more expensive kinds of tile, and in porcelain, etc. Used
in glass, feldspar makes the glass more resistant to impact,
bending, and sudden and drastic changes in temperature.
Much of the feldspar used in the United States has come
from North Carolina, New Hampshire, Connecticut, South
Dakota, and Colorado. Perhaps the world's most unusual
feldspar mine was in the Soviet Union, this particular mine
being in one gigantic feldspar crystal from which 2,000 tons
of feldspar were removed!

The potassium feldspars are *orthoclase* and *microcline,*
the sodium feldspar is *albite,* and the calcium feldspar is
anorthite. Oligoclase and *labradorite* have compositions between those of albite and anorthite, the series being isomorphous, that is, a change in chemical composition does
not affect the outward appearance of the mineral as far as
form is concerned. Members of the albite-oligoclase-labra-
dorite-anorthite series are known as the *plagioclase,* or soda-
lime, feldspars. Orthoclase is the only feldspar which is
monoclinic (see Fig. 11.1); all other feldspars are triclinic.

It is extremely difficult to distinguish between the feldspars on the basis of cleavage alone, as all feldspars either
have or seem to have two good cleavages at about right angles
to each other. Almost without exception, however, the plagioclase feldspars are twinned, and the twinning results in
parallel striations or lines on one of the two cleavage planes.

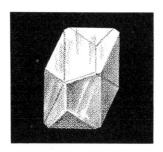

Fig. 11.1: Orthoclase feldspar crystal

The easiest way to identify a feldspar as either a plagioclase or nonplagioclase, then, is to find out if striations do exist, and this can be quickly determined by turning the piece of feldspar so that one face after the other reflects the light at different angles.

Amazonite. *Amazonite* (see Plate 5.F), a potash feldspar ($KAlSi_3O_8$), is a variety of microcline and looks much like jade. Amazonite is the feldspar gemstone most often found in the United States. Some of the states where good amazonite has been found are Colorado, Maine, Virginia, Massachusetts, New Mexico, North Carolina, Pennsylvania, and Texas.

Moonstone. *Moonstone* is a term which is applied to each of two different feldspars if they are of gemstone quality. One type of moonstone is glassy orthoclase ($KAlSi_3O_8$) which shows blue opalescence. The other moonstone (see Plate 6.A) is a variety of albite whose general formula is $NaAlSi_3O_8$. In either variety the outstanding characteristic is a bluish opalescence or sheen. This effect is of course accentuated by proper cutting of the stone. Moonstone has been found in Virginia, Colorado, California, North Carolina, Pennsylvania, Rhode Island, and Delaware. Some of the best moonstone collecting localities in the United States are some of the beaches in Rhode Island.

It would probably seem almost inevitable that if there is a moonstone there must also be a sunstone, and there is, discussed in following.

Sunstone. *Sunstone* is often described as *oligoclase*, a plagioclase (soda-lime) feldspar, which also contains iron mineral inclusions which impart a golden, sunlight effect to the feldspar. Such inclusions sometimes occur in other feldspars, however, giving the same effect, and some rockhounds call all of these materials "sunstone." Sunstone has been found in the United States in Pennsylvania, North Carolina, and Virginia.

Labradorite. *Labradorite* is a plagioclase (soda-lime) feldspar, often grayish in color, which commonly shows a play of brilliant colors, an effect apparently due to the interference of light due to twinning. As pointed out in Chapter 4, this effect can be seen by holding a 33⅓ rpm record so that a strong light sweeps across the face of the record, with the observer sighting in a direction almost parallel to the face. As its name indicates, most specimens of this feldspar come from Labrador. In the United States, good labradorite has been found in Texas, Utah, and New York State.

How to Recognize the Feldspar Gemstones. The first step in recognizing a feldspar gemstone is, of course, to identify the specimen as a feldspar of some kind. Smooth, glassy cleavage faces at right angles to each other and which cannot be scratched with a knife are the earmarks of feldspar. Then, having determined that you have a feldspar, the next step is to determine whether it is plagioclase.

As already brought out, plagioclase feldspar is usually twinned, resulting in parallel striations on cleavage faces. Therefore, if the specimen shows such striations it is a plagioclase. If it does not show striations on prominent cleavage faces it is almost certainly either orthoclase or microcline. Having thus determined whether the specimen is a plagioclase or a nonplagioclase, and assuming that it is of gem quality, the rockhound can now easily identify the specimen as being either amazonite, moonstone, sunstone, or labradorite. There are a few other feldspar gemstones besides those discussed in this chapter but the chances of finding most of these in the United States seem rather remote.

Where and How to Look for Feldspar Gemstones. Amazonite is found in pegmatites, hence the rockhound who looks for beryl, tourmaline, topaz, etc., should also keep his eyes open for amazonite. On the other hand, do not expect to find an

orthoclase gemstone—orthoclase "moonstone," for example
—in pegmatites since orthoclase gemstones in pegmatites
are rare occurrences. Good places to look for good orthoclase
specimens, including orthoclase gemstones, include porphyritic rocks, and veins.

The plagioclase gemstones—moonstone, sunstone, and
labradorite—are found in several types of igneous rocks.
The albite type of moonstone, as opposed to the orthoclase
type is found in pegmatites. Sunstone is found in coarse-
grained igneous rocks and in metamorphosed limestone,
while labradorite tends to make up its own rock structure.

The reader may remember a statement in Chapter 9 to
the effect that the best tourmaline and beryl specimens may
be expected to be found in "pockets" near the core of a pegmatite dike. It was also stated that finding the core is usually
easier said than done. Sometimes, however, the feldspar
minerals help us in locating at least the general position of
the core. It works this way: In a pegmatite structure, as one
goes from the core toward a wall of the dike, the transition
is commonly from feldspars rich in potassium to feldspars
rich in sodium and calcium. In other words, the gemstone
amazonite tends to form near the core in many pegmatites
while the albite variety of moonstone tends to form nearer
the walls of the dike. Thus, if we find only one feldspar in
a, say, poorly defined dike, we know, many times, whether
we are near a core or a wall. If we find two different feldspars, we know in which general direction the core lies. The
feldspars found do not of course have to be gemstone varieties. Although this relationship between feldspar types and
the relative positions of core and walls of a pegmatite dike
does not, of course, apply to all dikes, it does occur often
enough to have been of great value in the locations of many
cores and the associated pockets.

Feldspar mines are of course excellent places in which to
look for most of the feldspar gemstones. Feldspar mining
methods and subsequent sorting are not very selective and
the result is that some good material can usually be found
on the mine dumps. Pegmatite mining has a high economic
risk factor because of various mining difficulties usually en-

countered, the result being that many feldspar mines have long been inactive and forgotten. The rockhound who lives in or is going into pegmatite territory should make it a point to look up old records, as one brief item may lead him to a long-forgotten pegmatite and a possible bonanza in gemstones.

The Garnets

Chemical composition: The garnets are silicates. See description of each garnet type.
Chemical formula: See description of each garnet type.
Color: red, brown, green, yellow, black, white.
Luster: vitreous, subvitreous, resinous.
Diaphaneity: transparent to translucent.
Hardness: 6.1–7.5
Specific gravity: 3.2–4.3
Cleavage: none.
Fracture: conchoidal to rough.
Crystal system: isometric.

Garnet, some specimens of which are shown in Plate 6.B, is an extremely widely disseminated mineral, and if we include crystals of small size we could say that good garnet crystals occur in and are easily found in every one of the United States. There are six garnet minerals and they can be divided into these groups: four *aluminum* garnets, one *iron* garnet, and one *chromium* garnet.

Almandine. Sometimes called "almandite," *almandine* garnet ($Fe_3Al_2(SIO_4)_3$) has a hardness of 7.5. The typical color of almandine is deep red or deep violet red. Almandine of good quality has been found in North Carolina, Nevada, Idaho, New Hampshire, Colorado, Pennsylvania, and New York State, to name several states. Almandine is also used as an abrasive, as well as a semiprecious gemstone, the world's leading producer of abrasive garnet long having been a deposit in New York State.

Grossularite. *Grossularite*, a second aluminum garnet ($Ca_3Al_2(SiO_4)_3$), has a hardness of 7.3. The color of grossularite varies enough for that mineral to supply two gemstones. Golden-yellow grossularite is called *cinnamon-stone*, while orange-colored or reddish-yellow grossularite is called *essonite* (or *hyacinth*). Grossularite has been found in North Carolina, Nevada, Idaho, New Hampshire, Colorado, Pennsylvania, New York State, Maine, and other states.

Pyrope. *Pyrope* ($Mg_3Al_2(SiO_4)_3$), the third aluminum garnet to be discussed, has a hardness of 7.5, and its color ranges from deep red to a very dark red approaching black. A rose-red or purple form of pyrope is called *rhodolite*. Rhodolite is actually a mineral whose composition is a two-to-one ratio of pyrope and almandine, respectively. Good specimens of pyrope have been found in New Mexico, Arizona, Idaho, California, and North Carolina.

Spessartite. The fourth aluminum garnet, *spessartite* ($Mn_3Al_2(SiO_4)_3$), is capable of possessing a beautiful red color but, unfortunately, when it is found—it is rare—spessartite usually has a brown color. Spessartite has a hardness of 7.3. It has been found in Colorado, Pennsylvania, Connecticut, Virginia, and Utah.

Andradite. *Andradite* is the iron garnet ($Ca_3Fe_2(SiO_4)_3$) and it has a wide range of colors from wine to yellow to green to black. The emerald-green version of andradite is called *demantoid* and is the most valuable member of the garnet family. *Topazolite* is wine-yellow andradite. The hardness of andradite varies from 6.1 to 6.5. Localities where andradite has been found in the United States include areas in Pennsylvania, New Hampshire, Connecticut, Arkansas, and Colorado.

Uvarovite. The chromium garnet *uvarovite* ($Ca_3Cr_2(SiO_4)_3$) is emerald-green in color and has a glassy luster. The hardness of uvarovite is 7.5. In the United States, from fair to good uvarovite has been found in Arizona, California, New York State, Pennsylvania, and Texas.

How to Recognize Garnet. The most distinguishing feature of garnet is its isometric form with, usually, either twelve diamond-shaped, equal faces or twenty four trapezium-shaped, equal faces (see Fig. 11.2). Garnet usually occurs in crystals, and the crystal shape plus garnet's hardness and specific gravity make garnet an easily identifiable gemstone.

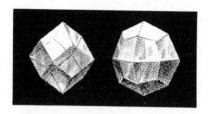

Fig. 11.2: Garnet crystals

Where and How to Look for Garnet. As a general picture we may think of the garnets and their associated host rocks as follows:

Alamandine and andradite: Mica schists.
Grossularite: Metamorphosed limestones.
Pyrope: Serpentine and peridotites.
Spessartite: Granitic rocks and schists.
Uvarovite: Serpentine, in association with chromium.

Looking at the above listed associations, it is apparent that the rockhound should be on the lookout for garnet whenever in a metamorphic region. Mica schists often weather to the point where they form glistening residual "boulders" or more or less isolated slabs of shiny, silvery-appearing rock standing, sometimes, at steep angles. Due to the same weathering, garnets often protrude from such rocks, like large warts. Often overlooked by some rockhounds is the fact that, in such areas, there are often more garnets lying around loose in the soil than there are garnets still embedded in those parts of the rock that are accessible.

If you find an exposure of garnet-bearing schist in, for example, a road cut, there could well be a concentration of garnets near the top of the cut, in any soil which may be there. Garnets underground seem to be highly unpopular with ants, so it is always a good idea to inspect ant hills for garnets. The ants may have already hauled some of the biggest garnets to the surface.

Because of the combination of hardness, a fairly high specific gravity, and lack of cleavage, garnet is commonly found in streams and stream deposits. A sluice box is efficient in recovering garnets of any size, and the *batea*, gold pan, or cone sieve can be used for smaller garnets. It is virtually impossible not to find garnets in stream gravel since the layer of black sand in a sluice box, batea, or gold pan, will almost inevitably contain many little garnet crystals whose often perfect shapes can be studied with the aid of a magnifying glass.

Jade: Nephrite

Chemical composition: calcium magnesium (iron) silicate.
Chemical formula: $Ca_2(Mg, Fe)_5(OH_2)(Si_4O_{11})_2$
Color: white to dark green; sometimes violet.
Luster: glassy to waxy.
Diaphaneity: transparent to translucent.
Hardness: 6.0–6.2
Specific gravity: 3.0–3.1
Cleavage: perfect prismatic.
Fracture: uneven to splintery.
Crystal system: monoclinic.

Jade: Jadeite

Chemical composition: sodium aluminum silicate.
Chemical formula: $NaAlSi_2O_6$
Color: various shades of green; brownish; white; violet; lilac.
Luster: glassy to silky.
Diaphaneity: translucent to opaque.
Hardness: 6.5–7.0
Specific gravity: 3.3–3.5
Cleavage: prismatic.
Fracture: very hard to fracture.
Crystal system: monoclinic.

As is apparent from the above, there are two minerals which are properly called "jade," a fact which is unknown to many people. One of the strangest facts concerning the two jades is that, although they look very much alike, their chemical compositions are very different.

Nephrite Jade. *Nephrite* jade is not often found in the place where it was formed, but is usually found in boulders and as stream-worn pebbles (see Plate 6.C). When nephrite jade is found in place, it is often found in serpentine (see Plate 6.D), in rounded boulderlike masses, and in schist and gneiss.

How to Recognize Nephrite Jade. The first-time jade hunter often has a hopeful mind's eye picture of green, waxy-appearing boulders scattered around on a hillside, but the truth is that any nephrite jade which may be in an area is often covered with a thin brownish or grayish crust which probably forms due to the weathering of the nephrite, and the formation of manganese and iron oxides. Once green jade is found, however, its color, specific gravity, luster, and hardness will identify it. Some minerals develop a weathered surface which looks much like the surface of unaltered jade, but a fresh fracture surface on true nephrite jade will at the most be glassy in appearance in sunlight and not sparkling. The fracture surface is best obtained by carefully chipping the specimen with the point of the rock hammer. If the fracture surface does not sparkle in the sunlight the specimen may be jade, but there is another observation to make. If the fracture surfaces are conchoidal and not rough, or if the surface chipped out by the point of the rock hammer is shaped like a crescent moon, then what you have probably found is a chalcedony of some kind, and not jade.

Where to Look for Nephrite Jade. One of the best ways in which to look for nephrite jade is to first test the stream gravel of an area. There are two reasons for this: (1) a mass of nephrite jade usually looks just like thousands of other boulders or boulderlike masses in an area, and (2) pebbles of jade found in stream gravel commonly have no "weather coats," in which case the jade is almost immediately recognized as such. It may then be possible to trace the float back to its source, using the methods outlined in Chapter 7, and this is preferable to walking or climbing through an untested field strewn with rocks, and hammering pieces off rocks to see if they are jade. In the United States, nephrite jade has been found in Alaska, Nevada, Wyoming, and California.

Jadeite. Like nephrite jade, *jadeite* is usually found in boulderlike masses and as waterworn pebbles, and when found in place, jadeite is also often found associated with serpentine. Jadeite is harder and heavier than nephrite and is the most prized of the two types of jade.

Jadeite tends to be spotty in color, sometimes to the point of being mottled and opaque. The valuable emerald-green variety of jadeite, however, known as "imperial green jade," is highly translucent and a two-inch square of this variety can sell for over $15,000.

Jadeite is searched for in much the same manner as is nephrite jade. The two jades may be distinguished from each other by difference in specific gravities and by the fact that jadeite is easily fusible beneath the blowpipe flame while nephrite jade is fusible with difficulty. Also, jadeite colors the flame yellow, due to the presence of sodium. Serpentine is sometimes confused with jade in the field, but serpentine is lighter in weight than either jade. In the United States, jadeite has been found in Oklahoma, Washington, and California.

Turquoise

Chemical composition: Hydrous aluminum phosphate, with copper.
Chemical formula: $CuO \cdot 3\,Al_2O_3 \cdot 2P_2O_5 \cdot 9H_2O$
Color: sky blue, bluish green, green.
Luster: waxy.
Diaphaneity: translucent on thin edge.
Hardness: 5–6
Specific gravity: 2.6–2.8
Cleavage: none.
Fracture: smooth.
Crystal system: triclinic.

Turquoise (see Plate 6.E) has been a gemstone since at least 1,000 years before the birth of Christ, having been mined by the Egyptians at about the same time that jade was being mined by the Chinese. The word "turquoise" apparently was derived to describe the fact that this gemstone was exported from Persia to Europe by way of Turkey, hence the medieval French *pierre turqueise,* or "Turkish stone."

Turquoise is one of the copper gemstones discussed in this book.

Crystals of turquoise are very rare and turquoise is usually found in kidney-shaped masses in highly metamorphosed igneous rocks, and in small veins and "stringers" in such rocks. Turquoise is porous and care should be taken against exposing turquoise to anything which might be absorbed by the mineral. Turquoise, although fairly hard, is very brittle and is therefore not normally found in good pieces in stream gravel.

Its rather unique combination of characteristics makes turquoise easily identifiable. If there is any doubt as to identity, turquoise will usually fly apart with sharp, cracking noises under the blowpipe flame. If a drop of hydrochloric acid is placed on a small quantity of powdered turquoise on the charcoal block, and then the powder is gently heated, a blue-green coloration of the flame will result due to the presence of copper.

Considering the difficulty of locating and sampling veins which might contain turquoise, and also considering that turquoise is not in general a high-priced or easily worked stone, it is little wonder that few rockhounds spend much time in looking for turquoise. On the other hand, if other copper minerals are found in an area, turquoise is often a possibility, too. In the United States, turquoise has been found in Arizona, New Mexico, Colorado, California, Nevada, Texas, Virginia, and, believe it or not, New Jersey.

"Bone turquoise," or "odontolite," is not turquoise but is fossil bone which, because it is fossilized and colored blue by iron, resembles and is often sold as turquoise. The two may be differentiated by the blowpipe test for copper.

Azurite, Malachite, and Chrysocolla

Azurite, malachite, and chrysocolla (see Plates 7.A through 7.D) are secondary ore minerals of copper and are also gemstones often of great beauty. These three minerals are found together so often that it is logical to present their characteristics in the same table:

Azurite

Chemical composition: basic copper carbonate.
Chemical formula: $Cu_3(OH)_2(CO_3)_2$
Color: azure blue.
Luster: glassy.
Diaphaneity: thin pieces are transparent.
Hardness: 3.5–4.0
Specific gravity: 3.8
Cleavage: two indistinct, one good.
Fracture: conchoidal.
Crystal system: monoclinic.

Malachite

Chemical composition: basic copper carbonate.
Chemical formula: $Cu_2CO_3(OH)_2$
Color: bright green.
Luster: glassy, silky, dull.
Diaphaneity: translucent to opaque.
Hardness: 3.5–4.0
Specific gravity: 3.9–4.0
Cleavage: one perfect.
Fracture: splintery.
Crystal system: monoclinic.

Chrysocolla

Chemical composition: hydrous copper silicate.
Chemical formula: $CuSiO_3 \cdot 2H_2O$
Color: green, greenish blue, blue.
Luster: glassy, shining, earthy.
Diaphaneity: often earthy and opaque.
Hardness: 2–4
Specific gravity: 2–2.5
Cleavage: none.
Fracture: conchoidal.
Crystal system: cryptocrystalline; may be orthorhombic.

Azurite often occurs in prismatic crystals and in radiating groups of spherical shape. Malachite commonly occurs in botryoidal form, and both azurite and malachite are often found in limestone. Chrysocolla, although a silicate, is often found with malachite and azurite. Chrysocolla usually sticks to the tongue, and this is perhaps its best known distinguishing characteristic. All three minerals should be looked for in the weathered zones of copper deposits, usually on or near the surface.

Although even many experienced rockhounds more or less regard these three minerals as being restricted to states such as Arizona, azurite, malachite, and chrysocolla have been and are still being found in many states. Much of the material found, of course, is not of gem quality and some of it is not much more than a stain on a rock surface. Be that as it may, azurite, malachite, and chrysocolla have been found in these states: Arizona, Georgia, Idaho, Maryland, Massachusetts, Michigan, Missouri, Nevada, New Hampshire, New Jersey, New Mexico, Oregon, Pennsylvania, South Dakota, Tennessee, Utah, Vermont, Virginia, Washington, Wyoming.

As an instance of the present occurrence of these minerals in a given state, a rockhound club recently made a journey to an old mine in Berkshire County, Massachusetts, which had furnished lead for bullets in the Revolutionary War. In addition to many other minerals found, the club members found azurite as a coating, chrysocolla as coatings, and malachite occurring in fine, needlelike crystals. Lists such as the above, and more general lists such as the partial list of gem material collecting localities in the United States, in Chapter 13, support the statement that "minerals are where you find them."

Chapter 12

Mineral Oddities
and Curiosities

Every year, rockhounds find and collect such diverse items as meteorites, fossils, glass manufactured by volcanos, stones which dinosaurs carried around inside themselves, a mineral which crystallizes in the form of a cross, and many more. Some rockhounds have even collected chunks of glassy rock which may have come from the moon. Items like the latter are, of course, not found every day in the field, but what is not found in the field can many times be purchased. As a result, some rockhounds specialize in mineral oddities and curiosities and have built up outstanding and valuable collections of the more exotic prizes of rockhounding, including fossils. This present chapter discusses some of these diverse specimens.

Geodes

A *geode* (see Plate 7.E) is essentially a roughly spherical, stonelike formation with a cavity which commonly contains crystals. It has been only within comparatively recent years that the formation of geodes has been thoroughly understood. Despite this, however, rockhounds have been enthusiastically collecting geodes for many years and, theory or no theory, have found many beautiful specimens. The story of geode formation, however, is one of Nature's most interesting stories and it should be known by anyone who searches for and collects these remarkable objects. More pragmatically, as will be seen, knowing how geodes form also helps us to find them.

How Geodes Form. The type of geode we will talk about is the most common type, formed in sedimentary rock. Strangely enough, the first part of the geode which forms is the cavity and this can result from the removal, by underground water, of plant or animal material which was buried in the sediments. This removal must occur before the sediments have hardened into rock, when the sediments are more or less water-soaked. The cavity fills with water as the removal of the organic material proceeds and, finally, the resulting cavity is filled with water.

As the sediments slowly change into rock, a shell of silica, essentially, is deposited around the water-filled pocket. The water thus trapped inside this shell has a relatively high salt content. On the other hand, the water in the sediments surrounding the silica wall will eventually have a much lesser salt content because of wholesale precipitation of solid material as a cement, the flushing out of salt as the water moves downward through the sediments, and the introduction of fresh water from the surface of the ground.

At this point an amazing thing happens. To equalize the pressures between the salty water inside the pocket and fresher water outside the pocket, the two fluids start to intermingle by osmosis, passing through the wall of silica which acts as a membrane. As the water molecules inside the pocket have more salt ions attached to them than the water molecules outside, they exert more pressure as they squeeze and pass through the silica "membrane." This results in an expansion of the pocket, the silica wall being pushed outward, much as a rubber balloon being inflated. The expansion continues until the internal and external pressures on the silica shell are equal, and at this point the growth ceases.

Eventually, the silica wall crystallizes into chalcedony. Later, solutions carrying minerals in dissolved form may seep through the cracks in the chalcedony wall and form crystals (often of some kind of quartz) in the geode, the crystals growing inward into the cavity. After untold centuries of weathering and erosion which strip away the less resistant rock, the geode is revealed to the rockhound as a rather uninteresting-appearing, roughly spherical rock whose usually drab outward appearance belies its interesting past, to say nothing of its interesting interior.

Finding Geodes. Knowing how geodes form, it is evident that as the silica wall is pushed outward, the wet sediments surrounding the geode must be deformed. If a geode which is fairly large has been thus formed in sediments whose beds are relatively thin, a sudden bowing up and bowing down of rock layers in the same spot may outline the position of the geode.

A similar bowing of strata, however, can occur with the growth of *concretions* (see Chapter 14). As concretions commonly grow from a very small size to very large sizes (by deposition of rock material around a nucleus), this bowing effect, when it occurs, is usually much more evident in the case of concretions than it is in the case of geodes. If, however, a spheroidal mass of rock is much lighter in weight than it appears it should be, the chances are that you have found a geode. Even if the rock does not seem of abnormally light weight, it may still be a geode as sometimes the cavities in geodes are almost completely filled with crystals. Sometimes a stone of suspiciously light weight is found which rattles when shaken. What has been found, commonly, is a geode in which crystals or pieces of lining have broken loose. Anything which could be a geode should be cut by a rock saw, as attempts to open geodes in the field usually result in ruined specimens. Some of the more famous geode collecting localities in the United States are in Colorado, Iowa, New Jersey, Oregon, South Dakota, Illinois, Missouri, Nebraska, and Utah.

Meteorites

Most astronomers believe that the birthplace of meteors is the region between Mars and Jupiter. Some scientists also suggest that asteroids, planetoids, meteors, etc., represent the debris formed when a tenth planet once orbiting between Mars and Jupiter blew up or otherwise disintegrated. Most people have at one time or another seen "falling stars" or "shooting stars," which are actually meteors which are literally burning up at a temperature of about 4,000°F as they hurtle through the earth's atmosphere. Meteors which finally impact the earth's surface are called *meteorites*, and many meteorites ultimately find their ways into rock and mineral collections.

Beliefs Concerning Meteors and Meteorites. Contrary to popular belief, most meteors which are seen blazing in our atmosphere are very small, their original size as they enter the atmosphere usually being about that of a grain of sand. Most meteors entering our atmosphere therefore burn up completely. Also contrary to popular belief, most meteorites are cold enough to handle immediately after they impact the earth's surface, as the intense heating is normally confined to the "skin" of the meteor.

Every now and then, meteors of various sizes do hit the earth but some of the older stories and pictorial representations concerning such events seem rather unbelievable. One old woodcut, for example, depicts the terrified inhabitants of a seventeenth-century village running around trying to dodge meteors which are falling all around them. Several apparently less agile villagers are shown being hit by meteors. Actually, very few people have been hit by meteors, at least in historic times, and few people have ever been close enough to a meteor to hear its sound of passage.

Kinds of Meteorites. There are three principle kinds of meteorites, the *stony* meteorites, the *iron* meteorites, and the *stony-iron* meteorites. The stony meteorites consist chiefly of silicate minerals and small amounts of iron. The iron meteorites, or *siderites,* are mainly composed of iron-nickel alloys with, usually, some cobalt and copper. In a surprisingly large number of cases, small diamonds are found in such meteorites. The stony-iron meteorites usually have a composition of approximately 50 percent metal and 50 percent stone.

How to Recognize Meteorites. Stony meteorites are usually difficult to recognize at first sight as being meteorites since their black, glassy surfaces turn brown upon weathering, and they usually look just about like any other rock, to the casual observer. Stony meteorites, however, are usually more or less rounded in shape and this feature and that of a fine-grained internal structure beneath a brown crust are principal identification characteristics.

Although the surfaces of iron meteorites also turn brown upon weathering, iron meteorites are usually much easier to identify. Iron meteorites usually have patterned indentations on their surfaces which look almost exactly as if they had been formed by the pressures of thumbs. Iron meteorites also often show a flowage or near-flowage pattern on their surfaces, due to heating. Sometimes the surfaces of iron meteorites are strongly fluted due to melting and flowage of surface material.

Finding Meteorites. Probably very few rockhounds get up on Saturday mornings to go on a field trip with the avowed intention of finding a few meteorites. Meteorites are just not that easy to find. As a matter of fact, most meteorite discoveries have been made by chance, many times in the form of a farmer plowing his field and turning up a meteorite. This brings up the point that meteorites can bury themselves to considerable depth and then somehow gradually get closer to the surface where some of them are eventually turned up.

This phenomenon of what is often referred to as a stone object "working its way up" is, of course, not restricted to meteorites, as anyone who has done any gardening in spring, in regions where temperatures fall below freezing in winter, well knows. As another example, hunters of Indian arrowheads and spearheads are often puzzled as to why they can go over a particular piece of ground one year and find nothing and then, one or two years later, find arrowheads in formerly barren spots. Loose mineral specimens—agates, for example—will do the same thing.

The reason for this "working up" of rock material in climates with cold winters is that solid rock conducts heat more rapidly than does an equivalent volume of soil grains. Thus as the soil water slowly freezes in winter and the soil expands, a rock object is thrust upward by the force of the ice crystals growing beneath it and eventually, perhaps after a number of years of this process, the object will reach the surface. The process is selective in that larger stone objects tend to move toward the surface while smaller objects tend to remain buried. In regions of cold winters, then, last year's apparently barren hunting ground may be next spring's site of discovery of a good-sized stone object, possibly a meteorite. If careful explorations were methodically carried out in the plains states, for example, in spring, it is almost certain that a number of meteorites would be found, and without too much trouble.

Tektites

Tektites are chunks of black glass whose origin has been argued for more than one hundred years. Most scientists who have studied tektites do agree that they were apparently formed by the impact of a meteor, the resulting blast hurling chunks of rock in all directions. Some experts believe that these meteors hit the moon, and that the rocks were blasted so far away that some of them were captured by the earth's gravity field, to impact the earth where they are found as tektites. Other scientists believe that the meteors hit the earth, the flying rock material finally being pulled back to earth.

At the time of writing, the moon theory as to the origin of tektites seems to a number of scientists to be the most acceptable, and if this theory is true, almost anyone can have their own collection of moon rocks. Tektites have been found in southeast Asia (Thailand tektites are sold in many places), the Philippines, in mud from the floors of the Pacific and Indian Oceans, and tektites have also been found in Texas and Georgia. Tektites are black, shiny and glassy and show the effects of aerodynamic heating and shaping as they hurtled through the atmosphere. As shown in Fig. 12.1, tektites vary in size and shape, and some tektites almost one foot in diameter have been found. Rockhounds in the field, in the United States, are not likely to find tektites, but tektites are extremely interesting items and they can be purchased at very nominal prices at some museums and observatories. Even if the moon theory of origin is correct, it's not everyone who owns a moon rock.

Obsidian

When molten rock material cools very quickly, a natural glass, or *obsidian*, is formed. This volcanic glass is usually black, its fracture is conchoidal, and it is translucent on a thin edge. Obsidian has a hardness of about 6.

Despite its dark appearance, obsidian has approximately

1 inch

Fig. 12.1: Tektites. Many scientists believe that these strange chunks of glass come from the moon. Tektites have been found in several regions of the world, including Texas and Georgia. (Courtesy of U.S. Geological Survey)

the same chemical composition as a granite. That is, if a given granitic magma solidifies far beneath the surface, a granite is formed. If, however, the same magma were to pour rapidly out onto the earth's surface, an obsidian could form, sometimes even in the shape of small mountains. If such a magma cools rapidly but not rapidly enough to become very shiny, the result is *pitchstone*, which has a dull luster. This term is also applied to partially altered obsidian. Small rounded pieces of obsidian which weather out of masses of altered obsidian are called "Apache Tears."

Obsidian was used by the American Indians for scrapers, arrowheads, and spearheads, etc., while the Mayans used obsidian for the same purposes, and also for mirrors and jewelry. Obsidian is found in a number of the western United States where one variety, which shows a beautiful play of colors, is called *rainbow obsidian*. Both rainbow obsidian and "Apache Tears" are highly popular with rockhounds, especially those rockhounds who do lapidary work.

Good obsidian is found in California, Oregon, Wyoming,

Utah, and Arizona, and rock shops in virtually every state offer it for sale. As a word of caution, be very careful when handling obsidian as its edges are often razor sharp. As a matter of fact, some Mayans made razors out of obsidian. When carrying obsidian in a vehicle, always wrap it with a *thick* layer of newspaper. Above all, never place unwrapped obsidian in a place in a vehicle where the obsidian can rub against anything and cut it.

Crosses of Stone

Staurolite, an iron-aluminum silicate, occurs in schists, usually in the form of reddish-brown or dark-brown crystals which may be translucent or opaque, the opaque variety being much more common. The luster of staurolite varies from vitreous to dull, but there is nothing dull about staurolite's crystal shape which is typically that of an X (see Plate 7.F) or a cross. These shapes are due to twinning, of course, and in a number of places such crosses are sold as good luck charms and curios. Names such as "fairy crosses" seem to have been first applied to staurolite crosses in Europe, it apparently having been believed that the "Little People" were the prime movers behind the crosses. In the United States, staurolite is found throughout New England and is found in Georgia, Virginia, New Mexico, North Carolina, and other states.

Within the last decade, the demand for these crosses has greatly exceeded the ready supply in some places, the result being that many imitations are now being sold. Some of these imitations are carved from fine-grained, brown mica-schists, while others are carved or molded from brown clay, baked, and then sold, more or less hot from the oven. As a small cross commands a good price these days, the buyer should make certain that he is getting real staurolite, if that is what the material is supposed to be.

First of all, the potential buyer should be suspicious of any cross whose surfaces are extremely smooth and un-blemished. Next, if the cross is being advertised as staurolite, ask the seller if you can test the cross for hardness. Staurolite has a hardness of from 7 to 7½, and a knife will scratch most imitations. If a knife is not handy, the cross should easily scratch glass. Also, although the arms of the cross need not be the same size, they should both be orthorhombic, that is, with three axes of unequal lengths meeting at right angles. These tests and observations can be made in a few seconds, but if the customer does not make them he may end up with a cross which was whittled out of soft rock, or baked in a large oven somewhere.

Fossils

Fossils often constitute some of the most interesting (and sometimes most valuable) specimens in a collection. Organic material which became a fossil may have been partially or completely replaced by a mineral substance, or perhaps no replacement at all took place. Fossils can also be footprints in sedimentary rocks, complete or partial skeletons, molds, imprints, etc. In short, any remains or records of past animal or plant life are fossils. The element of time must enter somewhere here, of course, because probably no one would regard a shellfish which died two weeks ago as a fossil, whereas one which died ten thousand years ago would be a fossil.

Just as not everything which glistens is gold, not everything which looks very old is a fossil. In a gold mining camp in California, for example, a strange-looking object was discovered deeply buried in some river sediments and was held in some reverence by the miners as a fossil until it was identified as the hind leg of a mule, complete with shoe.

Where to Look for Fossils. Most fossils are of course found in sedimentary rocks (see Fig. 12.2), and thus the fossil hunter explores in areas which are geologically very different than the areas of igneous and metamorphic rocks where most of the gemstone hunting is done in many states. In these sedimentary rock areas, the best places in general to look for fossils are in regions which have been dissected by streams. In such places, thousands of years of geologic history are often exposed on the sides of a single valley, in the form of strata and the fossils within the strata. Road cuts in sedimentary rock are often very good collecting sites for fossils, also, as are some quarries.

In some states, the hunting ground of the fossil collector

Fig. 12.2: Fossilized whale vertebra (top), two Indian artifacts, and four fossil shellfish surround a fish fossil. All of the fossils and the stone used to make the artifacts came from the same sedimentary formation, approximately 15 million years old. From the author's collection. (Photo by Armando Solis)

is also an excellent place in which to look for agate, flint, chert, geodes, and arrowheads, etc. Fig. 12.3, for example, shows a region of stream-dissected sedimentary rock in North Dakota which is one of the excellent rockhounding and Indian-artifact collecting areas in that state.

How to Collect Fossils. Many fossils are found weathering out of decomposing and disintegrating rock and in such cases all that is often needed is to literally pick up the fossil and walk away with it. Many fossils, though, are in solid rock and a great deal of care must be used in getting the specimen out of the rock.

The method used in extracting a particular fossil which is firmly embedded in rock depends largely upon the kind of fossil, the depth of embedding, the type of rock, its stratification, and possible cracks. If the fossil is firmly embedded, don't try to get it out without any host rock attached to it; take some host rock along with it, otherwise you may break the fossil. Another reason for including some host rock is that most fossils look better and are certainly more instructive if left in a matrix of the rock in which they were found impounded.

If the rock holding a fossil is a shale or a shaley sandstone, it is usually possible to split the rock along planes of bedding, using a thin chisel edge in conjunction with a hammer. Blows with the hammer, on the handle end of the chisel, should be of the order of careful taps until the character of the rock is established. When working in a soft shale a putty knife whose blade has been shortened is a good tool for separating thin strata. Sometimes it will be necessary to

Fig. 12.3: Look for fossils where sediments have been strongly dissected by streams. Road cuts through sedimentary rocks are also good fossil-hunting areas. (Photo courtesy of North Dakota Travel Division)

chisel a channel around the fossil, carrying the channel to a depth at least that of the width of the prism at its top; then the base of the prism can be cut through.

If no fossils are seen on rock surfaces, this by no means indicates that there are no fossils in the rock. Samples of the rock should be carefully split open and, considering that a fossil might be found in any layer, a given piece of rock should be split into several sections before trying another sample. The location of a good-sized fish or plant fossil is often indicated in shale by a slight separation between layers, and any separations between layers should therefore be carefully investigated.

Fossils which are substantially protruding from a rock surface can sometimes be safely removed from the matrix by chiseling, but it is important that the chisel edge always be directed *away* from the fossil, before striking the chisel with the hammer. If this precaution is not observed, a single blow may break the fossil into pieces. After any fossil has been collected, it should be carefully wrapped to prevent breakage.

Fossils in the United States. Fossils are found in varying quantities in every one of the contiguous United States and in Alaska. Wherever there are sedimentary rocks there are liable to be fossils and thus no rockhound need lack for interesting and instructive activity. Some states are especially well-endowed with sedimentary rocks and therefore with fossils. In Ohio, for example, fossils are found in every county in the state.

Important new discoveries of fossils are being made constantly and the rockhound should keep in mind that today's layer of soil may be eroded to reveal tomorrow's discovery. As an example, dinosaur tracks have been known in New England for many years but an extremely important and new discovery of dinosaur tracks was made there only a short time before this book went to press. Many discoveries of fossils have proven to be rewarding not only from a scientific standpoint, but also financially.

Fossil Gem Material. Although most fossils are obtained to add to a collection, some fossils can be made into striking gems, examples being petrified wood, fossil coral, fossil palm root, petrified dinosaur bones, fossil shark teeth, fossil whale-bone, and other material. Typically, such material which is sought for lapidary work has been agatized or calcified and will take a good polish. The color photograph (Plate 8.A) in this book of a piece of petrified whalebone is a specimen from the author's collection, and the polish which is evident resulted from merely rubbing the sawed surfaces against emery cloth, held flat on a floor, for approximately ten minutes.

Gastroliths. A *gastrolith* is one of the most unusual fossils which a rockhound can add to his collection. Dinosaurs, as an aid to their gastronomic processes, swallowed stones, much as chickens swallow gravel, dinosaurs and chickens not being too far removed from each other from the standpoint of ancestry. Considering that the gastric juices of a dinosaur must have verged upon the indescribable, it is little wonder that the stones in a dinosaur's gizzard would eventually become rounded and smooth. These "stomach stones," or gastroliths, are found with some fossil remains of dinosaurs. Some rounded and smooth stones which are not found with dinosaur remains may also be gastroliths but this would be hard to prove. Conversely, it is just as difficult to prove that such stones are not gastroliths. Therefore, unless the stones are found with dinosaur remains, they are not considered to be gastroliths. Another requisite is that only a few stones be found with a given dinosaur since, conceivably, an entire fossil skeleton could be virtually inundated with river gravel during a flood.

Gastroliths are prized items in many collections and these "stomach stones" have been found in several states. Don't buy "gastroliths" from just anyone, however. You might be buying something which could just as correctly be described as a "genuine Indian throwing-stone."

Chapter 13

Gemstones in the United States

The majority of people who for the first time see a list of U.S. gem material localities are usually surprised to discover that many of these gemstones are more or less "right in their own back yard." The list presented in this chapter is only a partial one, of gemstone localities in the United States, and is used with the permission of the United States Bureau of Mines. In some places, the author has made some additions to the list on the basis of new information which he received from several states and it is felt that the list is a good sampling of gemstones and of gemstone localities in the United States. It is, however, only a sampling, and the reader who is interested in a particular section of the country, or gemstone, is referred to the list of "guides" and other books in the bibliography.

Keep an open mind when looking for gemstones because, someday, someone is almost certainly going to rediscover some of the old "gemstone" mines which have apparently been lost. Fossil resin, *amber* (see Plate 8.B), for example, was once found near Nantucket, Massachusetts, near Camden, Harrisonville, and Trenton, New Jersey, and other places. *Danburite,* a wine-yellow gemstone, was once found near Danbury, Connecticut, but that "mine" has also been lost. Few diamonds have been found in the Great Lakes region in recent years, yet for every diamond ever found there, there are probably 1,000 more, many of these no doubt deeply buried in the glacial debris—but some may be close to the surface, too.

So, when you go on a field trip, you might find something valuable, you might rediscover an old gemstone mine, you might find only a few pieces of, say, milky quartz of not too good quality—or you might find quartz in the form of beautiful crystals of amethyst. You just never know, and therein lies one of the great attractions of rockhounding.

Partial List of Gem Material Localities in the United States

State and county   *Gem materials*

Alabama:

Clay .... Azurite, garnet, malachite, marcasite.
Cleburne .... Beryl, garnet, kyanite, malachite, marcasite.
Coosa .... Beryl, tourmaline.
Limestone .... Geodes.
Tuscaloosa .... Agate, chert, jasper, onyx.

Alaska: [1]

Cook Inlet-Susitna ... Soapstone.
Northwestern Alaska . Jade.
Southeastern Alaska .. Agate, garnet, jade.

Arizona:

Apache .... Agate, obsidian, peridot, petrified wood.
Cochise .... Agate, amethyst, azurite, malachite, shattuckite.
Coconino .... Agate, obsidian, petrified wood.
Gila .... Agate, amethyst, azurite, bloodstone, carnelian, chalcedony, chrysocolla, epidote, garnet, hypersthene, obsidian, opal, peridot, petrified wood, serpentine, turquoise.
Graham .... Agate, azurite, banded agate, chalcedony, malachite, obsidian, onyx, opal, petrified wood, turquoise.
Greenlee .... Agate, amethyst, azurite, chalcedony, chrysocolla, garnet, jasper, malachite, obsidian, onyx, opal, petrified wood, rose quartz, shattuckite, turquoise, variscite.
Maricopa .... Agate, amethyst, chalcedony, fire agate, jasper, marble, onyx, opal, petrified wood, plume agate.
Mohave .... Agate, chalcedony, chalk turquoise, jasper, petrified wood.

[1] Alaska has no county designation.

State and county   *Gem materials*

Arizona:
Navajo .... Garnet, petrified wood.
Pima .... Azurite, chalcedony, malachite, ob-
                   sidian, shattuckite.
Pinal .... Chalcedony, chrysocolla, obsidian,
                   peridot.
Yavapai .... Agate, carnelian, chalcedony, chryso-
                   colla, chrysoprase, jade, jasper,
                   moonstone, obsidian, onyx, petri-
                   fied wood, quartz crystal.
Yuma .... Agate, chalcedony, garnet, jasper,
                   obsidian, petrified wood, quartz
                   crystal, rhyolite, turquoise.

Arkansas:
Garland .... Novaculite, quartz crystal.
Hot Spring .... Quartz crystal, smoky quartz.
Montgomery .... Quartz crystal.
Pike .... Diamond.

California:
Alameda .... Agate.
Alpine .... Agate.
Amador .... Rhodonite.
Calaveras .... Agate, chalcedony, chrysoprase, petri-
                   fied wood, quartz crystal.
Colusa .... Travertine.
Contra Costa ..... Agate.
Del Norte .... Agate, jasper, petrified wood.
El Dorado .... Agate, garnet, idocrase, jasper, neph-
                   rite, petrified wood, vesuvianite.
Fresno .... Chert, jasper, petrified wood, smoky
                   quartz.
Humboldt .... Agate, jade, jasper, petrified wood.
Imperial .... Agate, andalusite, chalcedony, du-
                   mortierite, garnet, jasper, kyanite,
                   opal, petrified palm root, petrified
                   wood.
Inyo .... Agate, amethyst, bloodstone, epidote,
                   garnet, geode, jasper, obsidian,
                   onyx, opal, quartz crystal, tur-
                   quoise.

State and county   *Gem materials*

California:

Kern .... Actinolite, agate, colemanite crystal, jade, jasper, morrisonite, petrified wood, quartz crystal, rhodonite, rose quartz.

Lake .... Jasper, onyx, quartz crystal.

Los Angeles .... Agate, chalcedony, jasper, rhodonite.

Madera .... Chiastolite.

Marin .... Agate, jade, petrified whalebone.

Mariposa .... Quartz crystal.

Mendocino .... Agate, jade, jasper, opal, quartz.

Modoc .... Agate, jasper, obsidian.

Mono .... Geode, obsidian.

Monterey .... Agate, jadeite, jasper, nephrite, rhodonite, serpentine.

Napa .... Cinnabar, jasper, onyx, quartz crystal.

Nevada .... Opal, petrified wood.

Placer .... Jade.

Riverside .... Actinolite, agate, amazonite, aquamarine, beryl, calcite, chalcedony, corundum, diopside, epidote, fire agate, garnet, geode, idocrase, jasper, petrified wood, quartz crystal, rhodonite, rose quartz, rubellite, spinel, topaz, tourmaline.

Sacramento .... Agate, jade, opal.

San Benito .... Benitoite, diopside, garnet, jade, jadeite, natrolite, serpentine.

San Bernardino ...... Actinolite, agate, amethyst, aragonite, bloodstone, chalcedony, crawfordite, epidote, geode, jasper, moss agate, onyx, opalite, petrified wood, rhodonite, travertine, verde antique.

San Diego .... Beryl, garnet, kunzite, quartz crystal, rhodonite, topaz, tourmaline.

San Francisco .... Jasper, nephrite.

San Luis Obispo ..... Agate, jade, jasper, marcasite, onyx, quartz, sagenite.

San Mateo .... Petrified whalebone.

Santa Barbara .... Agate.

State and county   *Gem materials*

California (cont'd):

Santa Clara .... Agate, jasper.
Santa Cruz .... Agate, petrified whalebone.
Siskiyou .... Agate, californite, idocrase, jade, quartz crystal, rhodonite.
Solano .... Onyx, travertine.
Sonoma .... Actinolite, jasper.
Trinity .... Agate, jade, jasper, rhodonite.
Tulare .... Agate, chrysoprase, jade, quartz crystal, smoky quartz, thulite, topaz.
Tuolumne .... Agate, gold quartz, jasper, marble, petrified wood, pyrite.
Ventura .... Agate.

Colorado:

Chaffee .... Agate, aquamarine, beryl, jasper, onyx, petrified wood, phenacite.
Clear Creek .... Amazonite, garnet.
Custer .... Petrified wood.
Delta .... Jasper.
Douglas .... Amazonite, smoky quartz, topaz, petrified wood.
Elbert .... Petrified wood.
El Paso .... Agate, amazonite, garnet, phenacite, topaz, tourmaline, zircon.
Fremont .... Agate, coprolite, onyx, petrified wood, rose quartz, satin spar.
Garfield .... Oil shale, petrified wood.
Jefferson .... Amazonite, barite crystal, beryl, topaz, tourmaline.
Kiowa .... Agate.
Las Animas .... Rose agate.
Mesa .... Agate, amethyst, flint, petrified wood.
Mineral .... Agate, amethyst, jasper, petrified wood.
Moffat .... Agate.
Montrose .... Amazonite, coprolite, covellite, jasper, phenacite, smoky quartz, topaz.
Ouray .... Quartz crystal, rhodonite.
Park .... Agate, beryl, fluorite, jade, moss opal, petrified wood, topaz.
Rio Grande .... Agate, petrified wood.

State and county	*Gem materials*

Colorado (cont'd):

Saguache .... Agate, amethyst, jade, turquoise.

San Juan .... Feldspar, mica, quartz crystal, rhodonite.

San Miguel .... Jasper, petrified bone.

Sedgwick .... Agate, petrified wood.

Teller .... Agate, amazonite, amethyst, jade, petrified wood, phenacite, quartz crystal, siderite, smoky quartz, topaz, zircon.

Weld .... Agate, barite, petrified wood.

Connecticut:

Fairfield .... Albite, beryl, epidote, fluorite, mica, quartz crystal, scheelite, siderite, spodumene, topaz, tremolite, wolframite.

Hartford .... Amethyst, azurite, datolite, malachite, prehnite, quartz, smoky quartz.

Litchfield .... Calcite, fluorite, galena, garnet, graphite, kyanite, magnetite, opal, prehnite, pyrite, quartz, siderite, sphalerite, stilbite, tourmaline, tremolite.

Middlesex .... Actinolite, amblygonite, apatite, austinite, bertrandite, beryl, columbite, chrysoberyl, feldspar, fluorite, garnet, hiddenite, kunzite, lepidolite, mica, pollucite, rose quartz, spodumene, topaz, tourmaline.

New Haven .... Amethyst, barite, beryl, columbite, datolite, feldspar, garnet, prehnite, rose quartz, smoky quartz.

New London .... Garnet, kyanite, pyrite, quartz crystal, rose quartz.

Florida:

Hillsborough .... Agatized coral.

Lake .... Chalcedony.

Pinellas .... Agatized shark bone.

Georgia:

Brooks .... Agate.

Cobb .... Topaz.

State and county   *Gem materials*

Georgia:
  Elbert .... Smoky quartz.
  Forsyth .... Moonstone.
  Habersham .... Kyanite.
  Jones .... Agate.
  Lincoln .... Lazulite, rutile.
  Lumpkin .... Garnet.
  Morgan .... Amethyst.
  Paulding .... Garnet.
  Rabun .... Amethyst, garnet, quartz, rose quartz, ruby.
  Towns .... Ruby, sapphire.
  Troup .... Amethyst, aquamarine, rose quartz.
  Washington .... Opal.
  Wilkes .... Kyanite, lazulite, rutile.

Idaho:
  Benewah .... Garnet.
  Blaine .... Agate, petrified wood.
  Butte .... Agate, petrified wood.
  Canyon .... Agate, petrified wood, white plume agate.
  Lemhi .... Petrified wood.
  Nez Perce .... Agate, garnet, jasper, opal, petrified wood, sapphire.
  Owyhee .... Agate, jasper, petrified wood.

Illinois:
  Alexander .... Jasper.
  Hancock .... Agate, geodes, jasper.
  Hardin .... Fluorite.
  Pope .... Jasper.
  Pulaski .... Jasper.

Indiana:
  Morgan .... Garnet, sapphire.
  Scott .... Petrified wood.

Iowa:
  Des Moines .... Petrified wood.
  Henry .... Agate, jasper, petrified wood.
  Lee .... Geode, jasper.
  Muscatine .... Agate.
  Page .... Agate.

State and county	*Gem materials*

Kansas:

Cherokee	Marcasite, sphalerite.
Franklin	Petrified wood.
Wallace	Opal.
Wyandotte	Agate.

Kentucky:

Ballard	Jasper.
Elliott	Garnet.
Jefferson	Agate.

Louisiana:

Ouachita	Agate, jasper, petrified wood.
Vernon	Petrified wood.

Maine:

Androscoggin	Amblygonite, apatite, beryl, garnet, lepidolite, spodumene, pollucite, tourmaline.
Cumberland	Actinolite, beryl, columbite, garnet.
Franklin	Columbite, spodumene.
Hancock	Beryl.
Kennebec	Cancrinite, nephelite, sodalite, zircon.
Knox	Spodumene.
Oxford	Agate, amblygonite, amethyst, apatite, aquamarine, beryl, chrysoberyl, eosphorite, herderite, lepidolite, pollucite, quartz crystal, rose quartz, smoky quartz, spodumene, tourmaline.
Sagadahoc	Beryl, lepidolite, tourmaline.
Washington	Agate, jasper.

Maryland:

Allegany	Barite crystal, quartz crystal, siderite.
Baltimore	Antigorite, calcite crystal, garnet, jasper, quartz, serpentine, smoky quartz, tourmaline.
Calvert	Jasper.
Carroll	Azurite, malachite.
Cecil	Onyx, serpentine, williamsite.
Frederick	Onyx, malachite.
Garrett	Picrolite, serpentine, williamsite.
Hartford	Serpentine.
Washington	Cuprite.

| *State and county* | *Gem materials* |

Massachusetts:
Essex .... Smoky quartz, serpentine.
Hampden .... Amethyst, beryl, datolite, marcasite, prehnite, spodumene, tourmaline.
Hampshire .... Amethyst, beryl, datolite, galena, prehnite, pollucite, rhodonite, spodumene.
Middlesex .... Chiastolite, scheelite.
Plymouth .... Jasper.
Worcester .... Beryl, chiastolite, spodumene.

Michigan:
Dickinson .... Actinolite.
Emmet .... Agate, fossils, petoskey stone.
Houghton .... Agate, garnet.
Keweenaw .... Agate, chlorastrolite, domeykite, thomsonite.
Marquette .... Jasper, jaspillite.
Ontonagon .... Agate, datolite, malachite, tenorite.

Minnesota:
Carlton .... Agate, jasper.
Cook .... Agate, heulandite.
Lake .... Agate, thomsonite.
Morrison .... Garnet, staurolite.
Pipestone .... Catlinite.
St. Louis .... Agate.
Winona .... Agate.

Mississippi:
Copiah .... Agate.
Harrison .... Jasper.
Madison .... Petrified wood.
Wayne .... Petrified wood.

Missouri:
Bollinger .... Agate, jasper.
Cape Girardeau ...... Agate, jasper.
Clark .... Geode.
Crawford .... Amethyst.
Franklin .... Amethyst.
Jackson .... Amethyst.
Lewis .... Agate.
Madison .... Agate, jasper.

State and county   *Gem materials*

Missouri (cont'd):

St. Louis .... Agate, barite, galena, geode.

Wayne .... Agate, jasper.

Montana:

Beaverhead .... Corundum, quartz.

Custer .... Agate, sapphire.

Dawson .... Agate.

Deer Lodge .... Sapphire.

Fergus .... Sapphire.

Gallatin .... Agate, corundum, petrified wood, rose quartz.

Granite .... Sapphire.

Jefferson .... Amethyst, barite, tourmaline.

Judith Basin .... Sapphire.

Lewis and Clark ..... Garnet, ruby, sapphire, spinel.

Madison .... Garnet, jasper, onyx, orthoclase, quartz crystal, serpentine, tourmaline.

Meagher .... Agate.

Missoula .... Quartz.

Park .... Amethyst, arsenopyrite, garnet, iceland spar, petrified wood, travertine.

Powell .... Agate, amazonite, sapphire.

Prairie .... Agate, petrified wood.

Ravalli .... Fluorite.

Rosebud .... Agate.

Silver Bow .... Amethyst, epidote, fluorite, garnet, sapphire.

Yellowstone .... Agate, jasper.

Nebraska:

Cass .... Horn coral, petrified wood.

Dawes .... Chalcedony.

Gage .... Geode.

Jefferson .... Agate, jasper, petrified wood.

Lincoln .... Agate, jasper.

Nance .... Agate, jasper, petrified wood.

Saunders .... Agate, petrified wood.

Sioux .... Agate, chalcedony, petrified wood.

Nevada:

Clark .... Amethyst.

State and county	*Gem materials*

Nevada (cont'd):

Douglas .... Topaz.

Elko .... Agate, azurite, chalcedony, petrified wood.

Esmeralda .... Agate, chalcedony, petrified wood, turquoise.

Eureka .... Sulfur crystal.

Humboldt .... Agate, fire opal, jasper, petrified wood, rhodonite.

Lander .... Chert, turquoise.

Lincoln .... Agate, chalcedony, chrysocolla, jasper, malachite, petrified wood, quartz.

Lyon .... Agate, jasper, opal.

Mineral .... Obsidian, petrified wood, turquoise.

Nye .... Onyx, petrified wood.

Pershing .... Opal, petrified wood.

Washoe .... Agate, garnet, idocrase, jasper, obsidian, petrified wood, piedmontite.

White Pine .... Garnet.

New Hampshire:

Carroll .... Amethyst, danaite, phenacite, helvite, quartz crystal, smoky quartz, topaz.

Cheshire .... Amethyst, apatite, aquamarine, beryl, fluorite, garnet, quartz crystal, rose quartz, tourmaline, spodumene.

Coos .... Amethyst, quartz crystal, topaz.

Grafton .... Apatite, beryl, columbite.

Merrimack .... Beryl, garnet.

Rockingham .... Spodumene.

Sullivan .... Aquamarine, rose quartz.

New Jersey:

Bergen .... Natrolite.

Cape May .... Jasper, quartz crystal.

Mercer .... Albite, calcite, chabazite, datolite, natrolite, stilbite.

Middlesex .... Marcasite, petrified wood, pyrite.

Morris .... Carnelian, serpentine.

Passaic .... Agate, amethyst, carnelian, chabazite, datolite, heulandite, pectolite, prehnite.

State and county	Gem materials

New Jersey (cont'd):

Sussex .... Aragonite, corundum, garnet, pyrrhotite, rhodonite, spinel, tourmaline, willemite.

Union .... Calcite, chalcedony, prehnite, sphalerite, stilbite.

Warren .... Molybdenite.

New Mexico:

Bernalillo .... Agate.

Catron .... Agate.

Chaves .... Agate.

Eddy .... Agate, quartz crystal.

Grant .... Agate.

Hidalgo .... Agate, chalcedony, serpentine.

Luna .... Agate, carnelian, onyx, travertine.

Otero .... Turquoise.

Rio Arriba .... Agate, beryl, dumortierite, feldspar, petrified wood.

San Juan .... Agate, ricolite, petrified wood.

Santa Fe .... Beryl.

Sierra .... Agate, carnelian, fluorite, petrified wood.

Socorro .... Agate, chalcedony.

Valencia .... Agate, jasper, obsidian, petrified wood.

New York:

Dutchess .... Quartz crystal.

Erie .... Satin spar.

Essex .... Garnet, rose quartz, wollastonite.

Herkimer .... Quartz crystal.

Jefferson .... Hematite.

Madison .... Celestite.

Niagara .... Calcite.

Orange .... Quartz crystal, sunstone, tourmaline.

Putnam .... Magnetite, opal, serpentine.

Rockland .... Pink garnet, sphene.

St. Lawrence .... Calcite, hexagonite, pyrite, serpentine, sphalerite, talc, tremolite.

Saratoga .... Beryl.

Ulster .... Quartz crystal.

Warren .... Garnet.

Westchester .... Beryl, garnet, quartz, rose quartz.

State and county   *Gem materials*

North Carolina:

Alexander . . . . Hiddenite, quartz, rutile, sapphire.
Ashe . . . . Beryl, garnet, moonstone, rutile.
Avery . . . . : . . . . Epidote, unakite.
Buncombe . . . . Kyanite, moonstone.
Burke . . . . Amethyst.
Clay . . . . Ruby, sapphire.
Granville . . . . Jasper.
Haywood . . . . Emerald, sapphire.
Iredell . . . . Actinolite, rose quartz, sapphire.
Macon . . . . Garnet, rhodonite, ruby, sapphire.
Mitchell . . . . Actinolite, beryl, biotite, emerald, epidote, feldspar gems, garnet, rhodonite, unakite.
Orange . . . . Agate.
Rutherford . . . . Emerald.
Warren . . . . Amethyst.
Wilkes . . . . Agate.
Yancey . . . . Emerald, feldspar gems.

North Dakota:

Adams . . . . Petrified wood.
Billings . . . . Petrified wood.
McLean . . . . Petrified wood.
Morton . . . . Petrified wood.
Stark . . . . Chalcedony, jasper, quartz crystal.

Ohio:

Coshocton . . . . Flint, selenite crystal.
Franklin . . . . Petrified wood.
Gallia . . . . Petrified wood.
Licking . . . . Flint, jasper.
Lucas . . . . Fossils.
Montgomery . . . . Agate, gem granite.
Muskingum . . . . Jasper.
Ottawa . . . . Celestite, fluorite.
Wood . . . . Barite, calcite.

Oklahoma:

Canadian . . . . Agate, jasper, petrified wood.
Comanche . . . . Zircon.
Dewey . . . . Agate, chalcedony, jade, jasper, petrified wood.

State and county	Gem materials

Oklahoma (cont'd):

Greer	Alabaster.
Jackson	Quartz.
Major	Agate, jasper, petrified wood.
Ottawa	Sphalerite.
Pushmataha	Green quartz.

Oregon:

Baker	Agate, jasper, petrified wood.
Benton	Agate.
Coos	Fossil wood.
Crook	Agate, carnelian, geode, moss agate.
Curry	Jade.
Deschutes	Agate, carnelian, geode, jasper, moss agate.
Douglas	Agate.
Grant	Agate, petrified wood.
Harney	Agate, obsidian.
Jackson	Agate, bloodstone, jasper, petrified wood, rhodonite.
Jefferson	Agate, amethyst, geode, opal.
Lake	Geode, obsidian.
Lane	Agate, petrified wood.
Lincoln	Agate, agatized coral, bloodstone, jasper, petrified wood, sagenite, sardonyx.
Linn	Agate.
Malheur	Agate, geode, jasper, petrified wood.
Morrow	Agate, geode.
Polk	Agate, jasper, petrified wood.
Union	Agate.
Wallowa	Agate.
Wasco	Agate, amethyst, bloodstone, chalcedony, geode, jade, jasper, opal, quartz, sagenite.
Wheeler	Agate.

Pennsylvania:

Adams	Cuprite.
Bedford	Calcite, quartz, spar.
Berks	Calcite, epidote, feldspar, garnet, hematite, kyanite, magnetite, quartz crystal, unakite, zeolite.

State and county   *Gem materials*

Pennsylvania (cont'd):

Bucks .... Galena, sphalerite.

Carbon .... Autunite, carnotite.

Chester .... Anglesite, azurite, feldspar, garnet, goethite, hornblend, kyanite, magnetite, malachite, martite, phlogopite, pyromorphite, pyrite, pyrrhotite, quartz, quartz crystal, sphalerite, sulfur, stibnite, wulfenite.

Cumberland .... Phosphorite.

Delaware .... Actinolite, apatite crystal, deweylite, feldspar, garnet.

Lancaster .... Actinolite, aragonite, calcite, chalcedony, chromite, dolomite, hematite, malachite, marcasite, quartz crystal, pyrite, serpentine.

Lebanon .... Anthophyllite, apophylite, biotite, garnet, hematite, magnetite, serpentine.

Lehigh .... Calamine, corundum, goethite, greenockite, jasper, quartz crystal, sphalerite.

Monroe .... Quartz crystal.

Montgomery .... Calcite, galena, lead and copper minerals, natrolite, quartz crystal, sphalerite, stibnite, zeolite.

Northampton .... Calcite, graphite, gummite, limonite, serpentine, talc, uraninite.

Perry .... Travertine.

Schuylkill .... Chlorite, galena, pyrite, quartz crystal, siderite, sphalerite.

Somerset .... Quartz.

Westmoreland ...... Petrified wood, quartz.

York .... Limonite, pyrite.

Rhode Island:

Bristol .... Amethyst.

Newport .... Agate, cobbles with staurolite crosses, garnets (all on beaches of Conanicut Island).

Providence .... Amethyst, beryl, fluorite, quartz crystals.

State and county	Gem materials

Rhode Island (cont'd):

Washington .... Amazonite, amethyst, moonstone (all on Moonstone Beach, in South Kingstown).

South Carolina:

Anderson .... Amethyst, beryl, garnet, sapphire, tourmaline.

Chesterfield .... Topaz.

Florence .... Petrified wood.

Laurens .... Amethyst, corundum.

South Dakota:

Custer .... Agate, amblygonite, beryl, chalcedony, feldspar, garnet, jade, jasper, lepidolite, mica, petrified wood, quartz crystal, rose quartz, sillimanite, tourmaline.

Fall River .... Agate, chalcedony, jasper, petrified wood, vanadanite.

Harding .... Agate, petrified wood.

Lawrence .... Garnet, rose quartz.

Meade .... Gastroliths, geodes, petrified wood, selenite.

Pennington .... Agate, apatite, beryl, chalcedony, feldspar, galena, garnet, jasper, lepidolite, petrified wood, rose quartz, staurolite, tourmaline.

Shannon .... Agate, jasper, petrified wood.

Tennessee:

Bedford .... Agate.

Carter .... Unakite.

Coffee .... Agate.

Texas:

Brewster .... Agate, amethyst, carnelian, chalcedony, citrine, fire opal, jasper, labradorite, moonstone, novaculite, petrified wood, quartz.

Burnet .... Garnet, topaz.

Culberson .... Agate.

De Witt .... Agate, jasper, petrified wood.

Duval .... Agate, jasper, petrified wood.

State and county   *Gem materials*

Texas (cont'd):

El Paso .... Agate.
Fayette .... Petrified wood.
Gillespie .... Amythest, garnet, petrified wood,
                     topaz.
Gonzales .... Petrified wood.
Hildalgo .... Agate.
Hudspeth .... Agate.
Jeff Davis .... Adularia, agate, amethyst, carnelian,
                     chalcedony, citrine, jasper, moon-
                     stone, opal, petrified wood, quartz
                     crystal.
Lee .... Petrified wood.
Live Oak .... Agate, petrified wood.
Llano .... Amethyst, garnet, quartz crystal,
                     topaz, tourmaline.
McMullen .... Petrified wood.
Mason .... Amazonite, cassiterite, fluorite,
                     quartz, topaz.
Pecos .... Agate.
Potter .... Petrified wood.
Presidio .... Agate, amethyst, carnelian, chalced-
                     ony, citrine, jasper, moonstone,
                     opal, petrified wood, quartz crystal.
Reeves .... Agate, amethyst, carnelian, chalced-
                     ony, citrine, jasper, moonstone,
                     opal, petrified wood, quartz crystal.
Taylor .... Smoky quartz, topaz.
Terrell .... Agate.
Travis .... Topaz.
Trinity .... Petrified wood.
Walker .... Petrified wood.
Webb .... Agate, jasper.
Zapata .... Agate, jasper.

Utah:

Beaver .... Agate, obsidian, quartz crystal.
Box Elder .... Variscite.
Carbon .... Agate.
Emery .... Agate, chalcedony, obsidian, petrified
                     wood.
Garfield .... Agate, barite, dinosaur bone, onyx,
                     petrified wood, jasper.

State and county | *Gem materials*

Utah (cont'd):

Grand .... Agate, dinosaur bone, petrified wood, jasper.
Iron .... Agate, geode.
Juab .... Agate, geode, jasper, topaz.
Kane .... Agate, petrified wood.
Millard .... Fossils, jasper, obsidian.
Salt Lake .... Agate, onyx.
San Juan .... Garnet.
Sevier .... Agate.
Tooele .... Agate, geode, obsidian.
Utah .... Onyx, variscite.
Washington .... Agate, alabaster, azurite, jasper.
Wayne .... Agate, barite, dinosaur bone, jasper, petrified wood.

Vermont:

Addison .... Labradorite.
Chittenden .... Jasper.
Washington .... Serpentine.
Windham .... Kyanite, serpentine.
Windsor .... Actinolite, kyanite, pyrite, staurolite, talc.

Virginia:

Amelia .... Albite, amazonite, cleavelandite, garnet.
Madison .... Blue quartz, epidote, unakite.
Page .... Epidote, jasper, onyx.
Prince Edward ..... Amazonite, amethyst, kyanite.
Rockbridge .... Unakite.
York .... Shark teeth, whalebone.

Washington:

Benton .... Petrified wood.
Chelan .... Thulite.
Cowlitz .... Carnelian, sardonyx.
Douglas .... Jadeite, thulite.
Kittitas .... Agate, chalcedony, jasper, petrified wood.
Klickitat .... Agate, jasper, petrified wood.
Lewis .... Carnelian, sardonyx.
Snohomish .... Petrified wood.
Yakima .... Carnelian, sardonyx.

State and county	*Gem materials*

West Virginia:
   Hardy .... Aragonite, stilbite.
   Mineral .... Fossils.

Wisconsin:
   Ashland .... Agate, jasper.
   Bayfield .... Agate.
   Clark .... Agate, jasper.
   Douglas .... Agate.
   Iron .... Agate.

Wyoming:
   Albany .... Agate, petrified wood.
   Big Horn .... Agate.
   Carbon .... Agate, jade, jasper, petrified wood.
   Fremont .... Actinolite, agate, aventurine, garnet, jade, jasper, petrified wood, rhodonite, sapphire, serpentine.
   Goshen .... Jasper.
   Johnson .... Petrified wood.
   Lincoln .... Agate, petrified wood.
   Natrona .... Agate, amazonite, jade, petrified wood.
   Platte .... Agate.
   Sweetwater .... Agate, chalcedony, corundum, eden wood, jade, jasper, moss agate, petrified wood.
   Uinta .... Petrified wood.

Chapter 14

The Rockhound Tourist

A journey by car, from the one-day variety to a full-fledged vacation tour, always offers a number of opportunities for roadside rockhounding. There is always the temptation, for example, to pull the car over to the side of the road and investigate roadcuts for gemstones or fossils, or to take a gold pan or small sluice box down to an inviting-looking stream and try the gravel for gold or gemstones.

In addition to items such as gemstones, fossils, and gold, however, there are many other specimens which can be collected by the rockhound, usually in sites close to the road, and many hobbyists say that these specimens are some of the most interesting of all. These may be ore samples from an operating mine; slick, polished pieces of rock taken from a fault zone which cuts across the road; oddly shaped, wind-carved stones from the side of a desert road or an ocean beach or mountain highway; scratched and grooved rocks from a pile of glacier-deposited material a few feet from the road, and many more.

Notice that such specimens are not only interesting mementoes of a trip; they also serve as instructive reminders of the geological processes which formed, shaped, and placed the specimens. Thus, almost any trip can include thoroughly entertaining and informative journeys into the related worlds of rockhounding and geology, and all this usually only a few yards from a roadside.

Metal Mines and Ore Minerals

Mining companies are among the most hospitable organizations which rockhound tourists will encounter on their travels (see Fig. 14.1). Many mining companies offer free or nominally priced guided tours in parts of the mines, and many mines also offer the visitor free or nominally priced samples of the ore minerals being mined.

Fig. 14.1: From rockhound paradise to skiers' heaven. Many mines in the United States offer conducted underground tours in season. When the snow flies, this particular mine also whisks skiers aloft, in mine cages, to the snow-covered slopes on a Utah mountain. Notice the ore cars at the right. (Photo courtesy of U.S. Bureau of Mines)

An extremely good investment for rockhound tourists—or for any traveler, for that matter—would be the purchase, for thirty-five cents, of a 90-page booklet entitled *Mining and Mineral Operations in the United States, A Visitor's Guide,* written by the staff members of the United States Bureau of Mines. This generously illustrated publication may be obtained from the Superintendent of Documents, Government Printing Office, Washington D.C. 20402. If you send for the booklet, send check or money order, not stamps, and include its catalogue number (I 28.16/2:M 66).

The booklet lists, for each state included, "Mines You Can See from the Highway," "Mines You Can Visit," and "Ghost Towns and Historical Sites." Other information is included, such as the locations of mineral and mining museums, locations of quarries, where to write for more information, etc.

Ore and Ore Minerals. An *ore* is an aggregate of metallic minerals which can be mined at a profit. Thus, depending upon economic factors, today's ore may not be an ore a few years from now. Conversely, a concentration of minerals which is not an ore today may become an ore sometime in the future.

Most of the major metal mining regions of the world where the metals occur in veins are situated on the fringes of batholiths (see Chapter 6), and it was obviously magma from the batholiths which released the solutions which formed the veins. Some ores, however, such as certain ores of copper, zinc, and lead are found in contact metamorphic zones and some metals occur in disseminated deposits. Ores can also be of sedimentary origin, most ores of iron and some of aluminum and manganese being of this type. The iron ores of the Lake Superior region, for example, were originally sediments which were precipitated in a large body of water and then enriched by the subsequent removal of much of the worthless material, by natural processes. *Bauxite*, aluminum ore, is often concentrated by the decomposition of rocks like granite; it is also formed by the leaching of aluminum from sediments, with subsequent deposition in the form of impure aluminum hydroxides, these hydroxides constituting bauxite.

Most ore minerals occur as chemical compounds, the chief ores of copper, for example, being sulfides. Some metals also occur at times in uncombined form, that is, as native copper, native silver, etc. The often astonishing difference in appearance between the combined and uncombined forms of a metal is well-illustrated by the color photographs, in this book, of native copper (Plate 8.C) and some of the ore minerals of copper such as bornite and chalcopyrite (see Plate 8.D). Also, note the photographs (Plates 6.F, 7.A) of azurite and malachite, both gemstones of copper, and compare them with the photograph of native copper.

Many a rockhound will remember *galena*, the "crystal" of the crystal radio sets of some years ago. Galena (see Plate 8.E) is lead sulfide and is an ore mineral of lead. Galena often contains silver and, as a matter of fact, many ores commonly contain several metals. Almost any ore of copper, as an example, also contains at least small quantities of gold and silver. Galena is illustrated in the color photographs, as is *rhodonite* (see Plate 8.F), a minor ore of manganese and also a gemstone.

Common Ore Minerals. A selected list of metals and ore minerals appears below. The distinguishing characteristics of these ore minerals, and other information concerning them, can be determined by consulting both the determinative tables in Chapter 16 and the table of minerals immediately preceding the determinative tables. The explanation in Chapter 16 relative to the use of these tables should be read first, however.

Metals and Some of Their Ore Minerals

Metal	Ore Minerals
Aluminum	Bauxite.
Copper	Native copper, bornite, chalcopyrite, chalcocite, malachite.
Gold	Native gold.
Iron	Hematite, magnetite, limonite, siderite, pyrite, pyrrhotite.
Lead	Galena, cerussite, anglesite.
Silver	Native silver, argentite, cerargyrite.
Tin	Cassiterite.
Uranium	Uraninite, carnotite.
Zinc	Sphalerite, smithsonite.

Coal and Coal Mines

Coal is formed by plant material which dies and is covered over by a mixture of water and dirt, as in a bog or swamp. With only partial decay and partial burial, however, *peat* is formed. If the peat is completely but not deeply buried, and if there is no pressure applied other than that caused by the overlying sediments, the peat becomes *lignite*, or brown coal. If the peat is deeply covered and the area is strongly folded by geologic processes, a hard coal called *anthracite* is commonly formed. The coal intermediate in rank between lignite and anthracite is *bituminous* coal which results from sufficiently deep burial to form a soft coal which has a higher carbon content than that of lignite. In order of decreasing carbon content (and increasing water content) the coals are: anthracite, bituminous, subbituminous, and lignite.

Coal Mines. Due in part to the fact that lignite forms with only shallow burial, much of the latest lignite formed is found near the surface. Thus, in many areas the worthless overburden can be easily stripped from above the lignite. Much bituminous coal is also mined by strip operation.

The machinery involved in the strip mining and the open pit mining of lignite and bituminous coal is of tremendous size and is well worth seeing. In North Dakota, a machine which is used to remove the overburden from lignite at one particular mine is ten stories high and weighs 2,350 tons. In Illinois, visitors to a certain mine can see bituminous coal being scooped up by a shovel having a capacity of 180 cubic yards, the coal then being hauled away by a truck which carries 240 tons of coal on every trip to the processing plant.

Thirty-two of the fifty United States have appreciable deposits of coal and in many of these states coal is mined underground. Rockhound tourists will be interested to know that several underground coal mines scattered throughout the United States offer conducted tours for visitors. In a coal mine in Pennsylvania, for example, visitors travel far underground in electric cars, and children on the tour can "dig" their own bucket of coal and also meet "Big John," the legendary coal miner.

Where to Get Information about Roadside Mines

Information regarding "roadside" mines and mine tours, etc., in particular states can be obtained from the United States Bureau of Mines visitor's guide previously referred to, from state geologists, and from the United States Bureau of Mines offices listed in the following table. The table is arranged in terms of geographical areas, and the Bureau of Mines offices which handle inquiries for particular states are designated, with their addresses, opposite those states.

United States Bureau of Mines Offices

Area Number, and States	U.S. Bureau of Mines Office
Area I	
Connecticut, Maine, Maryland, Massachusetts, New Hampshire, New Jersey, New York, Ohio, Pennsylvania, Rhode Island, Vermont, Virginia, West Virginia	Federal Bureau of Mines Area Director Area I Mineral Resource Office 4800 Forbes Avenue Pittsburgh, Pa. 15213
Area II	
Alabama, Florida, Georgia, Kentucky, North Carolina, South Carolina, Tennessee	Federal Bureau of Mines Area Director Area II Mineral Resource Office 301 West Cumberland Knoxville, Tenn. 37902
Area III	
Illinois, Indiana, Michigan, Minnesota, Wisconsin	Federal Bureau of Mines Area Director Area III Mineral Resource Office East 58th St. at Mississippi River P.O. Box 1660 Twin City Airport, Minn. 55111
Area IV	
Arkansas, Kansas, Missouri, Oklahoma	Federal Bureau of Mines Area Director Area IV Mineral Resource Office 206 Federal Bldg. Bartlesville, Okla., 74004
Texas	Federal Bureau of Mines Area IV Mineral Resource Field Office 1114 Commerce Street Dallas, Texas 75202

Area Number, and States	U.S. Bureau of Mines Office

Area V

Colorado, Nebraska, North Dakota, South Dakota

Federal Bureau of Mines
Area Director
Area V Mineral Resource Office
Building 20, Denver Federal Center
Denver, Colo., 80225

Arizona

Federal Bureau of Mines
Area V Mineral Resource Field Office
8 West Paseo Redondo
Tucson, Arizona 85705

New Mexico

Federal Bureau of Mines
Area V Mineral Resource Field Office
Socorro, N.M. 87801

Utah

Federal Bureau of Mines
Area V Mineral Resource Field Office
1600 East First South St.
Salt Lake City, Utah 84112

Wyoming

Federal Bureau of Mines
Area V Mineral Resource Office
365 North Ninth St.
Laramie, Wyo., 82071

Area VI

California

Federal Bureau of Mines
Area Director
Area VI Mineral Resource Office
450 Golden Gate Avenue
San Francisco, Calif., 94102

Nevada

Federal Bureau of Mines
Area VI Mineral Resource Office
1605 Evans Avenue
Reno, Nevada 89505

Area Number, and States	U.S. Bureau of Mines Office
Area VII	
Idaho	Federal Bureau of Mines Area VII Mineral Resource Field Office 1430 North Washington Spokane, Wash., 99201
Montana, Oregon, Washington	Federal Bureau of Mines Area Director Area VII Mineral Resource Office Albany, Oregon 97321
Area VIII	
Alaska	Federal Bureau of Mines Area Director Area VIII Mineral Resource Office Juneau, Alaska 99801

Delaware, Hawaii, Iowa, Kentucky, and Louisiana are not included in the above list.

Hot Springs, Geysers, and Hot Spring Deposits

Hot springs and geysers furnish not only unusual sights for the rockhound tourist, but also unusual specimens. Not every rockhound can get to Yellowstone National Park every summer to see the geysers and to obtain samples of geyser-deposited and hot spring-deposited rock at the local rock shops, but one little known fact is that there are more than 1,000 hot springs in the United States. Another little known fact is that a geyser is merely a hot spring which erupts at intervals, and therefore the rocks deposited around both geysers and hot springs are of the same general types. So, if you can't get to Yellowstone—but by all means, see it some day if at all possible—visit some hot springs sometime, and collect some specimens of hot spring deposits.

Geysers. The kind of a hot spring known as a *geyser* apparently receives its heat from a body of subsurface, cooling rock, as do some hot springs, but the two kinds of hot springs have very different "plumbing" systems. Whereas a simple hot spring might be likened to a pan of water boiling or simmering on a stove, a geyser evidently has a much more complex structure, like a large tree root with several smaller roots branching away from the main root all along its length. The water enters the geyser structure through these twisted "roots." In these "roots," the water, heated by a nearby mass of cooling igneous rock, can exceed a temperature of 212°F without forming steam, because of the pressure of the column of water above. For example, as almost any camper knows, water will boil at a lower temperature in the mountains than at sea level because of decreased atmospheric pressure. Conversely, if the pressure is increased to one greater than pressure at sea level, water attains a temperature of 212°F without boiling or forming steam.

Eventually, however, when the temperature of the geyser water is considerably above its normal boiling point, steam does form and the water throughout the geyser starts to rise as each "root" starts to discharge steam and superheated water into the main "root." Time after time, commonly, the steam bubbles collapse and the column drops down, only to rise again as more steam bubbles quickly form. This procedure, analogous to the water going up and down in the stem of a coffee percolator before the "perking" begins, may continue for some time with thudding and rumbling noises from the geyser. Finally, enough water is pushed up so that some of it spills over the edge of the geyser basin. This loss of weight immediately reduces the pressure on the water still in the geyser, much of that water flashes into steam, and the geyser erupts. The geyser "roots" then start filling again, and the process is repeated.

Hot Springs. A spring whose water is at least 15°F warmer than the surrounding air is called a *hot spring,* or *thermal spring.* Hot springs in the eastern part of the United States apparently receive their heat from the *geothermal gradient,* the natural increase in heat with depth (approximately 1°F for every 60 feet). Hot springs in the western part of the United States, on the other hand, are believed to receive their heat, as in the case of our geysers, from intrusive igneous rocks which are cooling. The water of some hot springs is colored red or yellow by oxides of iron and such springs are often referred to as *paint pots*.

Deposits Formed by Hot Springs and Geysers. Springs of both the hot and cold varieties deposit salts around their vents or basins, the salt most commonly deposited being calcium carbonate in the form of *travertine* or *tufa*. *Mexican onyx* is a banded, crystalline form of travertine which can be polished, while tufa is a spongy limestone which often contains the remains of plant material which happened to be growing near the hot spring. Large chunks of tufa, complete with such inclusions, are sometimes sold to home owners as "volcanic rocks," for unusual landscaping items.

Hot spring deposits of a siliceous nature are known as *siliceous sinter*. Siliceous sinter can be formed by either non-erupting hot springs or by geysers and, if formed by geysers, is often termed *geyserite*. In some hot springs, mud more or less fills the basins and thus *mud volcanos* are formed.

Hot Springs in the United States. Many hot springs in the United States are well-known because of the curative effects attributed to their waters. It should be pointed out, however, that drinking the water from a hot spring is not always necessarily healthful and, as a matter of fact, should not be done unless the water has been tested and pronounced safe to drink. Water in hot springs commonly contains varying concentrations of sulfur and various salts with, sometimes, some metallic sulfides which are not only tangy but also highly toxic. As for bathing in the waters from hot springs, some people say that the waters are relaxing and healthful while some others say that such water gives them skin rashes. For most people, however, bathing in tested and approved waters would probably have no ill effect.

Geysers in the United States. In the United States, the one area of true geysers is in Yellowstone National Park. Rockhound tourists in California and Nevada, however, can see a related phenomenon in the form of steam wells which tap hot water or natural steam below the surface of the earth. The steam furnishes power which is then converted into electrical energy by turbines. One of these areas is approximately 75 miles north of San Francisco, off Highway 101. The other area is in the southern outskirts of Reno, and is easily seen from Highway 395 which, as a matter of fact, goes right through the "steam" field.

Collecting Specimens of Hot Spring Deposits. Specimens of hot spring or geyser deposits cannot of course be collected in national parks, etc., or in places such as state parks where such collecting is prohibited. Usually, however, it is possible to buy such specimens in shops within the parks and privately owned areas. In privately owned hot spring areas, permission to collect a few specimens in out-of-the-way or abandoned sites is commonly granted, sometimes on a fee basis.

Specimens of hot spring deposits are usually rather soft and they are usually fairly easily broken. The specimen should therefore be carefully wrapped before being stowed away in a vehicle.

Caves and Cave Deposits

The two types of caves most visited by tourists are the *lava cave* and the *limestone cave*. Lava caves are formed when moving lava freezes in its outer portions and the still-liquid lava inside this forming crust keeps on moving, thus creating a tunnel or long cave from which the lava has drained out.

The formation of lava caves and tunnels is well-understood but there is some difference of opinion among geologists as to how limestone caves are formed. Many geologists believe that most caves in limestone were formed beneath the water table: the irregular plane which separates totally saturated rock or soil from the partially saturated soil or rock material above it. Some other geologists believe that most of these caves were formed above the water table. At least one thing is certain: if you can walk into one of these caves, it is at least now above the water table, otherwise entrance would be by swimming. Another thing is certain, also: stalactites and stalagmites in caves form when the cave is above the water table, no matter where the cave was originally carved out by water.

Cave Deposits. *Stalactites* form on the roof of a cave which is above the water table, when lime-charged water which has been seeping through the limestone rock collects in various places on the roof (called the "back" by miners) and starts to evaporate. Calcium carbonate solidifies around the circumference of a given drop as evaporation proceeds until a circular ring of calcium carbonate is attached to the roof. Once this ring is formed it acts as a barrier to some of the water on the roof which would have formerly migrated to the center of the ring. Such water encounters the ring and starts to drip slowly around the circumference of the ring, and the ring thus becomes the base of an ever-lengthening hollow tube of calcium carbonate whose wall thickness also increases. This is why a loose stalactite, when viewed in a direction parallel to its length, shows concentric banding on the broken cross section. The hole in the center of the stalactite is often visible but sometimes it also has been filled with calcium carbonate, probably by water from the roof which dripped right into and through the stalactite.

Stalagmites are formed by calcium carbonate which forms on the cave floor and grows toward the roof. Stalagmites typically develop beneath stalactites, from water which drips down from the stalactites. *Pillars* are formed when stalactites and the stalagmites beneath them join. Some pillars, however, seem to be chiefly either stalactites or stalagmites. Confusion as to which, stalactite or stalagmite, grows from the roof and which from the floor can easily be dispelled by noting that the "c" in "stalactite" could represent "ceiling" while the "g" in "stalagmite" could stand for "ground." Having said that, it must be admitted that the original confusion, many times, lies in not remembering the words at all. Whether a stalactite or stalagmite, the process of formation is tortuously slow, a "fast" rate of deposition of calcium carbonate in caves being one cubic inch every 100 years.

The general term for cave deposits is *dripstone*, and some dripstone, as shown in Fig. 14.2, takes forms other than those of individual stalactites, stalagmites, or pillars. Some dripstone looks like stone curtains hanging down from the cavern roofs while other dripstone looks like a series of underground terraces. Some caves are closed off in places by fantastically shaped curtains of dripstone. Dripstone is often varicolored due to mineral matter coloring and one of the most spectacular sights that one is ever liable to see is a

Fig. 14.2: Dripstone in caves and caverns often assumes fantastic shapes. A fast rate of deposition in a particular structure is one cubic inch of calcium carbonate every hundred years. (Photo courtesy of Luray Caverns, Virginia)

cavern whose stalactites, stalagmites, curtains, terraces, and other formations have turned the underground into a fantasy of shapes and colors.

Obtaining Specimens of Dripstone. Permission may sometimes be obtained in privately owned caves to collect specimens in designated areas, usually for a fee. Many caves also sell such specimens. In addition to stalactites and stalagmites, travertine which will take a good polish is also found in some caves, and this material can be made into very attractive mementoes and display pieces for a collection, especially if it is banded or mottled with colors.

Stones Carved by Wind and Sand

Sand blasting is a common sight in our modern civilization, but Nature has been performing the same operation ever since the first strong wind hurled a grain of sand against a rock surface. Oddly shaped stones called *ventifacts,* resulting from abrasion by wind-driven sand can be found in probably every one of our fifty states.

Ventifacts can be recognized by two features: rather shiny or greasy-appearing surfaces which are often pitted or fluted, and facets which meet to form sharp edges (see Fig. 14.3). The number of facets on a ventifact can vary greatly and some of these facets are, no doubt, carved simultaneously, when the rock or pebble happens to be positioned so that it "splits" the blasts of wind-driven sand for a long time. Facets can also be carved due to a change in wind direction or a change in the position of the ventifact. This latter can be brought about by the wind undercutting the ventifact and removing some slope material just below the ventifact which then rolls or slides—possibly a combination of these—and thus exposes new surfaces to be faceted and polished.

Where to Look for Ventifacts. Look for ventifacts in deserts, on beaches, in glaciated regions, on the slopes and tops of mountains, and, in general, any place where sand has been blown with force, and for some time, against rocks or pebbles. Almost any loose, exposed rock is to some extent a ventifact, the only problem then is to find a really good ventifact. The presence of ventifacts in glacial rock material in the United States indicates that a period of drying, strong winds, and little vegetation followed the disappearances of the ice sheets. Some glacially transported stones which were obviously scratched and striated as they crunched against other stones in the moving glaciers were just as obviously cut and pitted by wind-driven sand, later, many of the pits being in the glacial striations. Ventifacts tell a number of fascinating stories and they are prized members of many collections.

Fig. 14.3: Pebbles and rocks pitted and faceted by windblown sand are called *ventifacts*. Ventifacts are found in every one of the United States. (Photo by M. R. Campbell, U.S. Geological Survey)

Stones Shaped and Scratched by Glaciers

Rock material carried and deposited by glaciers is called *drift,* a term which apparently stemmed from the old belief that such rock material had somehow drifted over much of the world during the Flood. *Till* is unsorted drift. *Stratified* drift is drift which usually has been sorted and stratified by meltwater from the glaciers.

Stones in till often show facets cut by the powerful grinding action generated as stones in the advancing glaciers slowly turned and crunched against each other or against bedrock. As would be expected, scratches and grooves are common in such specimens, and some specimens of till show faceting, scratches, and polished surfaces, all on the same specimen. It might appear, then, that a glaciated stone could be confused with a ventifact, or vice versa.

A stone which has been glaciated only, however, does not show the characteristic pits of ventifacts. Also, the edges between the facets of a glaciated stone are rounded while the edges between the facets of a ventifact are usually sharp.

Glaciated Areas in the United States. New England, New York State, the Great Lakes region, and parts of Pennsylvania, Illinois, Iowa, Kansas, Nebraska, Missouri, South Dakota, North Dakota, Montana, and Washington were all glaciated by continental glaciation (ice sheets) at least once during the last one million years. During that time (the Pleistocene epoch), mountain areas in Colorado, New Mexico, Utah, Wyoming, Idaho, Oregon, and California were also glaciated, by "spot" glaciation. Some glaciers still occupy portions of these areas as, for example, the glaciers on Mt. Shasta, Mt. Rainier, and many more. Alaska, of course, has many glaciers.

Rockhounds who look for specimens of faceted and striated glacial till—and good specimens are easily found—should keep in mind that glaciers carry these rocks for sometimes thousands of miles and that the stones in a deposit of glacial drift of any kind often constitute a sample of the many types of rock which the glacier ploughed over and ploughed past. Almost any kind of material might be found in glacial material, therefore, from stones of no apparent interest at all to stones which tell an interesting story. It may be that not one more diamond will ever be found in the glacial material of the Great Lakes region, although this seems very unlikely, but even if this were to be the case, many of the most interesting and widely traveled specimens which could possibly be added to a collection are now resting on the surface of the ground in the Great Lakes and other regions waiting to be picked up.

Fig. 14.4: Concretions are formed by underground deposition of material around a nucleus. Many concretions are of bizarre form and are collected by rockhounds as curiosities. These concretions are still in Kansas. (Photo by M. R. Mudge, U.S. Geological Survey)

Other Mineral Specimens

It would be virtually impossible to list the great numbers of different kinds of specimens which can be collected and which dramatically illustrate and serve as reminders of the major geological forces and operations which shaped, formed, and placed them. As a few more examples, however, some rockhounds collect soil samples and display them in small, transparent containers; some collect various kinds of sands; many collect *concretions* (see Fig. 14.4), nodules of sometimes almost unbelievable shape which form around a nucleus in sedimentary rock; and some specialize in rock material found on ocean or lake beaches. Many rockhounds add specimens of *fault gouge, fault breccia,* and *slickensides,* all of these being rock material which has been formed due to the great shearing and other forces in fault zones. Faults, incidentally, often cause (as surface expressions which

Correct Names of Gemstones

Incorrect Name	Correct Name
African jade	grossularite garnet
Arizona ruby	pyrope garnet
Arkansas diamond	quartz
Brazilian emerald	tourmaline
Brazilian ruby	tourmaline or topaz
California jade	idocrase
Cape ruby	pyrope garnet
Colorado jade	amazonite feldspar
Colorado ruby	pyrope garnet
Evening emerald	peridot
Herkimer diamond	quartz
Hot Springs diamond	quartz
Mexican onyx	calcite
Montana jet	obsidian
Oriental amethyst	sapphire or spinel
Oriental aquamarine	sapphire
Oriental emerald	sapphire
Oriental sapphire	corundum
Oriental topaz	corundum
Shanghai jade	steatite or talc
South African jade	grossularite garnet
Topaz *	quartz
Transvaal jade	grossularite garnet
Uralian emerald	demantoid garnet

* For the composition and description of real topaz, see Chapter 9 and Chapter 16.

can often be spotted from a car) such features as sudden changes in kinds of vegetation along an almost straight line which may be several miles long, a "notch" on the top of a hill or mountain, a sudden change in the direction of a river, a sudden change in rock types, and so on.

Variations on any one of the original possibilities of specimen collecting are common and this of course increases the number of possible specializations even more. Some rockhounds, for example, specialize in collecting the various ores of one metal while others may collect, say, the sulfide ores of many metals. On a vacation trip, however, most rock-hounds just collect interesting items as they happen to come along and then, at home, after adding the specimens to their collections, start thinking pleasant thoughts about their next rockhound tourist vacation.

Correct Names of Gemstones

Untold numbers of tourists return from trips every year with gemstones which were sold to them under incorrect names. On page 210 is a list of such gemstones, with both the incorrect and correct names. The list is not complete but it does include many of the gemstones sold under incorrect names in the United States.

Chapter 15

The Rockhound at Home

Unlike a number of outdoor hobbies, rockhounding does not come to a halt with a change in weather or season, or as soon as one gets home again from a day in the open. Many hobbyists, as a matter of fact, are just about as enthusiastic about "indoor rockhounding" as they are about the outdoor variety and this is easily understood when one considers the great number of interesting indoor activities of the rockhound hobby. Some of these activities are discussed in this chapter.

The Lapidary Workshop

A person who cuts and polishes gemstones and makes gems out of them is a *lapidary*. Thousands of rockhounds throughout the United States are lapidaries in the sense that they cut and polish stones which they have found themselves or which they have obtained by purchase or trade. Much of the work done by amateur lapidaries in the United States is astonishing in both scope and degree of accomplishment and the quality of the finished product often equals that attained by professionals in the art.

How Gemstones Are Cut and Polished. Much of the lapidary work done in the United States by rockhounds involves working with opaque or near-opaque material such as some cryptocrystalline varieties of quartz, and such material is commonly cut as a *cabochon*, that is, with at at least one main face being cut in the shape of a dome. To cut *en cabochon*, sawing (usually done with a diamond-edged disk) is the first process, followed by grinding and sanding in that order. Grinding is done on disks, and the sanding can be done on drums, disks, or belts. Polishing is done on a lap (disk), using polishing agents such as certain metallic oxides. A little-known fact is that a really good polish on some gems means that the surfaces of the polished faces were heated,

212

by the polishing, to a temperature where melting took place and a thin glaze was thus formed.

Another method of polishing is done by "tumbling," wherein pieces of gem material are put into a container which may be lined with an abrasive. The container is then activated, to "tumble" the stones. This process usually results in good polishes, and always in irregularly shaped, or *baroque*, gems.

Facet cutting is the ultimate test of the lapidary for several reasons. First, usually only transparent gemstones having a hardness of over 7 are faceted. Next, the number of facets required for some of the most common cuts varies from 16 to 104, the most popular cut (the *brilliant*), requiring 58 facets. Despite all of the reasons why such things can't be done by amateurs, however, many of our amateur lapidaries go right ahead anyway and turn out faceted gems which often rival those turned out in the gem-cutting capitals of the world.

Beginning Lapidary. Anyone who wants to start the lapidary phase of the rockhounding hobby is advised to "make haste slowly" and to consult with experienced amateur lapidaries before buying an appreciable amount of lapidary equipment and supplies. There are tricks to all trades, and United States amateur lapidaries, having thought up at least their share of ingenious procedures and substitutions, not only can give the beginner some priceless tips as to craftmanship but can also give money-saving and other valuable advice regarding the purchase of equipment and supplies.

The Home Laboratory

Many rockhounds set up their own home laboratories, many of these laboratories being of a size such that all of the equipment can be placed on a workbench or on a kitchen table. The equipment for a home laboratory includes items such as hardness testers, streak plates, mortars and pestles, and blowpipe equipment and supplies, etc. In addition, some rockhounds either make or buy some kind of a balance for determining specific gravity.

One feature of the home laboratory is a greater number of chemicals and reagents than is normally carried into the field. Also, the rockhound at home has a variety of open and closed glass tubes which are used with the chemicals in the qualitative analysis of specimens. A number of rockhounds, incidentally, have become so knowledgeable concerning the ramifications of the formations and compositions of certain minerals that some of these rockhounds act as consultants to mining companies and other organizations. For beginners who may be interested in setting up home laboratories, the third edition of Dana's *Minerals and How to Study Them* gives an elementary description, suitable for the beginner, of various chemical tests used in mineral identification, and a list of equipment and supplies for a simple laboratory.

Micromounts

The smaller a crystal is, the less flaws it is liable to have, and some crystals of very small size are used as *micromounts*. These tiny crystals are permanently mounted on their own pedestals, in small boxes, and are examined by low-power microscopes, just as larger specimens in a collection are examined with the unaided eye.

Micromounting has become so popular that special sections in rock and mineral shows are set aside for micromount displays. In addition, rockhound hobby magazines feature articles on micromounting from time to time, and at least one of these magazines prints a monthly column on micromounts.

Some micromounters make photomicrographs of their specimens and show the resulting color slides at rock and mineral shows and at rockhound club meetings. As formerly mentioned, a good micromount specimen is often worth much more, from the standpoint of price, than larger crystals of the same mineral.

The Rockhound Photographer

Professional photographers are the first to admit that minerals are extremely difficult to photograph but, even so, a number of rockhounds turn out some very creditable photographs of minerals, and some of these are really excellent. Figure 15.1, for example, a photograph of a crystal of altered borax, was made by a past president of the American Federation of Mineralogical Societies and certainly leaves little if anything to be desired, from both the artistic and factually expository viewpoints.

Photographic possibilities for the rockhound at home include photomicrography and the making of "stereopairs" of

Fig. 15.1: Many rockhounds combine the hobbies of rockhounding and photography, as is the case in this photograph of a sample of altered borax. Note the extremely sharp delineation of the crystal edges. (Photo by Vince Morgan)

specimens, to be viewed through a stereoscope of some kind, to bring out the three-dimensional effects. Some rockhounds build up collections of photographs to illustrate various geological features and phenomena such as the effects of glaciation, faults, unconformities, etc. Some rockhounds take such pictures in "stereo," also, and come up with some remarkable results which give the impression that the observer is right back in the field again.

The theory behind the stereoscopic effect is simple: your right eye sees one view of something, your left eye sees a slightly different view, and the brain fuses these views together into a three-dimensional image. Try this experiment, for example: place the tips of your index fingers together, holding your fingers parallel and about one foot in front of your eyes. Now, focus, not on your fingers, but on a wall or any object, your line of sight being just below or above your fingers. Now move your finger tips apart, very slowly, and before the finger tips are very far apart you will see a small "sausage" which seems to be floating in air, between your finger tips. This is the three-dimensional image mentioned above. Many geological features, including mineral crystals in rock matrix, can be dramatically recorded by three-dimensional photography, for many pleasant hours of later viewing. Some rockhounds even make slides which can be projected onto a screen and viewed in three dimensions by an audience.

The World of Ultraviolet

As many people know, a collection of minerals which fluoresce when exposed to ultraviolet radiation is one of the most spectacular sights imaginable. The theory behind the effect is simple: some of the electrons of such minerals are displaced, by the ultraviolet radiation, to other orbits, taking new energy with them. A particular displacement is momentary, however, and as the electrons are pulled back into their usual orbits they release their excess energy in the form of light. Minerals handle all this activity according to particular mineral composition and structure, and the different frequencies resulting cause the differences in color in these "color broadcasts." The process repeats over and over again and to the human eye appears to be continuous. The glowing due to fluorescence ceases when the source of excitation, the ultraviolet radiation, is removed. A display of fluorescent minerals is often set up so that normal light and ultraviolet light alternately flood the display as it is being viewed.

The Rockhound Library

The books, magazines, and other publications which deal either directly or indirectly with the hobby of rockhounding offer a wealth of information to the hobbyist. Included are books on geology, mineralogy, petrology, petrography, magazines dealing with the same subjects, and the various publications of states and the national government. The rockhound library can be as small or as large as one wishes to make it, and many rockhounds regard their libraries as one of the most valuable and interesting parts of the rockhounding hobby.

Collecting Old Books. Some rockhounds have built up good collections of books on geology and mineralogy, etc., which are now out of print and may be many years old. Some of these books, like the sixth edition of Dana's *Descriptive Mineralogy*, printed in 1872, are virtually priceless to rockhounds, but some of these old books can sometimes be picked up on the "rummage" tables of bookstores. The particular edition of Dana referred to, incidentally, contains a listing of mineral localities in the United States in 1872, plus descriptions of the minerals found in the various localities.

Although some of the geographic areas described in these old books have had at least their surfaces long since depleted of easily collected specimens—and perhaps of all surface specimens—the reader is once more reminded that the mere fact that there may now seem to be no specimens in a particular area does not necessarily mean that specimens will not be found in that area, possibly tomorrow, after erosion or perhaps after some energetic rockhound strips away some overburden. Also, even though many of the place names appearing in these old books have been changed, some enterprising detective work has enabled some rockhounds to rediscover some of these old locations which other people had given up for lost. Thus, some excellent "new" collecting localities have come into being, within recent years.

Modern Reference Books. The rockhound who purchases a few books on mineralogy and geology soon finds himself in the midst of a fascinating and never-ending process of learning. No one book or even a group of books can ever completely cover a particular subject and this is especially true for an activity like rockhounding, with its many facets of activity. In rockhounding, we use reference books on collecting, books on mineral identification, books on crystallography, books on mineral families, books on fossils, books dealing with rocks, and so on. It is virtually impossible to do anything in the way of rockhounding which, with a little reading, will not lead us to learn something interesting.

Take, for example, the activity of field collecting. Suppose that late in the day we find some lava rock. There are no apparently possible mineral-bearing cavities in the rock and, all in all, it looks just about like any other lava. Not having a specimen of this particular kind of rock, though, we take a sample and start for home.

That night, we open a book on geology and idly start reading about igneous rocks. We soon find out that as our exposure of lava cooled, a major part of its magnetism aligned itself in accordance with the magnetic field at that time, something like today's magnetic compass needles point toward our present magnetic pole. Our flow of lava, then, we realize, is essentially the host of many little compasses whose "needles"—actually a molecular or electron pattern—were frozen into position when the magma cooled. Reading further, we find that the plotting of ancient magnetic pole positions from these frozen "compasses" in rocks of different ages has solved problems all the way from determining the ages of former civilizations to supporting the theory of continental drift. We also now realize a remarkable thing: every igneous rock which we see—and some sedimentary rocks—have these little compasses in them which, with allowance for local magnetic attraction, once pointed toward the magnetic north pole, wherever it was when the rock was formed millions of years ago.

The particular path which we took, above, led us into the fields of archaeology and paleogeography but we might just as well have gone, in our reading, in any one of several different directions. For example, we might have wondered just how the ages of rocks are determined, and this would have almost certainly led us into reading about radioactive dating and isotopes, etc. Some reference books suggested for a library are listed in the bibliography.

Magazines. One of the best pieces of advice that can be given to any rockhound, especially beginners, is to add to his library at least one rockhound magazine. Many rock-hounds subscribe to several of these magazines. Although most of the magazines are nominally regional in character, they cover almost any section of the country to which a rockhound writer may have made a collecting trip. The magazines also feature articles on lapidary work, micro-mounts, fossils, ore minerals, etc., from time to time, and even the advertisements are found by beginners to be highly instructive. The rockhound hobby magazines are listed in the bibliography.

Regional Guides. A number of regional guides have been written for certain states and groups of states. Essentially, these guides tell how to get to specified collecting localities and what can be found in the way of minerals once you get there. The best of these guides also contain good maps and explicit instructions as to whom to contact to get onto pri-vate land, etc. A discussion of regional guides appears in the bibliography.

The Collection

There would be little point in taking considerable time to collect specimens, to then merely toss them into a box and forget them. On the other hand, there would probably be objections to covering something like the living room mantle with rocks, minerals, and fossils. Fortunately, however, min-eral collectors in the United States have brought home enough specimens during the last one hundred and fifty years to have the problems of mineral storage and display fairly well solved by now.

Trimming Specimens. Rock specimens, specimens of min-erals within rock, and fossil specimens in rock should be trimmed to an optimum size and shape before storing or displaying them. For example, suppose that in one specimen a small, perfectly formed crystal seems to be lost in a sea of matrix material. In such a case, the amount of matrix mate-rial should be drastically reduced and shaped so that the crystal becomes the center of attention.

It must be said, however, that the hand trimming of spec-imens has ruined many specimens and tempers. If you do insist on hand trimming your own specimens, then remember the cardinal rule: never chip or chisel *toward* the mineral or fossil specimen; always chip or chisel *away* from the specimen.

In general, however, the use of a mechanical device for trimming is recommended, especially if there is much of this to be done or if the possible ruination of a very good specimen is involved. If the rockhound cannot use or gain ready access to a mechanical trimmer, he is advised to have the trimming done for him at a rock shop or a stone mason's, or a similar place. In any kind of trimming—mechanical or hand—it is essential that safety goggles and gloves be worn, and that persons not wearing safety goggles be kept a safe distance from the operation.

Cleaning Specimens. All mineral specimens become dusty after a while, some become tarnished, and some become downright dirty. Before attempting to clean a specimen by liquids, the first thing to do is to get rid of dust by brushing or by using a blower of some kind. The brush used might be anything—and often is—from an artist's brush to a shaving brush. Blowers used by rockhounds also run the gamut, in this case from hair dryers to tank-type vacuum cleaners operating in reverse.

The cleaning of mineral specimens by solutions is both an art and a science in that some manual skill is required as is some appreciation of chemistry. Experimental or doubtful solutions should not be used on good specimens. Many water-insoluble minerals can be effectively cleaned by washing them with detergent soap and water, or with sodium bicarbonate and water, in either case following the washing process with thorough rinsing in clean water, and drying in clean air. On the other hand, water-soluble minerals will be ruined with such treatment. Tarnishes can often be removed by chemicals, but the removal of tarnish usually results in accelerated decomposition of such a specimen.

At this point the reader may be wondering just how to go about cleaning a specimen with some hope of success. It is true that solubility tables do appear in some mineralogy books and in chemical handbooks, but it is also true that the average person finds these tables not too easy to use when it comes to bathing a cherished specimen with a liquid. Some rockhounds have done just that, only to see the specimen suddenly become rather bilious in appearance or to see much of it immediately disappear in a swirl of bubbles. The safest way for a beginner to clean specimens is to contact experienced fellow rockhounds, or a rock shop or the mineralogy department of a museum, identify the mineral in question, and ask for information regarding how best to clean it. After cleaning, some specimens can be lacquered. A thin film of lacquer protects the surfaces of the specimen from mechanical damage and also retards oxidation and both the loss and gain of water.

Display and Storage of Specimens. Mineral specimens and fossil specimens are commonly put into either *display cabinets* or *storage cabinets.* In either case, specimens should be properly identified as to name and place of occurrence. The identification of storage specimens may be indirect in that these specimens are often numbered by means of gummed labels or by numbering on a small painted surface on the specimen. Corresponding with these numbers are numbers on a chart or list, and opposite each of these numbers are the data for a particular specimen.

When storing specimens, never put one specimen on top of and in either direct or indirect contact with another. This may cause breakage and, in some cases, the formation of galvanic cells which may cause staining and corrosion.

A common method of storing specimens is to place each specimen in its own shallow, topless cardboard container which is then placed in a cabinet drawer. Styrofoam or a similar substance can often be used to advantage, and many rockhounds always embed their good specimens in such a material before storing them. Incidentally, egg boxes are excellent storage boxes for specimens which are of the correct size for such storage receptacles. If a specimen is capable of taking on water from the air, or of losing water, it should be placed in an airtight container. Storage cabinets may be purchased, they may be built by modification of some household type of cabinet, or the rockhound who is handy with tools can build his own cabinets from "scratch."

Display cabinets may also be either purchased or built by the rockhound and they assume a wide variety of designs.

The main idea, of course, is to show off each specimen to its best advantage and to also protect the specimen at the same time. Transparent and translucent specimens can often be mounted on a simple pedestal made of wire and, if desired, can be made to receive special illumination. Opaque specimens can be mounted on transparent material and so lighted that the specimens appear to be floating in the air. This latter method of mounting and illuminating is very effective in the display of cabochons.

Adding to the Collection. Other than collecting specimens in the field, there are several other methods of adding to a collection or, in the case of lapidaries, obtaining new material for cutting or faceting. As one possibility, some rockhound hobby magazines have "swap columns" whereby a rockhound in, say, New York State, offers to swap some local or other material for, say, obsidian from any place. In addition, rockhound clubs often stage "swap" sessions at which members and guests trade material and specimens, and the mammoth and some of the lesser rockhound shows now have special areas where rockhounds from all over the United States—and often much of the world—meet each other and trade specimens and cutting material.

Much material and many specimens are of course sold outright, by dealers. Bargains can very often be picked up from advertisements in the rockhound hobby magazines, and rock shops usually carry a very good stock of both specimens and cutting material. Many rock shops hold sales from time to time and also often feature "grab bags," bagged material and specimens, sold at nominal prices and which may include a piece or a specimen of mineral which alone is worth the entire price paid.

Chapter 16

Determinative Tables
and How to Use Them

This chapter contains a set of determinative tables for the identification of the 150 most commonly sought or found gemstones and minerals in the United States. Table 16.1 lists these minerals and gemstones in alphabetical order and is keyed to the determinative tables and also to pertinent descriptive material in the preceding chapters.

The minerals listed in the determinative tables are separated into two major groups: those minerals having either metallic or submetallic luster, and those minerals having nonmetallic luster. The next subdivisions are made on the basis of hardness and, in the case of minerals having non-metallic lusters, further subdivision is made on the basis of a specimen either showing or not showing good cleavage. Thus, merely knowing the luster, approximate hardness, and (for specimens having nonmetallic lusters) the cleavage characteristics of a specimen will automatically enable us to screen out anywhere from 80 to 97 percent of the listed minerals and gemstones from further consideration. The remaining physical characteristics of the specimen will then usually serve to identify it among the relatively few remaining possibilities in the determinative tables.

The order of appearance of each mineral under a particular subheading, such as those occurring on the top of page 231 in the determinative tables, is based on increasing hardness. This, in conjunction with color makes the tables easy to use in identifying minerals. In the occasional case when two or more minerals have the same hardness, further subdivision is made on the basis of specific gravity.

Once a specimen is identified, Table 16.1 may be used to determine (1) whether the specimen may be a gemstone or an ore mineral, etc., and (2) the pages in this book in which the mineral may be discussed. In Table 16.1 the page number or numbers to the left of a semicolon refer to descriptive matter in preceding chapters; numbers to the right of a semicolon refer to description of the mineral in the determinative tables. Where only one page number appears, the reference is to the determinative tables.

The tables may also be used in another way. For example, suppose that we have heard something about a mineral called "lazurite" and we want to know something about that mineral. We turn to Table 16.1 and find that lazurite is described on page 256 of the determinative tables. From that page we quickly get an overall description of lazurite.

Some minerals often exhibit "weathered" hardnesses and cleavage patterns and are described in several places in the tables. When identifying minerals, use this key:

	PAGE
Metallic or submetallic luster	
Hardness less than 2½	231–234
Hardness 2½–5½	234–238
Hardness greater than 5½	238–240
Nonmetallic luster, hardness less than 2½	
Shows good cleavage	240–243
Does not show good cleavage	243–244
Nonmetallic luster, hardness 2½–3	
Shows good cleavage	244–246
Does not show good cleavage	246–247
Nonmetallic luster, hardness 3–5½	
Shows good cleavage	247–253
Does not show good cleavage	253–257
Nonmetallic luster, hardness 5½–7	
Shows good cleavage	257–260
Does not show good cleavage	260–266
Nonmetallic luster, hardness greater than 7	
Shows good cleavage	266–268
Does not show good cleavage	268–271

Table 16.1
The 150 Most Commonly Found or Sought Minerals and Gemstones in the United States

Mineral or Gemstone	Remarks	Page Reference
Achroite	Gemstone. Colorless tourmaline.	122; 266
Agate	Gemstone. Variety of chalcedony.	139; 265
Almandine	Gemstone. A garnet.	152; 268
Amazonite	Gemstone. Variety of feldspar.	149; 259
Amber	Gemstone. Fossil tree resin.	244
Amethyst	Gemstone. Variety of quartz.	136; 265
Amphibole	Series of rock-forming minerals. Nephrite (jade) is an amphibole.	251
Andalusite	Gemstone. Also used as a refractory.	153; 266
Andradite	Gemstone. A garnet. Varieties are *demantoid* and *topazolite*.	153; 268
Anglesite	Lead mineral.	245
Anhydrite	Calcium sulfate.	248
Apatite	Common rock-forming mineral containing phosphorus.	255
Aquamarine	Gemstone. Variety of beryl.	129; 271
Aragonite	Calcium carbonate.	249
Argentite	An ore of silver.	233
Arsenopyrite	An ore of arsenic.	239
Axinite	Gemstone with boron.	264
Azurite	Gemstone. Also a secondary ore of copper.	159; 254
Barite	Used in drilling muds in oil well drilling, plus many more applications. Barium sulfate.	248
Bauxite	An ore of aluminum.	253
Beryl	Chief source of beryllium. Gemstone varieties are *aquamarine* (green blue to blue green), *emerald* (grass green), *golden beryl* (golden yellow), and *morganite* (pink to rose red).	126; 271
Biotite	Common rock-forming mineral. A dark-colored mica.	243
Bloodstone	Gemstone. Variety of chalcedony.	141; 265

Mineral or Gemstone	Remarks	Page Reference
Borax	Used as antiseptic and flux.	246
Bornite	An ore of copper. "Peacock ore."	236
Calcite	A common mineral. Forms lime-stone.	247
Carnelian	Gemstone. Variety of chalcedony.	140; 265
Carnotite	Brilliant yellow ore of uranium.	241
Cassiterite	An ore of tin.	264
Celestite	Strontium sulfate.	248
Cerargyrite	An ore of silver.	243
Cerussite	An ore of lead.	247
Chalcedony	Fibrous form of cryptocrystalline quartz. Gemstone varieties are *agate, carnelian, chrysoprase, heliotrope (bloodstone)*, and *onyx*.	139; 265
Chalcocite	An ore of copper.	234
Chalcopyrite	An ore of copper.	236
Chert	A granular cryptocrystalline quartz.	141; 265
Chlorite	Common rock-forming group of minerals.	242
Chondrodite	Occurs in metamorphic iron zones.	263
Chromite	An ore of chromium.	239
Chrysoberyl	Gemstone. Contains beryllium.	130; 271
Chrysocolla	Gemstone. Found in copper de-posits.	159; 247
Chrysoprase	Apple green gemstone variety of chalcedony.	140; 265
Cinnabar	An ore of mercury.	238
Cinnamon stone	A gemstone variety of grossularite garnet.	152; 268
Citrine	A gemstone variety of quartz.	137; 265
Copper	"Native" copper.	235
Corundum	Aluminum oxide. Gemstone vari-eties are *ruby* and *sapphire*.	116; 267
Covellite	An ore of copper.	232
Datolite	Found in cavities in traprock.	256
Demantoid	Emerald-green variety of andradite garnet.	153; 268
Diamond	Gemstone and abrasive.	111; 268

Mineral or Gemstone	Remarks	Page Reference
Dolomite	Calcium magnesium carbonate.	252
Emerald	A gemstone variety of beryl.	127; 271
Enargite	An ore of copper.	235
Enstatite	A pyroxene. Found in igneous rocks and some meteorites.	258
Epidote	Common mineral, found in many types of rock. Usually green or greenish.	259
Essonite (or *hyacinth*)	A gemstone variety of grossularite garnet.	152; 268
Feldspar	Most abundant family of minerals. Gemstone varieties are *amazonite*, *labradorite*, *moonstone*, and *sunstone*.	147; 259
Flint	A granular cryptocrystalline quartz.	141; 265
Fluorite	Furnishes fluorine, also outstanding specimens for collections.	250
Galena	An ore of lead.	233
Garnet	Widely disseminated family of silicates. Gemstone varieties are *almandine*, *andradite*, *grossularite*, *pyrope*, *spessartite*, and *uvarovite*.	152; 268
Goethite	An ore of iron.	237
Gold	"Native" gold.	91; 235
Golden beryl	A gemstone variety of beryl.	130; 271
Goshenite	Colorless variety of beryl.	126
Graphite	Carbon. Furnishes "lead" for pencils. Also a lubricant.	232
Grossularite	This garnet furnishes two gemstones: *cinnamon stone* and *essonite* (or *hyacinth*).	152; 268
Gypsum	Calcium sulfate. Used for plaster of Paris, etc.	241
Halite	Common table salt is halite.	244
Heliotrope	A gemstone variety of chalcedony.	141; 265
Hematite	An ore of iron.	231
Hyacinth (or *essonite*)	A gemstone variety of grossularite garnet.	152; 268
Idocrase	"California jade" is green variety of idocrase.	264

Mineral or Gemstone	Remarks	Page Reference
Indicolite	Dark blue tourmaline.	122
Jadeite	Pyroxene jade.	156; 263
Jasper	A granular form of cryptocrystalline quartz.	141; 265
Kaolin	Clay. Used in ceramics.	242
Kyanite	Used as refractory and sometimes as gemstone. Aluminum silicate.	252
Labradorite	Feldspar gemstone.	150
Lazurite	Source of *lapis lazuli*.	256
Leucite	Commonly found in lavas. Potassium aluminum silicate.	262
Limonite	Hydrous ferric oxides which color soils and rocks.	231
Magnetite	Widespread magnetic iron oxide.	240
Malachite	Gemstone. An ore of copper.	159; 254
Marcasite	Iron sulfide.	240
Microcline	A feldspar. Gemstone variety is *amazonite*.	149; 259
Milky quartz	Typically occurs in veins.	137; 265
Molybdenite	An ore of molybdenum.	231
Moonstone	Gemstone variety of feldspar.	149; 259
Morganite	Gemstone variety of beryl.	130; 271
Muscovite	A mica. Common rock-forming mineral. Typically light colored.	242
Natrolite	A cavity mineral.	251
Nepheline	Commonly occurs in cavities.	262
Nephrite	Nephrite jade is the amphibole type of jade.	155; 263
Niccolite	An ore of nickel.	238
Obsidian	Volcanic glass.	166; 262
Olivine	Common rock-forming mineral of the darker rocks. Gemstone variety is *peridot*.	264
Onyx	Gemstone. Variety of chalcedony.	140; 265
Opal	Gemstone. Amorphous. Silicon dioxide with water.	142; 256
Orpiment	Orange-yellow ore of arsenic.	241
Orthoclase	A potassium feldspar. Very common mineral.	147; 259
Peridot	Gemstone variety of olivine.	264
Petrified Wood	Commonly *agatized*, *jasperized*, or *opalized*.	144; 265

Mineral or Gemstone	Remarks	Page Reference
Phlogopite	A brown mica.	242
Plagioclase	Group of soda-lime feldspars.	148; 259
Platinum	Found usually in sands and gravels.	237
Prehnite	A cavity mineral.	262
Pyrargyrite	"Dark ruby silver ore."	234
Pyrite	Iron sulfide. "Fool's gold."	240
Pyrolusite	An ore of manganese.	232
Pyrope	A garnet.	153; 268
Pyroxene	A group of silicates which includes *jadeite* and *spodumene*.	249
Pyrrhotite	Very widespread iron sulfide.	236
Quartz	Most common mineral in earth's crust. "Crystalline" varieties are *amethyst, tiger's eye, citrine, milky quartz, rose quartz, rock crystal, sagenite, smoky quartz,* and *aventurine*. The *chalcedony* varieties are *agate, onyx, carnelian, chrysoprase,* and *heliotrope (bloodstone)*. *Chert, jasper,* and *flint* are cryptocrystalline, nonchalcedonic varieties.	135; 265
Realgar	Orange-red ore of arsenic.	243
Rhodochrosite	Gemstone. Ore of manganese.	250
Rhodonite	Manganese gemstone.	258
Rock crystal	Quartz crystal.	138; 265
Rose quartz	Gemstone variety of quartz.	137; 265
Rubellite	Gemstone. Variety of tourmaline.	122; 266
Ruby	Gemstone. Variety of corundum.	116; 267
Rutile	Ore of titanium.	263
Sagenite	Quartz with inclusions, such as those of rutile, tourmaline.	138; 265
Sapphire	Gemstone. Variety of corundum.	116; 267
Scapolite	Found in metamorphic rocks, sometimes a gemstone.	251
Scheelite	Ore of tungsten.	255
Schorl	Black tourmaline.	122; 266
Serpentine	Common mineral, formed from another mineral by hot water alteration.	80; 247
Siberite	Violet-red to purple tourmaline.	122; 266

Mineral or Gemstone	Remarks	Page Reference
Siderite	Iron carbonate.	250
Sillimanite	Aluminum silicate. Sometimes a gemstone.	266
Silver	"Native" silver.	235
Smithsonite	Sometimes an ore of zinc.	251
Smoky quartz	Gemstone. Variety of quartz.	138; 265
Sodalite	Sodium aluminum silicate. Gemstone.	252
Spessartite	A garnet.	153; 268
Sphalerite	An ore of zinc.	250
Spinel	Magnesium aluminum oxide. Red spinel looks like ruby.	271
Spodumene	Lithium mineral. Gemstone varieties are *hiddenite* and *kunzite*.	132; 267
Staurolite	A silicate which often twins into an X or a cross.	168; 266
Stibnite	An ore of antimony.	232
Stilbite	A cavity mineral.	249
Sulfur	Used in manufacture of sulfuric acid.	244
Sunstone	A gemstone consisting of feldspar with shiny inclusions.	149; 259
Talc	Massive form is *soapstone*. Main constituent of talcum powder.	241
Tiger's eye	Golden-brown quartz. Gemstone.	136; 265
Topaz	Gemstone. Mineral which represents hardness of 8.0 on the Mohs scale.	124; 267
Topazolite	Wine-yellow variety of andradite garnet.	153; 268
Tourmaline	Gemstone; also used in instrumentation. Gemstone varieties are *rubellite*, *siberite*, and *indicolite*. *Schorl* is black tourmaline. *Achroite* is colorless tourmaline.	121; 266
Turquoise	A copper gemstone.	157
Uraninite	As *pitchblende*, an ore of uranium.	239
Uvarovite	Emerald-green garnet.	153; 268
Willemite	An ore of zinc.	257
Witherite	Barium carbonate.	249
Zircon	Widely disseminated mineral in granites. Also a gemstone.	270

Determinative Tables

Metallic or Submetallic Luster
Hardness less than 2½
(Leaves mark on paper)

Color: Brown black to yellow brown.
Hardness: 1+
Specific gravity: 3.6–4
Streak: Brown to yellow.
Distinguishing features. Crystal system: Earthy. Amorphous.
Name. Chemical composition. Chemical formula: **Limonite.** Ferrous oxides. $FeO(OH) \cdot nH_2O$
Associations. Remarks: "Iron stain" in rocks. Sometimes forms "bog iron ore."

Color: Reddish.
Hardness: 1+
Specific gravity: 5.2
Streak: Red to red brown.
Distinguishing features. Crystal system: Earthy when of this hardness. Hexagonal system.
Name. Chemical composition. Chemical formula: **Hematite.** Iron (ferric) oxide. Fe_2O_3
Associations. Remarks: All types of rocks. Most important ore of iron.

Color: Blue black.
Hardness: 1–1.5
Specific gravity: 4.7
Streak: Gray.
Distinguishing features. Crystal system: One good cleavage. Hexagonal system. Usually disseminated.
Name. Chemical composition. Chemical formula: **Molybdenite.** Molybdenum sulfide. MoS_2
Associations. Remarks: Granites and pegmatites. Ore mineral of molybdenum.

Color: Black.
Hardness: 1–2
Specific gravity: 2.3
Streak: Black.

Distinguishing features. Crystal system: Greasy feel. Hexagonal system. Usually in masses.

Name. Chemical composition. Chemical formula: **Graphite.** Carbon. C

Associations. Remarks: Found in metamorphic rocks. Used in pencils, and as a refractory and a lubricant.

Color: Gray to black.
Hardness: 1–2
Specific gravity: 4.7
Streak: Sooty black.

Distinguishing features. Crystal system: Often in fibrous masses. Uneven fracture. Tetragonal system.

Name. Chemical composition. Chemical formula: **Pyrolusite.** Manganese dioxide. MnO_2

Associations. Remarks: In veins and ore deposits. Ore of manganese.

Color: Blue, but usually tarnished.
Hardness: 1.5–2
Specific gravity: 4.6
Streak: Black.

Distinguishing features. Crystal system: Platy masses. Hexagonal system.

Name. Chemical composition. Chemical formula: **Covellite.** Copper sulfide. CuS

Associations. Remarks: Copper veins. An ore of copper.

Color: Steel gray.
Hardness: 2
Specific gravity: 4.5
Streak: Gray-black.

Distinguishing features. Crystal system: Sectile. One good cleavage. Subconchoidal fracture. Orthorhombic system.

Name. Chemical composition. Chemical formula: **Stibnite.** Antimony sulfide. Sb_2S_3

Associations. Remarks: Black "fossil ferns" along rock fissures are usually pyrolusite dendrites.

Color: Lead gray.
Hardness: 2–2.5
Specific gravity: 7.3
Streak: Gray black.

Distinguishing features. Crystal system: Sectile. Isometric system. Subconchoidal fracture.
Name. Chemical composition. Chemical formula: **Argentite.** Silver sulfide. Ag_2S
Associations. Remarks: An ore of silver. Found in ore veins.

Color: Steel gray.
Hardness: 2–2.5
Specific gravity: 7.3
Streak: Gray black.
Distinguishing features. Crystal system: Sectile. Subconchoidal fracture. Isometric system.
Name. Chemical composition. Chemical formula: **Argentite.** Silver sulfide. Ag_2S
Associations. Remarks: Ore veins. An ore of silver.

Color: Red.
Hardness: 2–2.5
Specific gravity: 8.1
Streak: Red.
Distinguishing features. Crystal system: Massive and in crusts. Adamantine or earthy luster. Rarely in crystals. Subconchoidal fracture. Hexagonal system.
Name. Chemical composition. Chemical formula: **Cinnabar.** Mercury sulfide. HgS
Associations. Remarks: Commonly associated with quartz and antimony. Ore of mercury.

Color: Lead gray.
Hardness: 2.5
Specific gravity: 7.6
Streak: Gray black.
Distinguishing features. Crystal system: Perfect cubic cleavage. Isometric system. Even fracture.
Name. Chemical composition. Chemical formula: **Galena.** Lead sulfide. PbS
Associations. Remarks: An ore of lead. Found in ore veins.

Color: Lead gray.
Hardness: 2.5–3
Specific gravity: 5.7
Streak: Gray black.
Distinguishing features. Crystal system: Sectile with some diffi-

culty. Conchoidal fracture. Orthorhombic system.

Name. Chemical composition. Chemical formula: **Chalcocite.** Copper sulfide. Cu_2S

Associations. Remarks: Ore veins, and disseminated. An ore of copper.

Metallic or Submetallic Luster
Hardness 2½–5½
(Can be scratched by knife)

Color: Red·to black.
Hardness: 2.5
Specific gravity: 5.8–5.9
Streak: Red.
Distinguishing features. Crystal system: Crystals or massive. Subconchoidal fracture. Fuses easily. Hexagonal system.
Name. Chemical composition. Chemical formula: **Pyrargyrite.** Silver antimony sulfide. Ag_3SbS_3
Associations. Remarks: Silver veins. "Dark ruby silver ore."

Color: Lead gray.
Hardness: 2.5
Specific gravity: 7.5
Streak: Black.
Distinguishing features. Crystal system: Perfect cubic cleavage. Even fracture. Isometric system.
Name. Chemical composition. Chemical formula: **Galena.** Lead sulfide. PbS
Associations. Remarks: Ore veins. An ore of lead. Often contains silver.

Color: Red.
Hardness: 2.5
Specific gravity: 8.1
Streak: Red.
Distinguishing features. Crystal system: Massive. Adamantine. Also in crusts. Fracture subconchoidal. Hexagonal system.
Name. Chemical composition. Chemical formula: **Cinnabar.** Mercury sulfide. HgS
Associations. Remarks: Quartz and antimony. Ore of mercury.

Color: Copper.
Hardness: 2.5–3
Specific gravity: 8.9

Streak: Copper red.
Distinguishing features. Crystal system: Malleable. Tarnishes black. Isometric system.
Name. Chemical composition. Chemical formula: **Copper.** Cu.
Associations. Remarks: In veins and volcanic rocks, sometimes in sedimentary rocks as an intrusion.

Color: Silver white but usually tarnished.
Hardness: 2.5–3
Specific gravity: 10–11
Streak: Silver white.
Distinguishing features. Crystal system: Malleable. Isometric system. Usually occurs in wirelike form.
Name. Chemical composition. Chemical formula: **Silver.** Ag
Associations. Remarks: Ore veins.

Color: Golden.
Hardness: 2.5–3
Specific gravity: 19.3 (when pure)
Streak: Gold yellow.
Distinguishing features. Crystal system: Malleable. Isometric system. Massive, disseminated, flakes, or nuggets.
Name. Chemical composition. Chemical formula: **Gold.** Au
Associations. Remarks: Quartz veins and gravels. A widely disseminated metal.

Color: Gray black.
Hardness: 3
Specific gravity: 4.4
Streak: Black.
Distinguishing features. Crystal system: Good prismatic cleavage. Uneven fracture. Orthorhombic system. Commonly in crystals.
Name. Chemical composition. Chemical formula: **Enargite.** Copper arsenic sulfide. Cu_3AsS_4
Associations. Remarks: Ore deposits. An ore of copper.

Color: Bronze, but usually tarnished to purple.
Hardness: 3
Specific gravity: 4.9–5.3
Streak: Black.
Distinguishing features. Crystal system: Purple tarnish is characteristic. Uneven fracture. Isometric system.

Name. Chemical composition. Chemical formula: **Bornite.** Sulfide of copper and iron. Cu_5FeS_4

Associations. Remarks: Copper ore veins and igneous intrusives. "Peacock ore."

Color: Yellow brown to black.
Hardness: 3.5–4
Specific gravity: 3.9–4.1
Streak: Brown.
Distinguishing features. Crystal system: Luster frequently resinous. Conchoidal fracture. Isometric system.

Name. Chemical composition. Chemical formula: **Sphalerite.** Zinc sulfide. ZnS

Associations. Remarks: In veins, commonly with galena. An ore of zinc.

Color: Brass yellow or golden.
Hardness: 3.5–4
Specific gravity: 4.1–4.3
Streak: Greenish black.
Distinguishing features. Crystal system: Crystals look like pyramids, or may be massive. Uneven fracture. Tetragonal system.

Name. Chemical composition. Chemical formula: **Chalcopyrite.** Sulfide of copper and iron. $CuFeS_2$

Associations. Remarks: In sulfide veins, and disseminated in igneous rocks. An ore of copper.

Color: Bronze.
Hardness: 4
Specific gravity: 4.6
Streak: Black.
Distinguishing features. Crystal system: Usually massive. Magnetic to some degree. Subconchoidal fracture. Hexagonal system.

Name. Chemical composition. Chemical formula: **Pyrrhotite.** Iron sulfide. FeS (approximate formula).

Associations. Remarks: Ore veins, pegmatites, contact-metamorphic deposits. Commonly associated with nickel.

Color: Steel gray.
Hardness: 4–4.5
Specific gravity: 14–19 (usually impure)
Streak: Gray.

Distinguishing features. Crystal system: Malleable. Usually found as grains or larger pieces in placer deposits. Isometric system.

Name. Chemical composition. Chemical formula: **Platinum.** Pt

Associations. Remarks: Placer deposits.

Color: Brown to black.

Hardness: 5–5.5

Specific gravity: 3.3–4.3

Streak: Brown yellow to yellow.

Distinguishing features. Crystal system: Fibrous, platy, or reniform. Brittle. Uneven fracture. Orthorhombic system.

Name. Chemical composition. Chemical formula: **Goethite.** Hydrogen iron oxide. $HFeO_2$

Associations. Remarks: In veins and weathered ore bodies. An ore of iron.

Color: Brown black to yellow.

Hardness: 5–5.5

Specific gravity: 3.6–4.0

Streak: Brown to yellow.

Distinguishing features. Crystal system: Massive. Amorphous. Fracture sometimes conchoidal.

Name. Chemical composition. Chemical formula: **Limonite.** Hydrous ferric oxides. $FeO(OH) \cdot nH_2O$

Associations. Remarks: "Iron stain" in rock, or crustlike. Sometimes form "bog iron ore."

Color: Copper colored.

Hardness: 5–5.5

Specific gravity: 7.8

Streak: Black.

Distinguishing features. Crystal system: Usually massive. Uneven fracture. Hexagonal system.

Name. Chemical composition. Chemical formula: **Niccolite.** Nickel arsenide. NiAs

Associations. Remarks: In ore veins, with silver, copper, and nickel. An ore of nickel.

Color: Blackish to brown red.

Hardness: 5.5–6.5

Specific gravity: 4.9–5.3

Streak: Red.

Distinguishing features. Crystal system: Massive, mamillary, or reniform. Fracture conchoidal to uneven. Hexagonal system.

Name. Chemical composition. Chemical formula: **Hematite.** Iron (ferric) oxide. Fe_2O_3

Associations. Remarks: All types of rocks. Most important iron ore.

Metallic or Submetallic Luster
Hardness greater than $5\frac{1}{2}$
(Cannot be scratched by knife)

Color: Brown to black.

Hardness: 5–5.5

Specific gravity: 3.6–4

Streak: Yellow brown.

Distinguishing features. Crystal system: Massive and somewhat earthy-appearing. Amorphous.

Name. Chemical composition. Chemical formula: **Limonite.** Hydrous ferric oxide. $FeO(OH) \cdot nH_2O$

Associations. Remarks: "Iron stain" in rock. Sometimes forms "bog iron ore."

Color: Brown to black.

Hardness: 5–5.5

Specific gravity: 4.3

Streak: Brownish yellow to yellow.

Distinguishing features. Crystal system: Fibrous, in radiating pattern. Brittle. Fracture uneven. Orthorhombic system.

Name. Chemical composition. Chemical formula: **Goethite.** Hydrogen iron oxide. $HFeO_2$

Associations. Remarks. In veins and weathered ore bodies. An ore of iron.

Color: Copper red.

Hardness: 5–5.5

Specific gravity: 7.8

Streak: Black.

Distinguishing features. Crystal system: Usually massive. Subconchoidal fracture. Hexagonal system.

Name. Chemical composition. Chemical formula: **Niccolite.** Nickel arsenide. NiAs

Associations. Remarks: In ore veins, with silver, copper, and nickel. An ore of nickel.

Color: Steel gray to blackish.
Hardness: 5–6
Specific gravity: 6.3–9.8
Streak: Brown black.
Distinguishing features. Crystal system: Submetallic luster. Brittle. Fracture conchoidal to uneven. Isometric system.
Name. Chemical composition. Chemical formula: **Uraninite.** Uranium dioxide. UO_2. Is always impure.
Associations. Remarks: Vein deposits and pegmatites.

Color: Black.
Hardness: 5.5
Specific gravity: 4.1–4.9
Streak: Brown.
Distinguishing features. Crystal system: Usually massive. Uneven fracture. Isometric system.
Name. Chemical composition. Chemical formula: **Chromite.** Ferrous chromic oxide. $FeCr_2O_4$
Associations. Remarks: In basic, as opposed to acidic, rocks. An ore of chromium.

Color: Black to reddish brown.
Hardness: 5.5–6
Specific gravity: 4.8–5.3
Streak: Red brown.
Distinguishing features. Crystal system: Reniform or mammilary. Crystals rare. Subconchoidal to uneven fracture. Hexagonal system.
Name. Chemical composition. Chemical formula: **Hematite.** Iron (ferric) oxide. Fe_2O_3
Associations. Remarks: All types of rocks. Chief ore of iron.

Color: Silver white.
Hardness: 5.5–6
Specific gravity: 5.9–6.2
Streak: Black.
Distinguishing features. Crystal system: Usually massive and granular. Uneven fracture. Garlic odor upon "sparking" with knife, hammer, etc. Monoclinic system.
Name. Chemical composition. Chemical formula: **Arsenopyrite.** Iron sulfarsenide. $FeAsS$
Associations. Remarks: Veins and igneous rocks.

Color: Black.
Hardness: 6
Specific gravity: 5.2
Streak: Black.
Distinguishing features. Crystal system: Very magnetic. Uneven
    fracture. Isometric system.
Name. Chemical composition. Chemical formula: **Magnetite.** Iron
    oxide. Fe_3O_4
Associations. Remarks: Intrusive igneous, and metamorphic
    rocks. Commonly in river and beach sands. "Black sand" of
    placer mining.

Color: Light brass yellow.
Hardness: 6–6.5
Specific gravity: 4.9
Streak: Black.
Distinguishing features. Crystal system: Crystals in "coxcomb"
    groups. Brittle. Fracture uneven. Orthorhombic system.
Name. Chemical composition. Chemical formula: **Marcasite.** Iron
    sulfide. FeS_2
Associations. Remarks: Sedimentary and metamorphic rocks,
    and in veins.

Color: Light yellow to brass yellow.
Hardness: 6–6.5
Specific gravity: 5.0
Streak: Black.
Distinguishing features. Crystal system: Massive or in crystals.
    Brittle. Conchoidal fracture. Isometric system.
Name. Chemical composition. Chemical formula: **Pyrite.** Iron
    sulfide. FeS_2
Associations. Remarks: All types of rocks and in veins. "Fool's
    gold."

Nonmetallic Luster
Hardness less than 2½
(Can be scratched by fingernail)
1. Shows good cleavage

Color: White, green.
Hardness: 1
Specific gravity: 2.7–2.8
Luster. Diaphaneity: Greasy to pearly. Translucent to opaque.
Distinguishing features. Crystal system: Foliated. Feels greasy.

Usually in flaky masses. Monoclinic system.

Name. Chemical composition. Chemical formula: **Talc.** Hydrous magnesium silicate. $Mg_3Si_4O_{10}(OH)_2$

Associations. Remarks: Metamorphic rocks. Source of talcum powder.

Color: Bright yellow.
Hardness: Usually impossible to determine. Approximately 1.
Specific gravity: 4.1
Luster. Diaphaneity: Opaque. Earthy.
Distinguishing features. Crystal system: Powdery. Sectile. Crystal system not determinable.
Name. Chemical composition. Chemical formula: **Carnotite.** Hydrous potassium uranium vanadate. Complex vanadate.
Associations. Remarks: Sedimentary rocks, principally sandstone. An ore of uranium.

Color: Orange yellow to lemon yellow.
Hardness: 1.5–2
Specific gravity: 3.5
Luster. Diaphaneity: Resinous or pearly. Transparent to opaque.
Distinguishing features. Crystal system: Perfect micaceous cleavage. Yellow streak. Monoclinic system.
Name. Chemical composition. Chemical formula: **Orpiment.** Arsenic trisulfide. As_2S_3
Associations. Remarks: In veins, with realgar. An ore of arsenic.

Color: Colorless, white. Also various tints, often brownish.
Hardness: 2
Specific gravity: 2.3
Luster. Diaphaneity: Glassy. Pearly on cleavage face. Transparent to opaque.
Distinguishing features. Crystal system: Commonly in tabular crystals. Monoclinic.
Name. Chemical composition. Chemical formula: **Gypsum.** Hydrous calcium sulfate. $CaSo_4.2H_2O$
Associations. Remarks: Sedimentary rocks. Used for "plaster of paris."

Color: White. Commonly stained.
Hardness: 2–2.5
Specific gravity: 2.6
Luster. Diaphaneity: Dull. Earthy. Opaque.

Distinguishing features. Crystal system: In earthy masses. Earthy smell when breathed upon. Monoclinic system.

Name. Chemical composition. Chemical formula: **Kaolin.** Hydrous aluminum silicates. $Al_2Si_2O_5(OH)_4$

Associations. Remarks: Alteration zones in soils and rocks. Used in ceramics.

Color: Green, black, brown, yellow.

Hardness: 2–2.5

Specific gravity: 2.6–3.0

Luster. Diaphaneity: Glassy to pearly. Transparent to opaque.

Distinguishing features. Crystal system: Thin sheets or flakes. Flexible but not elastic. Monoclinic system. Looks like mica.

Name. Chemical composition. Chemical formula: **Chlorite.** Complex silicate.

Associations. Remarks: Alteration areas in rocks, and in schists.

Color: White, yellow, green, amber.

Hardness: 2–2.5

Specific gravity: 2.8–3.0

Luster. Diaphaneity: Glassy to pearly. Transparent to translucent.

Distinguishing features. Crystal system: Thin sheets or flakes. Elastic. Monoclinic system.

Name. Chemical composition. Chemical formula: **Muscovite.** A mica. Complex silicate.

Associations. Remarks: Igneous and metamorphic rocks. Common rock-forming mineral.

Color: Light to dark brown.

Hardness: 2.5–3

Specific gravity: 2.7

Luster. Diaphaneity: Metallic or pearly on cleavage face. Translucent.

Distinguishing features. Crystal system: Thin flakes or sheets. Elastic. Monoclinic system.

Name. Chemical composition. Chemical formula: **Phlogopite.** A mica. Complex silicate.

Associations. Remarks: Typically in altered limestones and dolomite.

Color: Dark brown to black.

Hardness: 2.5–3

Specific gravity: 2.8–3.4
Luster. Diaphaneity: Adamantine luster. Opaque.
Distinguishing features. Crystal system: Thin flakes or sheets.
Elastic. Monoclinic system.
Name. Chemical composition. Chemical formula: **Biotite.** A
mica. Complex silicate.
Associations. Remarks: Igneous and metamorphic rocks. Common rock-forming mineral. "Black mica."

Nonmetallic Luster
Hardness less than 2½
(Can be scratched by fingernail)
2. Does not show good cleavage

Color: Colorless to gray.
Hardness: 1–1.5
Specific gravity: 5.5
Luster. Diaphaneity: Adamantine luster. Opaque.
Distinguishing features. Crystal system: Sectile. Waxy appearance. Conchoidal fracture. Isometric system.
Name. Chemical composition. Chemical formula: **Cerargyrite.**
Silver chloride. AgCl
Associations. Remarks: Weathered zones of ore deposits.

Color: White, brown, gray, yellow.
Hardness: 1–3
Specific gravity: 2.0–2.5
Luster. Diaphaneity: Dull. Opaque.
Distinguishing features. Crystal system: Earthy. Amorphous.
Name. Chemical composition. Chemical formula: **Bauxite.** Mixture of hydrated aluminum oxides. Formula varies.
Associations. Remarks: Weathered surface deposits. Ore of aluminum.

Color: Red to orange.
Hardness: 1.5–2
Specific gravity: 3.5
Luster. Diaphaneity: Resinous. Transparent to opaque.
Distinguishing features. Crystal system: Earthy. Fuses easily, with garlic odor. Monoclinic system.
Name. Chemical composition. Chemical formula: **Realgar.** Arsenic sulfide. AsS
Associations. Remarks: In veins, with orpiment. An ore of arsenic.

Color: Light yellow.
Hardness: 2
Specific gravity: 2.0–2.1
Luster. Diaphaneity: Resinous. Opaque.
Distinguishing features. Crystal system: Burns with blue flame. In crystals or crusts. Orthorhombic system.
Name. Chemical composition. Chemical formula: **Sulfur.** S
Associations. Remarks: Volcanic and sedimentary rocks, and around hot springs. Used in making sulfuric acid.

Color: Yellow, reddish, brownish.
Hardness: 2+
Specific gravity: 1+
Luster. Diaphaneity: Subvitreous. Transparent to translucent.
Distinguishing features. Crystal system: In lumps, etc. Conchoidal fracture. Not a mineral.
Name. Chemical composition. Chemical formula: **Amber.** Organic.
Associations. Remarks: In clays, etc. Fossil tree resin.

Nonmetallic Luster
Hardness greater than 2½ but less than 3
(Can be scratched by copper penny)
1. Shows good cleavage

Color: Colorless, white, pink, red, bluish.
Hardness: 2.5
Specific gravity: 2.1–2.5
Luster. Diaphaneity: Glassy. Transparent to translucent.
Distinguishing features. Crystal system: Cubic cleavage. Conchoidal fracture. Isometric system.
Name. Chemical composition. Chemical formula: **Halite.** Sodium chloride. NaCl
Associations. Remarks: Sedimentary beds and dried lake deposits. "Table salt."

Color: Colorless, white, gray.
Hardness: 2.8–3.0
Specific gravity: 6.4
Luster. Diaphaneity: Adamantine. Transparent to translucent.
Distinguishing features. Crystal system: Massive, or in tabular crystals. Conchoidal fracture. Orthorhombic system.

Name. Chemical composition. Chemical formula: **Anglesite.** Lead
   sulfate. $PbSO_4$
Associations. Remarks: Weathered lead ore deposits.

Color: Colorless, white, various tints.
Hardness: 3–3.5
Specific gravity: 3.0
Luster. Diaphaneity: Glassy or pearly. Transparent to translu-
   cent.
Distinguishing features. Crystal system: Three-directional cleav-
   age. Usually massive. Uneven fracture. Orthorhombic system.
Name. Chemical composition. Chemical formula: **Anhydrite.** Cal-
   cium sulfate. $CaSO_4$
Associations. Remarks: Sedimentary rocks and ore veins.

Color: Colorless, white, various tints.
Hardness: 3.0
Specific gravity: 2.7
Luster. Diaphaneity: Glassy. Transparent to translucent.
Distinguishing features. Crystal system: Cleavage in three direc-
   tions not at right angles. Conchoidal fracture. Hexagonal sys-
   tem. Effervesces rapidly in cold, dilute hydrochloric acid.
Name. Chemical composition. Chemical formula: **Calcite.** Cal-
   cium carbonate. $CaCO_3$
Associations. Remarks: All types of rocks.

Color: Colorless, white, reddish, brown, bluish.
Hardness: 3–3.5
Specific gravity: 3.9–4.0
Luster. Diaphaneity: Glassy. Transparent to translucent.
Distinguishing features. Crystal system: Three-directional cleav-
   age. Uneven fracture. Orthorhombic system.
Name. Chemical composition. Chemical formula: **Celestite.** Stron-
   tium sulfate. $SrSO_4$
Associations. Remarks: Sedimentary rocks. Gives crimson flame.

Color: Colorless, white, yellow, brown, reddish, bluish.
Hardness: 3–3.5
Specific gravity: 4.3–4.6
Luster. Diaphaneity: Glassy. Transparent to translucent.
Distinguishing features. Crystal system: Three-directional cleav-
   age. Pearly luster on one cleavage face. Uneven fracture. Or-
   thorhombic system.

Name. Chemical composition. Chemical formula: **Barite.** Barium sulfate. $BaSO_4$

Associations. Remarks: Sedimentary rocks and ore veins.

Nonmetallic Luster
Hardness greater than 2½ but less than 3
(Can be scratched by copper penny)
2. Does not show good cleavage

Color: White, brown, gray, yellow.

Hardness: 1–3

Specific gravity: 2.0–2.5

Luster. Diaphaneity: Dull. Opaque.

Distinguishing features. Crystal system: Earthy. Amorphous.

Name. Chemical composition. Chemical formula: **Bauxite.** Mixture of hydrous aluminum silicates. Composition varies.

Associations. Remarks: Weathered surface deposits. Ore of aluminum.

Color: Colorless, white, greenish, grayish.

Hardness: 2–2.5

Specific gravity: 1.7

Luster. Diaphaneity: Glassy. Transparent to translucent.

Distinguishing features. Crystal system: Easily fusible, with yellow flame. Soluble in water. Conchoidal fracture. Monoclinic system.

Name. Chemical composition. Chemical formula: **Borax.** Hydrous sodium borate. $Na_2B_4O_7 \cdot 10H_2O$

Associations. Remarks: Dry lake beds in deserts.

Color: White, commonly stained.

Hardness: 2–2.5

Specific gravity: 2.6

Luster. Diaphaneity: Dull. Opaque.

Distinguishing features. Crystal system: Earthy masses. Earthy smell when breathed upon. Monoclinic system.

Name. Chemical composition. Chemical formula: **Kaolin.** Hydrous aluminum silicate. $Al_2Si_2O_5(OH)_4$

Associations. Remarks: Alteration zones in rocks and soils. Used in ceramics.

Color: Green to blue.

Hardness: 2–4

Specific gravity: 2–2.5
Luster. Diaphaneity: Glassy to earthy. Opaque.
Distinguishing features. Crystal system: Massive. Tongue clings to specimen, usually. Conchoidal fracture. Cryptocrystalline.
Name. Chemical composition. Chemical formula: **Chrysocolla.** Hydrous copper silicate. $CuSiO_3.2H_2O$
Associations. Remarks: In upper portions of copper deposits. Sometimes an ore of copper.

Color: Green, white, brown, yellow, red, black.
Hardness: 2–5
Specific gravity: 2.2–2.6
Luster. Diaphaneity: Silky to greasy. Transparent to opaque.
Distinguishing features. Crystal system: Massive. Fibrous variety is chrysotile asbestos. Monoclinic system.
Name. Chemical composition. Chemical formula: **Serpentine.** Hydrous magnesium silicate. $Mg_3Si_2O_5(OH)_4$
Associations. Remarks: Dark-colored magnesium silicate rocks.

Color: Colorless, white, yellow, gray, brown.
Hardness: 3–3.5
Specific gravity: 6.5–6.6
Luster. Diaphaneity: Adamantine. Transparent to translucent.
Distinguishing features. Crystal system: Crystal lattices common. Conchoidal fracture. Orthorhombic system. Effervesces with nitric acid.
Name. Chemical composition. Chemical formula: **Cerussite.** Lead carbonate. $PbCO_3$
Associations. Remarks: Weathered parts of lead deposits.

Nonmetallic Luster
Hardness greater than 3, but less than 5½
1. Shows good cleavage

Color: Colorless, white, various tints.
Hardness: 3
Specific gravity: 2.7
Luster. Diaphaneity: Glassy. Transparent to translucent.
Distinguishing features. Crystal system: Crystals cleave in three directions not at right angles. Conchoidal fracture. May be fibrous or granular. Hexagonal system.
Name. Chemical composition. Chemical formula: **Calcite.** Calcium carbonate. $CaCO_3$

Associations. Remarks: All rocks. Effervesces rapidly in hydrochloric acid.

Color: Colorless, white, various tints.
Hardness: 3–3.5
Specific gravity: 3.0
Luster. Diaphaneity: Glassy to pearly. Transparent to translucent.
Distinguishing features. Crystal system: Three-directional cleavage. Usually massive. Splintery fracture. Orthorhombic system.
Name. Chemical composition. Chemical formula: **Anhydrite.** Calcium sulfate. $CaSO_4$
Associations. Remarks: Sedimentary rocks and ore veins.

Color: Colorless, white, reddish, brown, bluish.
Hardness: 3–3.5
Specific gravity: 3.9–4.0
Luster. Diaphaneity: Glassy. Transparent to translucent.
Distinguishing features. Crystal system: Cleavage in three directions. Uneven fracture. Orthorhombic system.
Name. Chemical composition. Chemical formula: **Celestite.** Strontium sulfate. $SrSO_4$
Associations. Remarks: Sedimentary rocks. Gives crimson flame.

Color: Colorless, white, yellow, bluish, brown, reddish.
Hardness: 3–3.5
Specific gravity: 4.3–4.6
Luster. Diaphaneity: Glassy. Transparent to translucent.
Distinguishing features. Crystal system: Three-directional cleavage. Pearly luster on one face. Uneven fracture. Orthorhombic system.
Name. Chemical composition. Chemical formula: **Barite.** Barium sulfate. $BaSO_4$
Associations. Remarks: Sedimentary rocks and ore veins.

Color: Colorless, white, yellowish, green.
Hardness: 3–3.5
Specific gravity: 4.3–4.6
Luster. Diaphaneity: Glassy. Translucent.
Distinguishing features. Crystal system: Crystals and crusts. Effervesces in cold hydrochloric acid. Colors flame green. Uneven fracture. Orthorhombic system.

Name. Chemical composition. Chemical formula: **Witherite.**
Barium carbonate. $BaCO_3$
Associations. Remarks: Found in galena ore veins. Alters to
barite by weathering.

Color: White, yellow, brownish, red.
Hardness: 3.5–4
Specific gravity: 2.1–2.2
Luster. Diaphaneity: Glassy. Transparent to translucent.
Distinguishing features. Crystal system: Crystals often in "wheat-
sheave bundles." Fracture uneven. Monoclinic system.
Name, Chemical composition. Chemical formula: **Stilbite.** Hy-
drous calcium, sodium, aluminum silicate. Complex silicate.
Associations. Remarks: Cavities and caves. A "zeolite." Zeolites
are used in water softeners.

Color: Colorless, white, pink.
Hardness: 3.5–4
Specific gravity: 2.8–2.9
Luster. Diaphaneity: Glassy or pearly. Transparent to translu-
cent.
Distinguishing features. Crystal system: Interlocked crystals and
massive. Conchoidal fracture. Hexagonal system.
Name. Chemical composition. Chemical formula: **Dolomite.** Cal-
cium magnesium carbonate. $CaMg(CO_3)_2$
Associations. Remarks: Sedimentary rocks and some ore veins.
Slow effervescence with cold hydrochloric acid.

Color: Colorless, white, light yellow.
Hardness: 3.5–4
Specific gravity: 2.9–3.0
Luster. Diaphaneity: Glassy. Transparent to translucent.
Distinguishing features. Crystal system: Usually in slender radi-
ating crystals or tabular shapes. Effervesces in cold hydro-
chloric acid. Subconchoidal fracture. Orthorhombic system.
Name. Chemical composition. Chemical formula: **Aragonite.** Cal-
cium carbonate. $CaCO_3$
Associations. Remarks: Hot springs deposits. Ore veins. Some
sediments.

Color: Red, pink, brown, gray.
Hardness: 3.5–4
Specific gravity: 3.5–3.6
Luster. Diaphaneity: Glassy or pearly. Transparent to translu-
cent.

Distinguishing features. Crystal system: Usually in cleavable masses. Conchoidal fracture. Hexagonal system.

Name. Chemical composition. Chemical formula: **Rhodocrosite.** Manganese carbonate. $MnCO_3$

Associations. Remarks: Ore veins. Contact metamorphic deposits. An ore of manganese.

Color: Yellow, brown, reddish, black.
Hardness: 3.5–4
Specific gravity: 3.9–4.1
Luster. Diaphaneity: Resinous. Transparent to opaque.
Distinguishing features. Crystal system: Often in good crystals. Conchoidal fracture. Isometric.
Name. Chemical composition. Chemical formula: **Sphalerite.** Zinc sulfide. ZnS
Associations. Remarks: In sulfide ore veins. An ore of zinc.

Color: White, brown, gray.
Hardness: 3.5–4
Specific color: 3.9–4.1
Luster. Diaphaneity: Glassy or pearly. Transparent to translucent.
Distinguishing features. Crystal system: Massive or in cleavable aggregates. Conchoidal fracture. Hexagonal system.
Name. Chemical composition. Chemical formula: **Siderite.** Iron carbonate. $FeCO_3$
Associations. Remarks: Ore veins and in some sedimentary rocks and pegmatites. Commonly alters to limonite.

Color: Colorless, white, violet, brown, green.
Hardness: 4
Specific gravity: 3.0–3.3
Luster. Diaphaneity: Glassy. Transparent.
Distinguishing features. Crystal system: Cubic crystals have octahedral cleavage. Conchoidal fracture. Isometric system.
Name. Chemical composition. Chemical formula: **Fluorite.** Calcium fluoride. CaF_2
Associations. Remarks: Ore veins, also sedimentary rocks and pegmatites.

Color: White, brown, greenish, bluish, pink.
Hardness: 5
Specific gravity: 4.3–4.5
Luster. Diaphaneity: Glassy or subglassy. Translucent.

Distinguishing features. Crystal system: Commonly botryoidal. Conchoidal fracture. Hexagonal system.

Name. Chemical composition. Chemical formula: **Smithsonite.** Zinc carbonate. $ZnCO_3$

Associations. Remarks: Zinc ore deposits.

Color: Colorless, white.
Hardness: 5–5.5
Specific gravity: 2.2
Luster. Diaphaneity: Glassy. Transparent to translucent.

Distinguishing features. Crystal system: Commonly in slender crystals in a radiating, fan-shaped pattern. Fracture uneven across crystal. Orthorhombic system.

Name. Chemical composition. Chemical formula: **Natrolite.** Hydrous sodium aluminum silicate. $Na_2Al_2Si_3O_{10} \cdot 2H_2O$

Associations. Remarks: Cavities and caves. Sometimes in "stringer" veins.

Color: Colorless, white, brown, pink, green.
Hardness: 5–6
Specific gravity: 2.5–2.7
Luster. Diaphaneity: Glassy. Transparent to translucent.

Distinguishing features. Crystal system: Large crystals common. Subconchoidal fracture. Tetragonal system.

Name. Chemical composition. Chemical formula: **Scapolite** (series). Complex silicates. Formulas vary.

Associations. Remarks: Metamorphic rocks. Frequently fluorescent.

Color: Green, black, white.
Hardness: 5–6
Specific gravity: 3.0–3.3
Luster. Diaphaneity: Glassy. Transparent to translucent.

Distinguishing features. Crystal system: Slender crystals. Crystal cross section is wedge-shaped. Fracture subconchoidal to uneven, conchoidal. Several systems.

Name. Chemical composition. Chemical formula: **Amphibole** (group). Complex silicates.

Associations. Remarks: Various rock types. Nephrite (jade) is an amphibole.

Color: Green, black, white.
Hardness: 5–7
Specific gravity: 3.1–3.3
Luster. Diaphaneity: Glassy. Transparent to translucent when in splinters.

Distinguishing features. Crystal system: Short, stubby crystals. Crystal cross section is rectangular. Fracture subconchoidal, conchoidal, uneven. Several systems.

Name. Chemical composition. Chemical formula: **Pyroxene** (group). Silicates, some complex. Formulas vary.

Associations. Remarks: Various rocks. *Jadeite, spodumene,* and *rhodonite* are pyroxenes.

Color: White, bluish, greenish, gray.
Hardness: 5–7
Specific gravity: 3.6–3.7
Luster. Diaphaneity: Glassy. Transparent to translucent.
Distinguishing features. Crystal system: Always in crystal "blades." Hardness 5 along blade and 7 across blade. Fracture splintery across crystal. Triclinic system.
Name. Chemical composition. Chemical formula: **Kyanite.** Aluminum silicate. Al_2SiO_5
Associations. Remarks: Gneisses and schists. Used as refractory (spark plugs, etc.).

Color: Blue, white, green, gray, pink.
Hardness: 5.5–6
Specific gravity: 2.2–2.3
Luster. Diaphaneity: Glassy. Transparent to translucent.
Distinguishing features. Crystal system: Commonly in blue masses. Conchoidal to uneven fracture. Isometric system.
Name. Chemical composition. Chemical formula: **Sodalite.** Sodium aluminum silicate containing chlorine. $Na_4Al_3Si_3O_{12}Cl$
Associations. Remarks: Basic igneous rocks. After heating, fluoresces orange under long wave ultraviolet light.

Color: Pink, red, black.
Hardness: 5.5–6.0
Specific gravity: 3.5–3.7
Luster. Diaphaneity: Glassy. Transparent to translucent.
Distinguishing features. Crystal system: Usually massive but good crystals not uncommon. Uneven to splintery fracture. Triclinic system.
Name. Chemical composition. Chemical formula: **Rhodonite.** Manganese Silicate. $MnSiO_3$
Associations. Remarks: Metamorphic rocks and in ore veins. A pyroxene.

Nonmetallic Luster
Hardness greater than 3 but less than 5½
2. Does not show good cleavage

Color: White, brown, gray, yellow.
Hardness: 1–3
Specific gravity: 2–2.5
Luster. Diaphaneity: Dull. Opaque.
Distinguishing features. Crystal system: In earthy masses. Amorphous. Earthy fracture.
Name. Chemical composition. Chemical formula: **Bauxite.** Mixture of hydrous aluminum silicates. Composition varies.
Associations. Remarks: Weathered surface deposits. Ore of aluminum.

Color: Green, white, yellow, brown, red, black.
Hardness: 2–5
Specific gravity: 2.2–2.6
Luster. Diaphaneity: Silky to greasy. Transparent to opaque.
Distinguishing features. Crystal system: Massive. Fibrous variety is chrysotile asbestos. Monoclinic system.
Name. Chemical composition. Chemical formula: **Serpentine.** Hydrous magnesium silicate. $Mg_3SiO_5(OH)_4$
Associations. Remarks: In dark-colored magnesium silicate rocks.

Color: Colorless, white, various tints.
Hardness: 3
Specific gravity: 2.7
Luster. Diaphaneity: Glassy. Transparent to translucent.
Distinguishing features. Crystal system: Cleavage in three directions not at right angles. May be fibrous or granular. Conchoidal fracture. Hexagonal system.
Name. Chemical composition. Chemical formula: **Calcite.** Calcium carbonate. $CaCO_3$
Associations. Remarks: All types of rocks. Effervesces rapidly in cold hydrochloric acid.

Color: Colorless, white, light yellow.
Hardness: 3.5–4
Specific gravity: 2.9–3.0
Luster. Diaphaneity: Glassy. Transparent to translucent.
Distinguishing features. Crystal system: Usually in slender radiating crystal "needles," or in tabular form. Effervesces in cold

hydrochloric acid. Subconchoidal fracture. Orthorhombic system.

Name. Chemical composition. Chemical formula: **Aragonite.** Calcium carbonate. $CaCO_3$

Associations. Remarks: Ore veins. In some sediments.

Color: Blue.

Hardness: 3.5–4

Specific gravity: 3.8

Luster. Diaphaneity: Glassy. Transparent to translucent.

Distinguishing features. Crystal system: Fanlike aggregates. Also slender crystals. Sometimes botryoidal. Conchoidal fracture. Monoclinic system.

Name. Chemical composition. Chemical formula: **Azurite.** Basic copper carbonate. $Cu_3(OH)_2(CO_3)_2$

Associations. Remarks: Weathered portions of copper ore deposits. Associated with malachite.

Color: White, brown, gray.

Hardness: 3.5–4

Specific gravity: 3.8–3.9

Luster. Diaphaneity: Glassy or pearly. Transparent to translucent.

Distinguishing features. Crystal system: Massive or in cleavable aggregates. Conchoidal fracture. Hexagonal system.

Name. Chemical composition. Chemical formula: **Siderite.** Iron carbonate. $FeCO_3$

Associations. Remarks: Ore veins. Some sedimentary rocks and pegmatites.

Color: Light to dark green.

Hardness: 3.5–4

Specific gravity: 3.9–4.0

Luster. Diaphaneity: Commonly silky. Translucent.

Distinguishing features. Crystal system: Fibrous. Sometimes mammillary. Effervesces in cold acid. Splintery fracture. Monoclinic.

Name. Chemical composition. Chemical formula: **Malachite.** Basic copper carbonate. $Cu_2CO_3(OH)_2$

Associations. Remarks: Weathered parts of copper ore deposits. An ore of copper. Associated with azurite.

Color: White, brown, green.

Hardness: 4.5–5

Specific gravity: 5.9–6.1
Luster. Diaphaneity: Adamantine. Transparent to translucent.
Distinguishing features. Crystal system: Commonly in good crystals. Also in grains. Uneven fracture. Tetragonal system.
Name. Chemical composition. Chemical formula: **Scheelite.** Calcium tungstate. $CaWO_4$
Associations. Remarks: Contact metamorphic zones. Sometimes in veins. Often in placer deposits. An ore of tungsten.

Color: Colorless, white, green, brown, violet.
Hardness: 5
Specific gravity: 3.1–3.2
Luster. Diaphaneity: Glassy. Transparent to translucent.
Distinguishing features. Crystal system: Massive. Also in hexagonal prisms. Conchoidal fracture. Hexagonal system.
Name. Chemical composition. Chemical formula: **Apatite.** Calcium fluophosphate. $Ca_5(Cl,F)(PO_4)_3$
Associations. Remarks: Common rock-forming mineral. Occurs in many rocks.

Color: White, brown, greenish, bluish, pink.
Hardness: 5
Specific gravity: 4.3–4.5
Luster. Diaphaneity: Glassy or subglassy. Transparent.
Distinguishing features. Crystal system: Commonly botryoidal. Conchoidal fracture. Hexagonal system.
Name. Chemical composition. Chemical formula: **Smithsonite.** Zinc carbonate. $ZnCO_3$
Associations. Remarks: In zinc ore deposits.

Color: Colorless, white.
Hardness: 5–5.5
Specific gravity: 2.2
Luster. Diaphaneity: Glassy. Transparent to translucent.
Distinguishing features. Crystal system: Thin, prismatic crystals. Also massive and as nodules. Orthorhombic system. Fracture uneven across crystal.
Name. Chemical composition. Chemical formula: **Natrolite.** Hydrous sodium aluminum silicate. $Na_2Al_2Si_3O_{10} \cdot 2H_2O$
Associations. Remarks: Cavities and caves. Sometimes in "stringer" veins.

Color: Violet blue to greenish blue.
Hardness: 5–5.5

Specific gravity: 2.4–2.5
Luster. Diaphaneity: Glassy. Translucent.
Distinguishing features. Crystal system: Usually in granular masses. Uneven fracture. Isometric system.
Name. Chemical composition. Chemical formula: **Lazurite.** Sodium aluminum silicate with sulfur. Composition varies.
Associations. Remarks: Metamorphosed limestones.

Color: Colorless, white, greenish, reddish.
Hardness: 5–5.5
Specific gravity: 2.8–3.0
Luster. Diaphaneity: Glassy (sometimes like porcelain). Transparent to translucent.
Distinguishing features. Crystal system: Usually in broad crystals. Monoclinic system. Fracture conchoidal to uneven.
Name. Chemical composition. Chemical formula: **Datolite.** Basic calcium boron silicate. $Ca_2B_2(SiO_4)_2(OH)$
Associations. Remarks: Cavities and caves.

Color: Colorless or any color.
Hardness: 5.2–6.5
Specific gravity: 1.9–2.2
Luster. Diaphaneity: Glassy to resinous. Transparent to translucent.
Distinguishing features. Crystal system: May assume almost any habit. Amorphous. Conchoidal fracture.
Name. Chemical composition. Chemical formula: **Opal.** Silicon dioxide, with water. $SiO_2 \cdot nH_2O$
Associations. Remarks: Hot springs deposits, volcanic rocks, sediments. Some varieties are "precious" opal.

Color: Colorless, white, brown, pink, gray, green.
Hardness: 5–6
Specific gravity: 2.5–2.7
Luster. Diaphaneity: Glassy. Transparent to translucent.
Distinguishing features. Crystal system: Large crystals common. Subconchoidal fracture. Tetragonal system.
Name. Chemical composition. Chemical formula: **Scapolite** (series). Complex silicates. Formulas vary.
Associations. Remarks: Metamorphic rocks. Often fluoresces orange or yellow.

Color: Black, white, green, orange, gray, brown.
Hardness: 5.5

Specific gravity: 3.9–4.2

Luster. Diaphaneity: Glassy to resinous. Transparent to translucent.

Distinguishing features. Crystal system: Radiating and fibrous. Also massive. Fracture conchoidal to uneven. Hexagonal system.

Name. Chemical composition. Chemical formula: **Willemite.** Zinc silicate. Zn_2SiO_4

Associations. Remarks: Oxidized portions of zinc veins.

Color: Blue, white, green, gray, pink.

Hardness: 5.5–6

Specific gravity: 2.2–2.3

Luster. Diaphaneity: Glassy. Transparent to translucent.

Distinguishing features. Crystal system: In blue masses. Conchoidal to uneven fracture. Isometric system.

Name. Chemical composition. Chemical system: **Sodalite.** Sodium aluminum silicate with chlorine. $Na_4Al_3Si_3O_{12}Cl$

Associations. Remarks: Basic igneous rocks. After heating, fluoresces orange under long wave ultraviolet light.

Nonmetallic Luster
Hardness greater than 5½ but less than 7
1. Shows good cleavage

Color: Green, black, white.

Hardness: 5–6

Specific gravity: 3.0–3.3

Luster. Diaphaneity: Glassy. Transparent to translucent.

Distinguishing features. Crystal system: Slender crystals. Crystal cross sections are wedge-shaped. Several systems. Fracture subconchoidal or conchoidal, also uneven.

Name. Chemical composition. Chemical formula: **Amphibole group.** Complex silicates.

Associations. Remarks: Various rock types. Nephrite (jade) is an amphibole.

Color: Green, black, white.

Hardness: 5–7

Specific gravity: 3.1–3.3

Luster. Diaphaneity: Glassy. Transparent to translucent.

Distinguishing features. Crystal system: Stubby crystals. Crystal cross section is rectangular. Several systems. Fracture subconchoidal, conchoidal, uneven.

Name. Chemical composition. Chemical formula: **Pyroxene group.** Silicates, some complex. Formulas vary.

Associations. Remarks: Various rocks. Jadeite, spodumene, and rhodonite are pyroxenes.

Color: White, bluish, greenish, gray.
Hardness: 5–7
Specific gravity: 3.6–3.7
Luster. Diaphaneity: Glassy. Transparent to translucent.
Distinguishing features. Crystal system: Always in crystal "blades." Hardness 5 along blade and 7 across blade. Fracture splintery across crystal. Triclinic system.

Name. Chemical composition. Chemical formula: **Kyanite.** Aluminum silicate. Al_2SiO_5

Associations. Remarks: Gneisses and schists. Used as refractory (spark plugs, etc.).

Color: Green, bronze, brown to black.
Hardness: 5.5
Specific gravity: 3.2–3.9
Luster. Diaphaneity: Glassy to silky. Transparent to translucent, in thin pieces.
Distinguishing features. Crystal system: Usually massive or fibrous. Good crystals rare. Uneven fracture. Orthorhombic system.

Name. Chemical composition. Chemical formula: **Enstatite.** Magnesium silicate. $Mg_2Si_2O_6$

Associations. Remarks: Igneous rocks. A pyroxene.

Color: Pink to red to black.
Hardness: 5.5–6
Specific gravity: 3.5–3.7
Luster. Diaphaneity: Glassy. Transparent to translucent.
Distinguishing features. Crystal system: Usually massive but crystals are not uncommon. Splintery fracture. Triclinic system.

Name. Chemical composition. Chemical formula: **Rhodonite.** Manganese silicate. $MnSiO_3$

Associations. Remarks: Metamorphic rocks and in ore veins. A pyroxene.

Color: White, flesh, green, red, gray.
Hardness: 6
Specific gravity: 2.5–2.6

Luster. Diaphaneity: Glassy. Transparent to translucent.

Distinguishing features. Crystal system: In cleavable masses. Also grains. Orthoclase feldspar is monoclinic. Microcline feldspar is triclinic. Both have conchoidal fracture.

Name. Chemical composition. Chemical formula: **Orthoclase and microcline (feldspars).** The "potassium" feldspars. Both have same composition: $KAlSi_3O_8$ (potassium aluminum silicate).

Associations. Remarks: Igneous and metamorphic rocks. Some veins.

Color: White, yellow, gray, black.

Hardness: 6

Specific gravity: 2.6–2.8

Luster. Diaphaneity: Glassy. Transparent to translucent.

Distinguishing features. Crystal system: In cleavable masses. Also grains. Crystals and fragments striated on some faces. Conchoidal fracture. Triclinic system.

Name. Chemical composition. Chemical formula: **Plagioclase feldspars.** Series of sodium and calcium aluminum silicates. Formulas vary.

Associations. Remarks: Igneous and metamorphic rocks. The "soda-lime" feldspars.

Color: Green black. Green to brown.

Hardness: 6–7

Specific gravity: 3.4

Luster. Diaphaneity: Glassy. Pearly on cleavage face. Transparent to translucent.

Distinguishing features. Crystal system: Long, slender crystals common. Also as films on rocks. Uneven fracture. Monoclinic system.

Name. Chemical composition. Chemical formula: **Epidote.** Hydrous calcium iron silicate. Group, so formulas vary.

Associations. Remarks: Metamorphic and igneous rocks. Very common mineral.

Color: White, gray, pink, greenish, yellow.

Hardness: 6.5–7

Specific gravity: 3.1–3.2

Luster. Diaphaneity: Glassy. Transparent to translucent.

Distinguishing features. Crystal system: In flattened, striated crystals. Monoclinic system. Fracture is uneven.

Name. Chemical composition. Chemical formula: **Spodumene.** Lithium aluminum silicate. LiAlSi$_2$O$_6$
Associations. Remarks: Pegmatites.

Nonmetallic Luster
Hardness greater than 5½ but less than 7
2. Does not show good cleavage

Color: Violet blue to greenish blue.
Hardness: 5–5.5
Specific gravity: 2.4–2.5
Luster. Diaphaneity: Glassy. Translucent.
Distinguishing features. Crystal system: Usually in granular masses. Isometric system. Fracture conchoidal to uneven.
Name. Chemical composition. Chemical formula: **Lazurite.** Sodium aluminum silicate with sulfur. Formula varies.
Associations. Remarks: Metamorphosed limestones.

Color: Colorless, white, greenish, reddish.
Hardness: 5–5.5
Specific gravity: 2.8–3.0
Luster. Diaphaneity: Glassy (sometimes like porcelain). Transparent to translucent.
Distinguishing features. Crystal system: Usually in broad crystals. Monoclinic system. Fracture conchoidal to uneven.
Name. Chemical composition. Chemical formula: **Datolite.** Basic calcium boron silicate. Ca$_2$B$_2$(SiO$_4$)$_2$(OH)
Associations. Remarks: Cavities and caves.

Color: May be almost any color.
Hardness: 5–6
Specific gravity: 1.9–2.2
Luster. Diaphaneity: Glassy to resinous. Transparent to translucent to almost opaque.
Distinguishing features. Crystal system: May assume almost any habit. Amorphous. Conchoidal fracture.
Name. Chemical composition. Chemical formula: **Opal.** Silicon dioxide, with water, SiO$_2 \cdot n$H$_2$O
Associations. Remarks: Hot spring deposits, volcanic rocks, sediments. Some varieties are "precious" opal.

Color: Colorless, white, pink, brown, gray, green.
Hardness: 5–6
Specific gravity: 2.5–2.7

Luster. Diaphaneity: Glassy. Transparent to translucent.

Distinguishing features. Crystal system: Large crystals common. Tetragonal system. Subconchoidal fracture.

Name. Chemical composition. Chemical formula: **Scapolite** (series). Complex silicates. Formulas vary.

Associations. Remarks: Metamorphic rocks. Frequently fluoresces orange or yellow.

Color: Blue, bluish, green, greenish blue.

Hardness: 5–6

Specific gravity: 2.6–2.8

Luster. Diaphaneity: Porcelainlike. May be translucent on thin edges.

Distinguishing features. Crystal system: Reniform masses. Crystals rare. Triclinic system. Smooth fracture.

Name. Chemical composition. Chemical formula: **Turquoise.** Hydrous basic aluminum phosphate with copper. Complex.

Associations. Remarks: Veins in desert climates. Also found near some copper deposits in more humid climates.

Color: Black, white, green, orange, gray, brown.

Hardness: 5.5

Specific gravity: 3.9–4.2

Luster. Diaphaneity: Glassy to resinous. Transparent to translucent.

Distinguishing features. Crystal system: Radiating masses. Fibrous. Also massive. Hexagonal system. Fracture conchoidal to uneven.

Name. Chemical composition. Chemical formula: **Willemite.** Zinc silicate. $ZnSiO_4$

Associations. Remarks: In oxidized portions of zinc veins.

Color: Blue, white, green, gray, pink.

Hardness: 5.5–6

Specific gravity: 2.2–2.3

Luster. Diaphaneity: Glassy. Translucent to transparent.

Distinguishing features. Crystal system: Commonly in blue masses. Isometric system. Fracture conchoidal to uneven.

Name. Chemical composition. Chemical formula: **Sodalite.** Sodium aluminum silicate with chlorine. $Na_4Al_3Si_3O_{12}Cl$

Associations. Remarks: Basic (as opposed to acidic) igneous rocks. After heating, fluoresces orange under long wave ultraviolet light.

Color: Gray, white, colorless.
Hardness: 5.5–6
Specific gravity: 2.4–2.5
Luster. Diaphaneity: Glassy to dull. Transparent to translucent.
Distinguishing features. Crystal system: Usually as embedded crystals in dark rocks. Crystals look like garnets. Tetragonal system. Also pseudoisometric. Conchoidal fracture.
Name. Chemical composition. Chemical formula: **Leucite.** Potassium aluminum silicate. $KAlSi_2O_6$
Associations. Remarks: Lavas.

Color: White, gray, reddish, greenish.
Hardness: 5.5–6
Specific gravity: 2.5–2.6
Luster. Diaphaneity: Greasy. Transparent to translucent.
Distinguishing features. Crystal system: Usually massive. Subconchoidal fracture. Hexagonal system.
Name. Chemical composition. Chemical formula: **Nepheline.** Sodium potassium aluminum silicate. $(Na,K)(Al,Si)_2O_4$
Associations. Remarks: Intrusive igneous rocks. Pegmatite dikes. Any rock which contains nepheline cannot contain quartz.

Color: Black, brown, greenish, reddish.
Hardness: 6
Specific gravity: 2.3–2.6
Luster Diaphaneity: Glassy. Transparent to translucent.
Distinguishing features. Crystal system: Is "volcanic glass," hence no crystals. Conchoidal fracture.
Name. Chemical composition. Chemical formula: **Obsidian.** Is not a mineral but is a rock of approximately the same composition as a granite.
Associations. Remarks: Often makes up its own rock structure. Found in western states.

Color: Green, white, gray.
Hardness: 6–6.5
Specific gravity: 2.8–2.9
Luster. Diaphaneity: Glassy. Translucent to nearly transparent.
Distinguishing features. Crystal system: Reniform or botryoidal. Also stalactitic. Orthorhombic system. Uneven fracture.
Name. Chemical composition. Chemical formula: **Prehnite.** Hydrous calcium aluminum silicate. $Ca_2Al_2Si_3O_{10}(OH)_2$
Associations. Remarks: Cavities and caves.

Color: White, green, violet
Hardness: 6–6.2 (nephrite). 6.5–7 (jadeite)
Specific gravity: 3.3 (approximate)
Luster. Diaphaniety: Glassy to silky. Nephrite is transparent to translucent to nearly opaque. Jadeite is translucent to opaque.
Distinguishing features. Crystal system: In rounded masses. Monoclinic system. Fracture of nephrite is uneven. Fracture of jadeite is splintery.
Name. Chemical composition. Chemical formula: **Jadeite** and **nephrite** are the two kinds of jade. Nephrite is an amphibole, jadeite a pyroxene.
Associations. Remarks: Metamorphic rocks. Streams and stream gravel.

Color: Yellow, brown, orange, red.
Hardness: 6–6.5
Specific gravity: 3.1–3.2
Luster. Diaphaneity: Glassy. Transparent to translucent.
Distinguishing features. Crystal system: In grains. Actually a mixture of two minerals, one orthorhombic, the other monoclinic. Subconchoidal fracture.
Name. Chemical composition. Chemical formula: **Chondrodite.** Magnesium fluosilicate. Actually a mixture of two minerals.
Associations. Remarks: Crystalline limestones.

Color: Large crystals are usually black. Thin crystals usually reddish brown.
Hardness: 6–6.5
Specific gravity: 4.2–4.3
Luster. Diaphaneity: Adamantine to submetallic. Transparent to translucent in thin pieces.
Distinguishing features. Crystal system: Commonly occurs in long, thin crystals which are striated and often form lattices. Tetragonal system. Subconchoidal to uneven fracture.
Name. Chemical composition. Chemical formula: **Rutile.** Titanium oxide. TiO_2
Associations. Remarks: Metamorphic and intrusive igneous rocks. Streak is light brown. An ore of titanium.

Color: Yellowish to brown to black.
Hardness: 6–7
Specific gravity: 6.8–7.1
Luster. Diaphaneity: Adamantine to greasy. Transparent to translucent.

Distinguishing features. Crystal system: Rounded surfaces common. Sometimes in prismatic crystals. Tetragonal system. Fracture subconchoidal to uneven.

Name. Chemical composition. Chemical formula: **Cassiterite.** Tin oxide. SnO_2

Associations. Remarks: Veins and pegmatites. Placer deposits. An ore of tin.

Color: Almost any color.
Hardness: 6.5
Specific gravity: 3.3–4.5
Luster. Diaphaneity: Glassy. Transparent to translucent.
Distinguishing features. Crystal system: Commonly in prismatic crystals. Also massive. Tetragonal system. Fracture conchoidal to uneven.
Name. Chemical composition. Chemical formula: **Idocrase.** Hydrous calcium, iron, magnesium silicate. Composition varies slightly.
Associations. Remarks: Contact metamorphic zones in limestone. Formerly called *vesuvianite.* Green variety is *californite.*

Color: Green, brown, gray.
Hardness: 6.5–7
Specific gravity: 3.3–3.4
Luster. Diaphaneity: Glassy. Transparent to translucent.
Distinguishing features. Crystal system: Granular or granular masses. Conchoidal fracture. Orthorhombic system.
Name. Chemical composition. Chemical formula: **Olivine** (series). Series with magnesium silicate and iron silicate as the end members.
Associations. Remarks: In the darker-colored rocks. Common rock-forming mineral.

Color: Green, brown, yellow, gray, yellow orange.
Hardness: 6.5–7
Specific gravity: 3.3–3.4
Luster. Diaphaneity: Glassy. Transparent to translucent.
Distinguishing features. Crystal system: Wedgelike crystals, often of large size. Triclinic system. Conchoidal fracture.
Name. Chemical composition. Chemical formula: **Axinite.** Aluminum, calcium, iron, manganese hydrous borosilicate. Composition varies slightly.
Associations. Remarks: In veins in intrusive igneous rocks. Contact metamorphic areas.

Color: Almost any color.
Hardness: 7
Specific gravity: 2.7
Luster. Diaphaneity: Glassy to waxy. Transparent to translucent to almost opaque.
Distinguishing features. Crystal system: Often botryoidal. Crystals not evident. Massive appearance. Conchoidal fracture.
Name. Chemical composition. Chemical formula: **Chalcedony.** Silicon dioxide. SiO_2
Associations. Remarks: Commonly found in cavities. Has several gemstone varieties.

Color: Almost any color.
Hardness: 7
Specific gravity: 2.7
Luster. Diaphaneity: Glassy to waxy. Subtranslucent to opaque. Less translucent than chalcedony.
Distinguishing features. Crystal system: Crystals not evident. Massive appearance. Conchoidal fracture.
Name. Chemical composition. Chemical formula: **Jasper, chert, flint.** Impure silicon dioxide.
Associations. Remarks: Jasper and chert are often found in cavities and veins in igneous rocks. Flint often found in bedded limestone.

Color: Colorless, white, various colors and tints.
Hardness: 7
Specific gravity: 2.6
Luster. Diaphaneity: Glassy. Transparent to translucent.
Distinguishing features. Crystal system: In good crystals or may be massive or drusy. Hexagonal system. Conchoidal fracture.
Name. Chemical composition. Chemical formula: **Quartz.** Silicon dioxide. SiO_2
Associations. Remarks: In virtually all rocks. Common vein mineral and common rock-forming mineral. Many gemstone varieties.

Color: Almost any color.
Hardness: 7–7.5
Specific gravity: 3.0–3.3
Luster. Diaphaneity: Glassy. Transparent to translucent.
Distinguishing features. Crystal system: Prismatic crystals have "spherical triangle" cross section. Conchoidal to uneven fracture. Hexagonal system.

Name. Chemical composition. Chemical formula: **Tourmaline.** Complex series containing boron, silicon, aluminum, and other elements. Formulas vary.

Associations. Remarks: Metamorphic and igneous rock. Pegmatite dikes furnish best crystals.

Color: Brown to black.
Hardness: 7–7.5
Specific gravity: 3.6–3.7
Luster. Diaphaneity: Glassy. Transparent to translucent.
Distinguishing features. Crystal system: Commonly twinned, to form X or cross. Subconchoidal fracture. Orthorhombic system.

Name. Chemical composition. Chemical formula: **Staurolite.** Iron aluminum silicate. $FeAl_4Si_2O_{10}(OH)_2$
Associations. Remarks: Schists and gneisses.

Color: Brown, green, red, pink.
Hardness: 7.5
Specific gravity: 3.1–3.2
Luster. Diaphaneity: Glassy. Transparent to translucent.
Distinguishing features. Crystal system: Crystals often have nearly square cross sections. Orthorhombic system. Conchoidal fracture.

Name. Chemical composition. Chemical formula: **Andalusite.** Aluminum silicate. Al_2SiO_5
Associations. Remarks: Contact metamorphic areas. Metamorphic rocks. The variety *chiastolite* shows a crosslike pattern which changes shape throughout the length of the crystal.

Nonmetallic Luster
Hardness greater than 7
1. Shows good cleavage

Color: White, gray, brown, greenish.
Hardness: 6–7.5
Specific gravity: 3.2
Luster. Diaphaneity: Glassy to satiny. Transparent to translucent.
Distinguishing features. Crystal system: Usually in long, thin crystals. Orthorhombic system. Splintery or conchoidal fracture.

Name. Chemical composition. Chemical formula: **Sillimanite.** Aluminum silicate. Al_2SiO_5

Associations. Remarks: Gneisses, schists, contact metamorphic deposits.

Color: White, gray, greenish, pink, yellow.
Hardness: 6.5–7
Specific gravity: 3.1–3.2
Luster. Diaphaneity: Glassy. Transparent to translucent.
Distinguishing features. Crystal system: Flattened, striated crystals. Monoclinic system. Uneven fracture.
Name. Chemical composition. Chemical formula: **Spodumene.** Lithium aluminum silicate. $LiAlSi_2O_6$
Associations. Remarks: Pegmatites. Gemstone varieties are rare and valuable.

Color: Colorless, white, bluish, pinkish, yellow, brownish.
Hardness: 8
Specific gravity: 3.4–3.6
Luster. Diaphaneity: Glassy. Transparent to translucent.
Distinguishing features. Crystal system: Commonly in crystals. Orthorhombic system. Conchoidal fracture.
Name. Chemical composition. Chemical formula: **Topaz.** Aluminum fluosilicate. $Al_2SiO_4(F,OH)_2$
Associations. Remarks: Cavities in granites, etc. Veins. Pegmatites. Replacement deposits.

Color: Colorless. Almost any color.
Hardness: 9
Specific gravity: 4.0
Luster. Diaphaneity: Adamantine. Transparent to translucent.
Distinguishing features. Crystal system: Six-sided, barrel-shaped crystals. Also in plates. May be disseminated. Hexagonal system. Fracture conchoidal or uneven.
Name. Chemical composition. Chemical formula: **Corundum.** Aluminum oxide. Al_2O_3
Associations. Remarks: Igneous and metamorphic rocks. Sapphire and ruby are gemstone varieties.

Color: White, black. Various tints and colors.
Hardness: 10
Specific gravity: 3.5
Luster. Diaphaneity: Adamantine. Transparent.
Distinguishing features. Crystal system: Crystals in streams usually have dull luster. Isometric system.

Name. Chemical composition. Chemical formula: **Diamond.** Carbon. C

Distinguishing features. Crystal system: Crystals in stream gravel. Has four directions of cleavage and is brittle.

Nonmetallic Luster
Hardness greater than 7
2. Does not show good cleavage

Color: White, green, violet.

Hardness: 6.5–7 (jadeite). 6–6.2 (nephrite)

Specific gravity: 3.3 (approximate)

Luster. Diaphaneity: Glassy to silky. Jadeite is translucent to opaque. Nephrite is transparent to translucent to nearly opaque.

Distinguishing features. Crystal system: In rounded masses. Monoclinic system. Fracture of nephrite is uneven. Fracture of jadeite is splintery.

Name. Chemical composition. Chemical formula: **Jadeite** and **nephrite** are the two kinds of jade. Nephrite is an amphibole, jadeite a pyroxene. The two jades have different compositions.

Associations. Remarks: Metamorphic rocks. Streams and stream gravel.

Color: Yellowish to brown to black.

Hardness: 6–7

Specific gravity: 6.8–7.1

Luster. Diaphaneity: Adamantine to greasy. Transparent to translucent.

Distinguishing features. Crystal system: Rounded surfaces common. Sometimes in prismatic crystals. Tetragonal system. Fracture subconchoidal to uneven.

Name. Chemical composition. Chemical formula: **Cassiterite.** Tin oxide. SnO_2

Associations. Remarks: Veins and pegmatites. Placer deposits. An ore of tin.

Color: Brown, red, green, yellow, black, white.

Hardness: 6.1–7.5

Specific gravity: 3.5–4.3

Luster. Diaphaneity: Glassy. Transparent to translucent.

Distinguishing features. Crystal system: Typically occurs in crystals having twelve faces or whose faces are trapeziums or trapezoids. Isometric system. Conchoidal fracture.

Name. Chemical composition. Chemical formula: **Garnet**

(group). Aluminum silicates and calcium silicates, each containing several other elements. Compositions vary.

Associations. Remarks: Igneous and metamorphic rocks. One of the most commonly found mineral groups. Often found in stream gravel.

Color: Green, brown, yellow, gray, yellow orange.
Hardness: 6.5–7
Specific gravity: 3.3–3.4
Luster. Diaphaneity: Glassy. Transparent to translucent.
Distinguishing features. Crystal system: Wedgelike crystals, often of large size.
Name. Chemical composition. Chemical formula: **Axinite.** Aluminum, calcium, iron, manganese hydrous borosilicate. Complex.
Associations. Remarks: Veins in intrusive igneous rocks. Contact metamorphic areas.

Color: Green, brown, gray.
Hardness: 6.5–7
Specific gravity: 3.3–3.4
Luster. Diaphaneity: Glassy. Transparent to translucent.
Distinguishing features. Crystal system: Granular or in granular masses. Orthorhombic system. Conchoidal fracture.
Name. Chemical composition. Chemical formula: **Olivine** (series). Series having magnesium silicate and iron silicate as end members. Compositions vary.
Associations. Remarks: A common rock-forming mineral. Found in the darker rocks. Gem variety is *peridot.*

Color: Colorless, white, various colors and tints.
Hardness: 7
Specific gravity: 2.6
Luster. Diaphaneity: Glassy. Transparent to almost opaque.
Distinguishing features. Crystal system: Massive or in crystals.
Name. Chemical composition. Chemical formula: **Quartz.** Silicon dioxide. SiO_2
Associations. Remarks: Virtually all kinds of rocks. Most common rock-forming mineral. Several gemstone varieties.

Color: Almost any color. Colorless, black.
Hardness: 7–7.5
Specific gravity: 3–3.2
Luster. Diaphaneity: Glassy. Transparent to opaque.
Distinguishing features. Crystal system: Prismatic crystals with

a spherical triangle cross section. Hexagonal system. Conchoidal fracture.

Name. Chemical composition. Chemical formula: **Tourmaline** (series). Complex series with a "base" of boron, silica, and aluminum. Compositions vary.

Associations. Remarks: Metamorphic and igneous rocks. Pegmatites furnish the best crystals.

Color: Brown to black.
Hardness: 7–7.5
Specific gravity: 3.6–3.7
Luster. Diaphaneity: Glassy. Translucent to almost transparent.
Distinguishing features. Crystal system: Crystals commonly twinned to form an X or a cross. Orthorhombic system. Subconchoidal fracture.
Name. Chemical composition. Chemical formula: **Staurolite.** Iron aluminum silicate. $FeAl_4Si_2O_{10}(OH)_2$
Associations. Remarks: Gneisses and schists.

Color: Brown, green, red, pink.
Hardness: 7.5
Specific gravity: 3.1–3.2
Luster. Diaphaneity: Glassy. Transparent to translucent.
Distinguishing features. Crystal system: Crystals have nearly square cross sections. Orthorhombic system. Conchoidal fracture.
Name. Chemical composition. Chemical formula: **Andalusite.** Aluminum silicate. Al_2SiO_5
Associations. Remarks: Contact metamorphic areas. Metamorphic rocks. The variety *chiastolite* shows, in its crystal cross section, a crosslike pattern which changes shape throughout the length of the crystal.

Color: Brown, gray, red, colorless. Almost any tint is possible.
Hardness: 7.5
Specific gravity: 4.7
Luster. Diaphaneity: Adamantine. Transparent to translucent.
Distinguishing features. Crystal system: Usually in short, prismatic crystals. Tetragonal system. Conchoidal fracture.
Name. Chemical composition. Chemical formula: **Zircon.** Zirconium silicate. $ZrSiO_4$
Associations. Remarks: Granitic rocks and pegmatites. Sands and gravel.

Color: Red, blue, black, brown, green.

Hardness: 7.5–8
Specific gravity: 3.6–4
Luster. Diaphaneity: Glassy. Transparent to opaque.
Distinguishing features. Crystal system: Often in octahedral crystals. Isometric system. Conchoidal fracture.
Name. Chemical composition. Chemical formula: **Spinel.** Magnesium aluminum oxide. $MgAl_2O_4$
Associations. Remarks: Igneous intrusives and metamorphic rocks. Red spinel looks much like ruby.

Color: White, yellow, blue, green, pink, colorless.
Hardness: 7.5–8
Specific gravity: 2.6–2.8
Luster. Diaphaneity: Glossy. Transparent to translucent.
Distinguishing features. Crystal system: Prismatic. May be massive. Hexagonal system. Conchoidal fracture.
Name. Chemical composition. Chemical formula: **Beryl.** Beryllium aluminum silicate. $Be_3Al_2(SiO_3)_6$
Associations. Remarks: Pegmatites. Has several gemstone varieties, including emerald.

Color: Yellow, green, green yellow, brown.
Hardness: 8.5
Specific gravity: 3.5–3.8
Luster. Diaphaneity: Glassy. Transparent.
Distinguishing features. Crystal system: In crystals which show "V" striations on one face. Crystals commonly twinned, to look like heart or arrowhead. Orthorhombic system. Fracture conchoidal to uneven.
Name. Chemical composition. Chemical formula: **Chrysoberyl.** Beryllium aluminum oxide. $BeAl_2O_4$
Associations. Remarks: Pegmatite dikes. A valuable gemstone.

Color: Colorless. Almost any color.
Hardness: 9
Specific gravity: 4
Luster. Diaphaneity: Adamantine. Transparent to translucent.
Distinguishing features. Crystal system: Six-sided, barrel-shaped crystals. Also in plates. May be disseminated. Hexagonal system. Fracture conchoidal or uneven.
Name. Chemical composition. Chemical formula: **Corundum.** Aluminum oxide. Al_2O_3
Associations. Remarks: Igneous and metamorphic rocks. Ruby and sapphire are gem varieties.

Appendix

The Common Chemical Elements of Mineralogy and Their Symbols

Element	Symbol	Element	Symbol
Aluminum	Al	Molybdenum	Mo
Antimony	Sb	Nickel	Ni
Arsenic	As	Nitrogen	N
Barium	Ba	Oxygen	O
Beryllium	Be	Phosphorus	P
Bismuth	Bi	Platinum	Pt
Boron	B	Potassium	K
Cadmium	Cd	Radium	Ra
Calcium	Ca	Selenium	Se
Carbon	C	Silicon	Si
Chlorine	Cl	Silver	Ag
Chromium	Cr	Sodium	Na
Cobalt	Co	Strontium	Sr
Copper	Cu	Sulfur	S
Fluorine	F	Tellurium	Te
Gold	Au	Thorium	Th
Hydrogen	H	Tin	Sn
Iron	Fe	Titanium	Ti
Lead	Pb	Tungsten	W
Lithium	Li	Uranium	U
Magnesium	Mg	Vanadium	V
Manganese	Mn	Zinc	Zn
Mercury	Hg	Zirconium	Zr

Suggested Books
and Magazines
for Rockhounds

Physical Geology

Leet, L. Don, and Judson, Sheldon. *Physical Geology.* 4th ed. Englewood Cliffs, N.J.: Prentice-Hall, Inc., 1971. A widely used and readable text, used in college courses.

Minerals and Mineralogy

Dana, Edward Salisbury. *Dana's Minerals and How to Study Them.* 3rd edition, revised by Cornelius S. Hurlbut, Jr. New York: John Wiley and Sons, Inc., 1949. Inexpensive but excellent book which describes minerals and their occurrences. Has chapters on crystallography and blowpipe analysis and also has a set of determinative tables.

Desautels, Paul E. *The Mineral Kingdom.* New York: Grosset and Dunlap, Inc., 1968. A beautiful book with many illustrations including 140 color plates. Interesting and well written. Also expensive, but worth it.

Dietrich, Richard V. *Mineral Tables. Hand-specimen Properties of 1500 Minerals.* New York: McGraw-Hill Book Company, 1969. Just about the only book of its kind. Paperback.

Morrissey, C. J. *Mineral Specimens.* New York: American Elsevier Publishing Company, 1968. Contains 100 color photographs of minerals, plus technical data concerning each mineral shown. Plates are six inches square. Expensive but elegant.

Pough, Frederick H. *A Field Guide to Rocks and Minerals.* 3rd ed. Boston: Houghton Mifflin Company, 1960. Thorough treatment of mineral descriptions. Many photographs, some of these in color. A classic reference for rockhounds.

Gemstones and Gems

Kraus, Edward H. and Slawson, Chester B. *Gems and Gem Materials.* 5th ed. New York: McGraw-Hill Book Co., Inc., 1957. One of the classics on gems and gemstones. Virtually complete and very readable.

Kunz, George Frederick. *Gems and Precious Stones of North America.* 2nd edition, 1892. Reprinted 1968 with an introduction by Edward Olsen. New York: Dover Publications, Inc., 1968. Perhaps *the* popular classic on gems and gemstones, republished for lucky new generations. Up until now, it was extremely difficult to buy copies of this work. The lists of old-time gemstone locations will get many a rockhound to wondering just what treasures may be buried "in his own backyard."

MacFall, Russell P. *Gem Hunter's Guide.* 4th ed. New York: Thomas Y. Crowell Co., 1969. State-by-state listing and mapping of gemstone locations in the United States. Also contains list of museums and state guides. Diamonds and pearls are treated in some detail.

Smith, G. F. Herbert. *Gemstones.* 13th ed. New York: Pitman Publishing Corporation, 1958. Systematic and readable.

Whitlock, Herbert P. *The Story of the Gems.* New York: Emerson Books, Inc., 1956. Extremely interesting treatment of gemstone occurrences, the history of gemstones and gems, and the elements of gemstone cutting.

Rocks and Minerals

Fenton, C. L. and M. A. *The Rock Book.* New York: Doubleday & Co., 1940. One of the most interesting and informative books on rocks ever published. Extremely well written, with eye-catching illustrations.

Pearl, Richard M. *Rocks and Minerals.* Revised ed. New York: Barnes & Noble, Inc., 1956. "The entire range of the mineral kingdom is presented in popular language. . . ." says the back cover of this excellent paperback, and that sums up this book very well. Also available in clothbound edition.

Zim, Herbert S. and Shaffer, Paul R. *Rocks and Minerals.* New York: Golden Press, Inc., 1957. Excellent for beginners, especially the younger ones. Very inexpensive paperback.

Fossils

Matthews, William H., III. *Fossils.* New York: Barnes & Noble, Inc., 1962. Good, generously illustrated paperback. Also available in clothbound edition.

Simpson, George G. *Life of the Past.* New Haven: Yale University Press, 1953. Excellent, slanted especially toward the beginner.

Spencer, E. W. *Basic Concepts of Historical Geology.* New York: Crowell, 1962. Readable presentation of the principles behind the story of historical geology.

Prospecting

Sinkankas, John. *Gemstones and Minerals. How and Where to Find Them.* Princeton: D. Van Nostrand Company, Inc., 1961. Includes chapters on rock types, prospecting tips, field features of mineral deposits, tools, and collecting practices. No individual treatments of gemstones and minerals but it is an excellent overall reference for the mineral and gemstone hunter.

Von Bernewitz, M. W. *Handbook for Prospectors and Operators of Small Mines.* 4th ed. Revised by H. C. Chellson, 1943. New York: McGraw-Hill Book Co., Inc., 1943. An old book but a famous one. A practical work and one which "reads easy."

Rockhound Hobby Magazines

Earth Science. P.O. Box 550-GM, Downers Grove, Illinois 60515. Official magazine of the Midwest Federation of Mineralogical and Geological Societies. Published bimonthly.

Gems and Minerals. P.O. Box 687, Mentone, California 92359. Official magazine of the American Federation of Mineralogical Societies, the California Federation of Mineralogical Societies, the Northwest Federation of Mineralogical Societies, and the Texas Federation of Mineralogical Societies. Published monthly.

Lapidary Journal. P.O. Box 2369, San Diego, California 92112. Many articles on field trips as well as on lapidary. Every April, the *Rockhound Buyer's Guide* is published by this magazine and is a fascinating education in itself. *Lapidary Journal* is published monthly.

Rocks and Minerals. Box 29, Peekskill, N.Y. 10566. Official magazine of the Eastern Federation of Mineralogical and Lapidary Societies. Published monthly.

Regional Guides

Regional guides such as *Eastern Gem Trails, Appalachian Gem Trails,* and *Midwest Gem Trails* are paperbacks which describe gemstone collecting localities and tell how to get to collecting sites. Such guides usually contain maps, with more or less detailed travel instructions. Similar guides have been published for individual states, and for groups of two or three states. If the rockhound cannot find a guide for a particular region at his bookstore, a letter to a rockhound magazine, or to a rockhound club in that area, will usually bring an answer. The book departments of some of the hobby magazines, incidentally, keep some of these guides in stock, for sale.

A different type of a guide—and a heart-warming one—is the "mineral collecting locality"—or similar—department featured in some of the rockhound hobby magazines wherein information on collecting sites is sent in or offered by various readers. For example, in one issue of *Rocks and Minerals,* a professor in Illinois lists his name and address and offers to take visiting rockhounds to localities for ores, geodes, and crystals; a rockhound in New York State offers information on collecting localities in New York, New Jersey, Pennsylvania, Connecticut, Massachusetts, Vermont, and New Hampshire; and a rockhound in the state of Washington offers information concerning localities where several types of minerals can be found.

Index